The New York Times

TAME CROSSWORDS

The New York Times

TAME CROSSWORDS

150 Easy Puzzles

Edited by Will Shortz

ST. MARTIN'S GRIFFIN NEW YORK

THE NEW YORK TIMES TAME CROSSWORDS.

Printed in the United States of America. For information, address St. Martin's Press, 175 Fifth Avenue, New York, NY 10010.

www.stmartins.com

ISBN-13: 978-0-312-54168-2
ISBN-10: 0-312-54168-6

First Edition: March 2009

10 9 8 7 6 5 4 3 2 1

749 10 min

ACROSS

1 Exiled Ugandan Idi ___
5 Home of the N.F.L.'s Buccaneers
10 Nile reptiles
14 "This ___ be!"
15 Criminal's "a k a" name
16 Post-Christmas store event
17 Anglican body
19 "Wheel of Fortune" action
20 Former Roxy Music member Brian
21 Point a gun
22 Hornswoggled
23 Discover
25 Oration
28 Question when you can't tell two things apart
32 Number of Little Pigs
35 Egg layers
36 Kanga's kid in "Winnie-the-Pooh"
37 Shot in the arm
38 Duracell size
39 Like a score of 10 of a possible 10
41 Attys.' org.
42 Baseball glove
43 Not just mean
44 Jewish high holy day
48 Top secret?
49 The "I" of Canada's P.E.I.
53 Shady spot
55 Excellent service?
56 Whisper sweet nothings
57 Profound
58 Youth groups . . . with a hint to 17-, 28- and 44-Across
62 Autobahn auto
63 Chili con ___
64 Suit to ___
65 Seat for two or more
66 Has a bawl
67 Salon applications

DOWN

1 Needed a chiropractor, say
2 The Pine Tree State
3 Gold brick
4 To the ___ degree
5 South Seas getaway
6 Homecoming attendee, for short
7 Old space station
8 ___-10 Conference
9 Louisville Slugger wood
10 Per se
11 September birthstones
12 Ballet bend
13 E-mail command
18 Sign of prestige
22 Morning moisture
24 Flock females
25 Put away, as a sword
26 Something beaten at a party in Mexico
27 Letter before tee
29 ___ longue
30 Jacket
31 Fit to be a saint
32 Skiers' lift
33 Tramp
34 Entree carved by a chef
39 "I'll be right there!"
40 Roald who wrote "James and the Giant Peach"
42 Treasure seeker's aid
45 Fanfare
46 "Ben-___"
47 Specialized markets
50 Less than 90°
51 Prestigious prize awarded every December
52 Prescribed amounts
53 Commotions
54 Seized vehicle
55 "Rule, Britannia" composer
58 Agcy. that can fine TV stations
59 Crew's control?
60 Geller with a psychic act
61 Fall behind

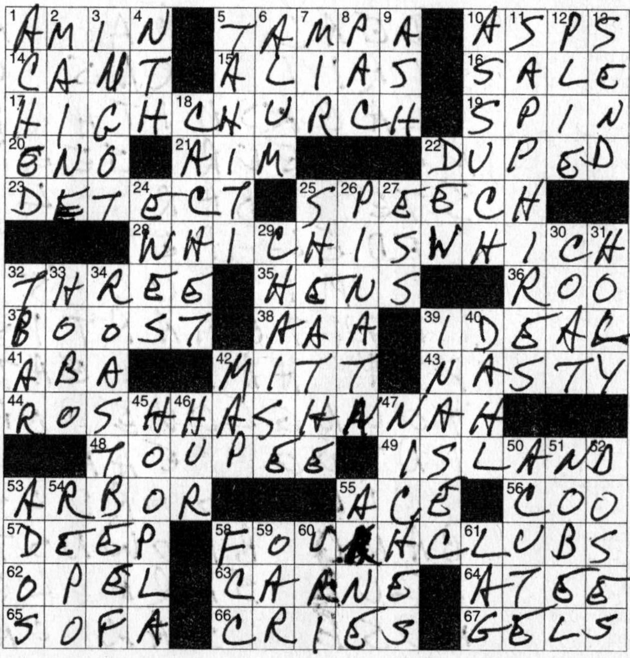

by Randall J. Hartman

2

ACROSS

1 Perfect
6 Farm sound
9 Highly excited
13 Wispy clouds
14 Ash containers
16 Let go
17 Singers Clint + Patti
19 Couple in the news
20 Ache reliever
21 They may be sown
23 Fr. holy woman
24 It's jumped in a high jump
26 As high as you can possibly go
29 Pulitzer-winning biographer Leon
32 Singers Tom + Johnny
35 Where Kofi Annan earned his master's deg.
37 Says lovingly
38 Copacabana Beach locale
39 Classic film company . . . or a description of 17-, 32-, 46- and 65-Across?
43 Pharmaceutical watchdog grp.
44 Show subtitled "The American Tribal Love-Rock Musical"
45 "___ my shorts!": Bart Simpson
46 Singers Neil + Courtney
49 D.E.A. agent
52 "___ Deep" (1999 Omar Epps film)
53 Suffix with Caesar
55 Yale student
57 Midwestern tribe
60 Perched
63 Like Yul Brynner, famously
65 Singers James + Sly
67 Blue, in Bogotá
68 ___ Lee cakes
69 Poet Federico García ___
70 Prominent part of a Groucho disguise
71 "Wailing" instrument
72 Vows

DOWN

1 Cold war weaponry
2 Widen, as a pupil
3 Got rid of marks
4 Paths of pop-ups
5 Simile part
6 Accused's bad break
7 Uris hero
8 "Farm" dwellers
9 Vinegary
10 1960s sitcom with the catchphrase "Sorry about that, Chief"
11 Uplifting poem
12 Cameo, e.g.
15 Any ship
18 40-Down, e.g.
22 Heavenly
25 Cut again, as a turkey
27 Mother goddess in Egyptian mythology
28 Howe'er
30 British record label
31 John of "3rd Rock From the Sun"
33 Rocky hill
34 Bag with handles
36 Bluish hue
39 Tempura ___ (Japanese dish)
40 Vessel in "Twenty Thousand Leagues Under the Sea"
41 God, to Galileo
42 Where to board a train: Abbr.
43 Post-it note abbr.
47 Brain, slangily
48 Q-tip target
50 "So's your old man!," e.g.
51 Grip tightly
54 Sine qua ___
56 "An invasion of armies can be resisted; an invasion of ___ cannot be resisted": Hugo
58 They may be crunched
59 Lima ladies: Abbr.
61 Norway's capital
62 Ancient Greek walkway
63 No-smoking ordinance, e.g.
64 ___ dye
66 ". . . ___ mouse?"

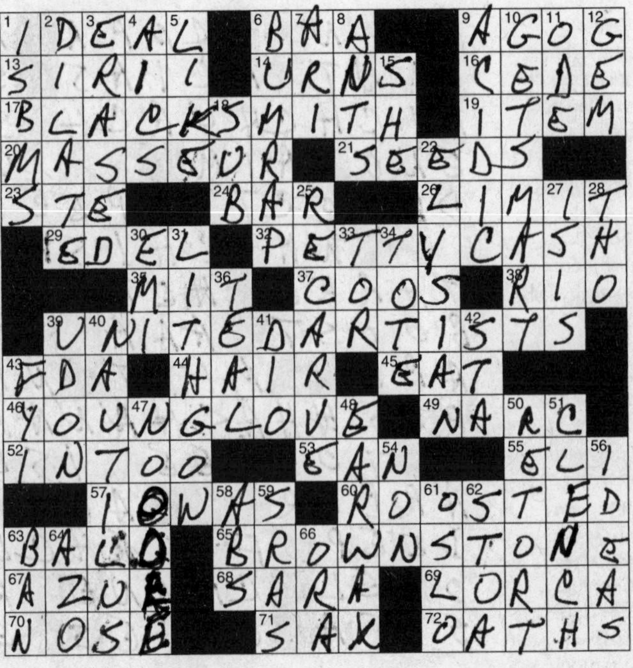

by Caleb Madison

8:19

10 MIN

ACROSS

1 The pyramids, for pharaohs
6 "Hey . . . over here!"
10 PBS newsman Lehrer
13 "The Cat and the Curmudgeon" author Cleveland ___
14 Inventor Elias
15 Absolutely the best
16 Place not generating rent
19 Feeling tied up, as a stomach
20 Rock band follower
21 "The first ___, the angel did say . . ."
23 Worked at, as a trade
24 Guarantees that mean nothing
30 Point again, as a gun
31 Crimped, as hair
32 Hit CBS drama with two spinoffs
35 Formal entrance
36 Euphoric
38 Pretend to be, as at a Halloween party
39 Without a prescription: Abbr.
40 Pal for Spot or Rover
41 Increase
42 Win that brings little actual gain
46 Avis competitor
48 Post-it, e.g.
49 Brandy cocktail
52 Warms up again
57 Contents of guns used in training exercises
59 Offerings to the poor
60 Dust Bowl migrant
61 New York footballer
62 Bad: Prefix
63 Baby boomers' kids, informally
64 Groups of buffalo

DOWN

1 Rikki-tikki-___
2 Neighbor of Yemen
3 Make fun of
4 Kellogg's Raisin ___
5 Roget's listing
6 "Star Trek" weapon
7 Soak (up)
8 Booty
9 Ariz., e.g., before 1912
10 Portrayer of Frank Sinatra on "Saturday Night Live"
11 Concave belly button
12 Rationed (out)
15 Stubborn as ___
17 Feature of many a sports car
18 ___-turvy
22 Scuttlebutt
24 Therefore
25 Vegetarians avoid it
26 1998 Robin Williams title role
27 Common Father's Day gift
28 Off one's rocker
29 Climbing vine
33 Suffix with dino-
34 1960s Bill Cosby TV series
36 Baseball great Hodges
37 Words before "You may kiss the bride"
38 London hrs.
40 Group watched by Little Bo Peep
41 A pair of deuces beats it
43 Black cats and broken mirrors, by tradition
44 Whirlpool or tornado
45 Anatomical passage
46 Equally awful
47 Eli ___ and Company
50 Slip ___ (blunder)
51 Clean up leaves, e.g.
53 Actress McClurg
54 Food thickener
55 Care for, with "to"
56 Fleet that was permanently retired in 2003
58 ___ Tin Tin

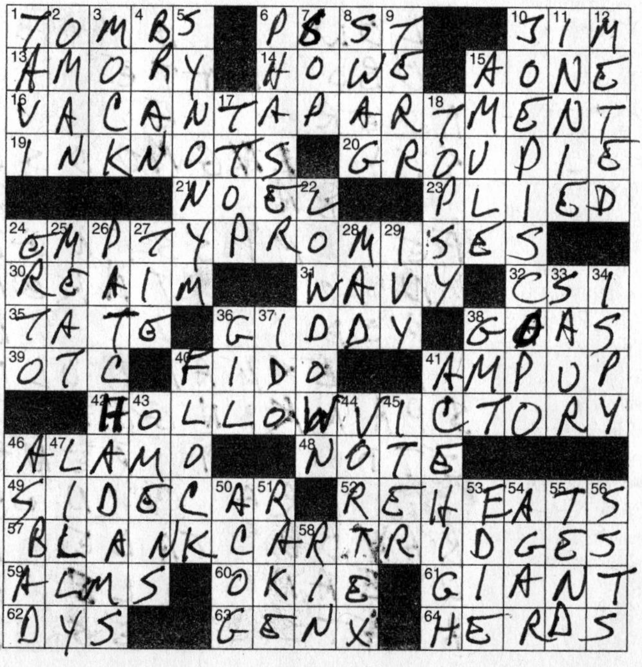

by Mike Nothnagel

4

830

ACROSS

1 Break ground, in a way
5 Spill the beans
9 Come to an end
14 Boxcar hopper
15 After the buzzer
16 "The usual," e.g.
17 Active sort
18 Salem's state: Abbr.
19 Fare payer
20 Antlered salon employee?
23 Woodworker's groove
24 Actress Vardalos
25 Curly poker
28 Make darts, say
31 Lost bobcat?
34 Heebie-jeebies
36 Grab some Z's
37 Teed off
38 Train alternative
39 Vintner's valley
40 One with a pitch
43 Passé
45 Wildebeest who doesn't spare the rod?
47 Future alums: Abbr.
48 Approx. takeoff hr.
49 Here, in Haiti
50 Broadway musical with the song "Will I?"
52 Unwelcome porcine party attendee?
57 Crawfish's home
60 Tall story
61 Like some chatter
62 Continental divide?
63 Building extensions
64 Parks of Montgomery
65 Cops' rounds
66 European deer
67 Tiny amount

DOWN

1 Profs' degs.
2 Rioter's take
3 Toe the line
4 Word before class or war
5 Mrs. Bumstead
6 Slow movements, in music
7 "Up and ___!"
8 Showy blooms
9 Prom accessory
10 Toledo's lake
11 Throw in
12 Comprehend
13 Slip up
21 Big name in pet foods
22 Barnyard sound
25 Chatty avians
26 Even (with)
27 Nationals living abroad, informally
28 Genève's land
29 Wholly absorbed
30 Li'l fellow
32 Attacked by a jellyfish
33 Come to earth
35 Yemeni port
38 Something to slide on
41 Vail trails
42 Easily split mineral
43 Unity
44 Pulmonary organ
46 It's between the headlights
51 Rival of a 'Vette
52 Fur
53 Saintly sign
54 What wavy lines signify in the comics
55 As well
56 Gather in
57 Short do
58 1 or 11, in twenty-one
59 Roll call vote

by Billie Truitt

5

1033

ACROSS

1 Irons or Woods
6 Iridescent gem
10 Classic clown
14 Old Big Apple restaurateur
15 Put blacktop on
16 Word repeated before "pants on fire"
17 Strap-on leg supports
19 Sister of Prince Charles
20 Reason for an R rating
21 Apple seeds' location
22 Film critic Gene
24 Without slack
25 Lady's partner
26 Cavalry cry
29 Experts with the ends of 17- and 55-Across and 10- and 24-Down
33 Eagle's nest
34 Cornmeal bread
35 Biblical flood survivor
36 Lame gait
37 Michelangelo masterpiece
38 Event proceeds
39 Fox's "American ___"
40 Away from the storm
41 Cancel, at Cape Canaveral
42 Rifle and revolver
44 Poisonous atmosphere
45 Part of a birthday celebration
46 Waste reservoir
47 Football refs
50 Mitchell who sang "Big Yellow Taxi"
51 "___ the season . . ."
54 "Peek-___, I see you!"
55 Mincemeat, e.g.
58 Gullet
59 Bones: Lat.
60 22-Across's longtime partner
61 Middle of many a steering wheel
62 Wed. follower
63 Things to salve

DOWN

1 Seeks info
2 Chaplin prop
3 "Jurassic Park" giant, informally
4 Poem often titled "To a . . ."
5 Chest protector
6 Some psychedelic designs
7 Show worry in the waiting room, maybe
8 "___ Maria"
9 Decreased
10 It sets things off
11 Sound piggish
12 Western writer Grey
13 Baseball's Hershiser
18 Rakish sort
23 Bank statement abbr.
24 Feat for Secretariat
25 Three wishes granter
26 Sacramento's state: Abbr.
27 Title heroine played by Shirley Temple in 1937
28 Knight's protection
29 Hawks' opposites
30 Goes up, up, up
31 Jazz great Art
32 "Come Back, Little ___"
34 ___ d'Or (Cannes award)
37 Appearing and disappearing feature on Jupiter
41 "Fresh as a daisy" and others
43 Org. that helps with tow service
44 Tax-exempt investment, for short
46 To date
47 2007 Masters champion Johnson
48 Longest Spanish river
49 Wild hog
50 Bach's "___, Joy of Man's Desiring"
51 Level
52 Legal memo starter
53 Some noncoms: Abbr.
56 Approximately: Suffix
57 Debt-incurring Wall St. deal

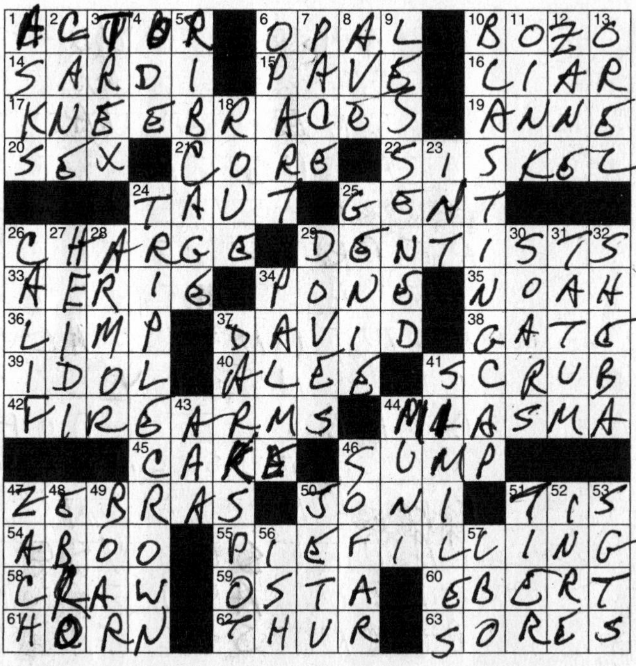

by Mark Sherwood

6

ACROSS

1 "Fall" guy
5 Three, it's said
10 Saks sack, say
14 Fries or slaw
15 Slot machine fruit
16 Enterprise alternative
17 E.S.L. class, perhaps?
20 Our base system
21 Word before fee or group
22 Main line
23 Harris's ___ Rabbit
24 It'll curl your hair
26 They're not original
29 Save for a rainy day
33 Diva's delivery
34 With 44-Down, "Wuthering Heights" actress
35 Title role for Will Smith
36 Seedy hangout across the Atlantic?
40 Web address ending
41 Down-and-out
42 Demon's doing
43 Bank receipts
45 Go to bat for
47 Makes verboten
48 Depend
49 Primp
52 Supreme Court count
53 Everyday article
56 Hip-hop critics?
60 Cookie with its name on it
61 Get off one's behind
62 Et ___
63 Hammer part
64 Meal with readings
65 1995 Physics Nobelist Martin L. ___

DOWN

1 Part of T.A.: Abbr.
2 Parcheesi pair
3 Mideast's Gulf of ___
4 Loo sign
5 Winds up
6 Direct, as for info
7 Actor Epps
8 Took all the marbles
9 Double-helix material
10 Puget Sound city
11 Frequent word from ham operators
12 TV control
13 "Cómo ___ usted?"
18 Lira's replacement
19 OPEC, e.g.
23 Kid you might feel like smacking
24 Kegger, e.g.
25 First name in scat
26 Did a 10K, e.g.
27 Eat away
28 Locker photo, maybe
29 Thrills
30 Give up
31 Chipmunk of pop music
32 Give up
34 Track team schedule
37 Out of one's mind
38 Ja's opposite
39 Go against
44 See 34-Across
45 Less astute
46 Gen. Robt. ___
48 Shampoo bottle instruction
49 Telephone on a stage, e.g.
50 Pink inside
51 Blunted blade
52 Reason to be barred from a bar . . . or the theme of this puzzle
53 Start to communicate?
54 "Aquarius" musical
55 Disney's "___ and the Detectives"
57 Carrier to Bergen
58 Opposite of post-
59 Bill (Bojangles) Robinson's forte

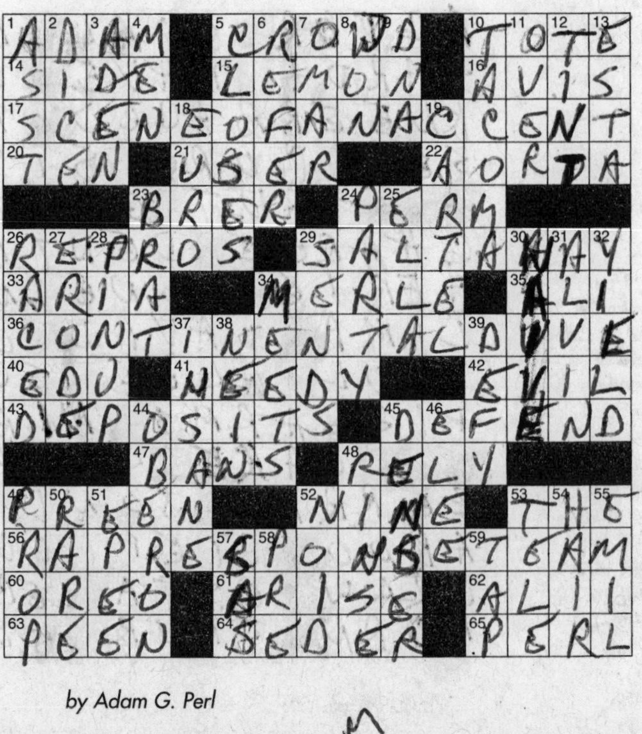

by Adam G. Perl

ACROSS

1 Calves' meat
5 Group of eight
10 Evil organization in "Get Smart"
14 Folkie Guthrie
15 Conductor Zubin
16 Shrek, for one
17 Knots
18 Keep an ___ (watch)
19 "Man, oh, man!"
20 Church bell ringer
22 Heater or repeater
24 Japanese maker of watches and calculators
26 Request
27 Weight of diamonds
30 Runs a cloth across furniture, say
32 Happy ___ clam
35 Event with ukulele entertainment
36 Revolutionary pattern of the moon
38 The "A" of A&E
39 Sex researcher Hite
40 Seep
41 Non-oil painting method
43 Fashion's ___ Saint Laurent
44 Stealthy
45 Soothed or smoothed
46 Treaty of ___-Litovsk, 1918
47 Guy's partner
48 "Ditto!"
50 TV Guide info
53 Shabby
57 Olympic sport from Japan
58 Lone Ranger's companion
60 Countess's husband
61 Upon
62 Available from a keg
63 The Beatles' "Lovely ___"
64 Beauty mark
65 View again
66 Iditarod vehicle

DOWN

1 Winery containers
2 Toledo's lake
3 "I'll take Potpourri for $200, ___"
4 The Civil War, for the Confederacy
5 Portents
6 1970s Dodgers All-Star Ron
7 What the starts of 22-, 36-, 41- and 50-Across comprise
8 Yours: Fr.
9 Predecessor of Katie Couric
10 Telly Savalas role
11 Golden ___ (senior)
12 City near Provo
13 "Oh yeah? ___ who?"
21 Grain in Cheerios
23 Gas brand in Canada
25 Some potatoes
27 Talons
28 Hearing-related
29 Dilapidated
31 Walked with a purpose
32 Upon
33 Assesses, as a situation, with "up"
34 "This is only ___"
36 Lazy person's stairs?
37 Trigger man?
42 Deciphered
46 It can be constricting
47 Search with the hands
49 Figure of speech
50 Jaguar or Mustang
51 Golden deity, say
52 Clock chime, e.g.
54 What a donkey gets at a children's party
55 Commedia dell'___
56 Trash bag brand
57 Musical free-for-all
59 ___ kwon do

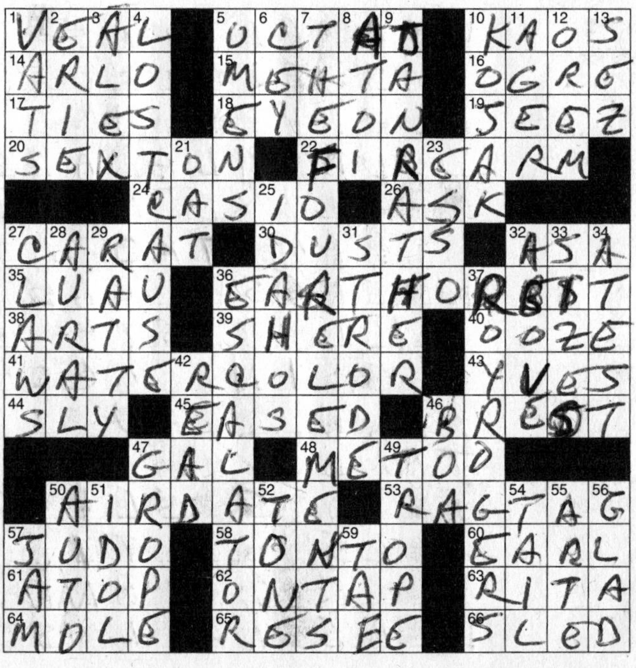

by Barry Boone

8

ACROSS
1 Sci-fi's "Doctor ___"
4 PG or R
10 From the start
14 Suffers from
15 "The Tempest" king
16 "Later"
17 Like many planetary orbits
19 Clarinet type
20 Ebony, e.g.
21 Like
22 Ranch visitor
24 Uneaten part of an apple
26 Long March participants
29 Airer of Congressional proceedings
32 Bout stopper, for short
34 Far from wimpy
35 Question posed by a 1987 children's best seller
38 Fighter for Jeff Davis
39 Western pal
40 Sample
41 Open widely
42 Old spy org.
43 This puzzle's answer to 35-Across (spelled out four times)
45 Pub serving
47 A, in Austria
48 Composer Camille Saint-___
49 Indian oven
51 It turns the tide
53 Commotions
54 Equinox mo.
55 Bargain
59 Bargain event
61 Building seen on a nickel
64 Moselle tributary
65 French satellite launcher
66 West of "My Little Chickadee"
67 Gum globs
68 City with a view of Vesuvius
69 Do zigzags, maybe

DOWN
1 "That was close!"
2 Symbol of sanctity
3 Nobel Institute city
4 Grammy category
5 Rite site
6 Light perfume
7 Pizarro foe
8 Code-cracking org.
9 Israel's Meir
10 Maine's ___ National Park
11 1990s–2000s sitcom shrink
12 Absorb, as a loss
13 Wine and dine
18 It may be swiped
23 Man, in 68-Across
25 Canadian "loonie" denomination
26 Material used in casting
27 It's "mightier," in a saying
28 Gets over drunkenness, with "up"
29 Breakfast cereal pioneer
30 Cascades peak
31 Purchase of one who's looking for love
33 Whole-grain cereal brand
36 RR stop
37 Boxing Day mo.
41 Starbucks size
43 Langston Hughes poem
44 Bear, in Bolivia
46 Jersey parts?
50 Ottoman Turk leader
52 Speak one's mind
54 Salon sound
56 "Slippery" trees
57 Wings: Lat.
58 MGM mogul Marcus
59 Phila.-to-Miami dir.
60 Tow-providing org.
62 ". . . man ___ mouse?"
63 These, in Tours

by Pete Muller

9

ACROSS

1 50%
5 Goya's "The Naked ___"
9 Pet adoption org.
13 Jai ___
14 Yale of Yale University
16 Where a horseshoe goes
17 *Sightseer's guide
19 Plus
20 Passover meals
21 One of the U.S. Virgin Islands
23 Hooded jacket
26 Variety
27 1950, on a cornerstone
30 *Creation made with a bucket and shovel
35 "Are you in ___?"
37 Stinks to high heaven
38 D.D.E.'s political rival
39 Spanish wine beverage
41 Has high hopes
43 CPR provider
44 Shenanigan
46 Mall unit
47 *One who puts the pedal to the metal
50 River of Hades
51 Opposite of paleo-
52 ___ Gay (W.W. II bomber)
54 Quits yapping
58 British society magazine
62 Arizona tribe
63 *The worst player wins it
66 Cupid
67 Longtime Yankees skipper
68 Big do
69 Here today, ___ tomorrow
70 Saucy
71 "Split" soup ingredients

DOWN

1 They may be thrown into the ring
2 Skin soother
3 Praise
4 *Hose company hookup
5 Gentlemen: Abbr.
6 PC key
7 Beam in a bar?
8 Solvers' shouts
9 Predatory types
10 Ralph Lauren label
11 Mozart's "___ Fan Tutte"
12 Crazy like ___
15 Slight improvements in business activity
18 Songwriter Gershwin
22 Necklace fasteners
24 Sport in which belts are awarded
25 "Wheel of Fortune" purchase
27 Grandma ___, American folk artist
28 Muscle malady
29 Three-card scam
31 Church official
32 Fortuneteller's card
33 Suspicious
34 Beloved of Elizabeth I
36 Swaps
40 Iffy
42 Warning cry . . . or a hint to the beginnings of the answers to the five starred clues
45 "___ Mine" (Beatles song)
48 Whole
49 "Maybe later"
53 Once around the track
54 Retro cut
55 ___ sapiens
56 Second word in many a fairy tale
57 Inside info
59 Long, long sentence
60 Cornell of Cornell University
61 Vintage vehicles
64 Valuable rocks
65 "Man, it's cold!"

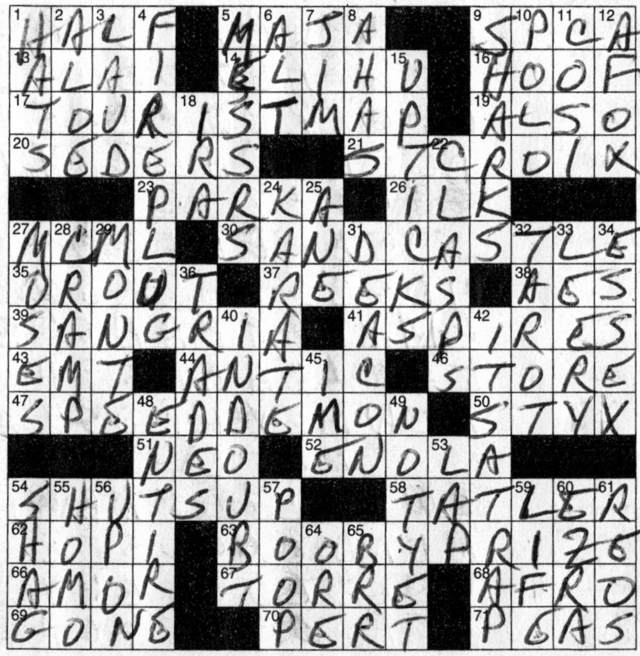

by Paula Gamache

10

ACROSS

1 Sportswriters' pick, for short
4 Serves at a restaurant
11 Masseur's workplace
14 "Look at that!"
15 Pennsylvania railroad city
16 Proof-ending abbr.
17 Oklahoma Indian
18 18th-century Parisian design
20 Scout's doing
22 Flyers' org.
23 Ocean motions
24 Joan at Woodstock
26 Slanty type: Abbr.
28 Beef cut
34 Charlton Heston role of 1956
35 Missouri river
36 Classic Jaguar
37 Holds the title to
38 ___ fatty acid
39 Board game turn
40 "___ Beso" (1962 hit)
41 Verbal flourishes
42 "The Republic" philosopher
43 Aggies' home
46 Rock's Clapton
47 Reagan's "evil empire"
48 1940s computer
51 The "one" of a one-two
53 Bumpkin
56 Surprises for buyers . . . or what 18-, 28- and 43-Across contain
60 ___ Ben Canaan of "Exodus"
61 Luau instrument, informally
62 In an imprecise way
63 Bronzed, at the beach
64 Govt. narcotics watchdog
65 Heavenly gateman
66 Silly Putty container

DOWN

1 State of mind
2 Privilege of those 18 and over
3 "Poetry Man" singer
4 Realm of Ares
5 Mourning of the N.B.A.
6 Prickly heat symptom
7 Shed item
8 Part of Ascap: Abbr.
9 "The Plastic ___ Band—Live Peace in Toronto 1969" (1970 album)
10 Tennis great Ilie
11 3 ft. by 3 ft.
12 Old Cosmos great
13 Sidewalk stand quaffs
19 Arcade flub
21 Broad valleys
25 Ambulance letters
26 Argumentative comeback
27 Glad rags
28 Use a divining rod
29 Kind of skiing
30 Violinist Stern
31 American in Paris, e.g.
32 "Go fly ___!"
33 Lotto relative
34 Big name in faucets
38 It's hailed by city dwellers
39 Web address punctuation
41 Bygone Toyotas
42 Qt. halves
44 Honey drink
45 Understated
48 Israel's Barak
49 Greek goddess of victory
50 Something to think about
51 "No way, ___!"
52 Play ___ (enjoy some tennis)
54 Mountain climber's grip
55 Word before snake or crab
57 "Just the opposite!"
58 Whistle blower, at times
59 Neighbor of Turk.

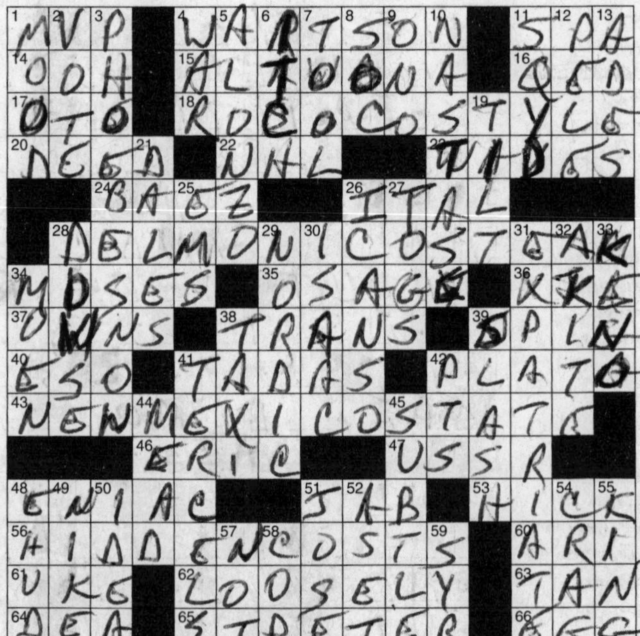

by Barry C. Silk

11

ACROSS

1 Hullabaloos
5 Wood for a model plane
10 Where eggs are laid
14 ___ I.R.A. (investment)
15 Arctic ___
16 Poison ivy symptom
17 Voice below soprano
18 Follow persistently, as a celebrity
19 One G
20 1960s weather song by Peter, Paul and Mary
23 Sacagawea dollar and others
24 Cuts into cubes
25 Secret matters
28 Wrigglers, to a fisherman
30 Co. honchos
31 Viewpoint
33 Star pitcher
36 1960s weather song by the Beatles
40 Bull or cow in the forest
41 Openly declares
42 Encircle
43 Dateless
44 Animals with brown summer fur
46 Clear jelly used as a garnish
49 "___ Gavotte," "My Fair Lady" tune
51 1960s weather song by the Cascades
57 Rani raiment
58 Prospero's servant in "The Tempest"
59 Mallorca or Menorca, por ejemplo
60 Red sky in the morning, e.g.
61 New Orleans's Vieux ___
62 Fur trader's fur
63 Eliot of the Untouchables
64 "To ___ sleep, perchance to dream": Hamlet
65 Back talk

DOWN

1 Qatari, e.g.
2 Barbie or Ken
3 Director Preminger
4 Cabinet for displaying wares
5 Neighbor of Croatia
6 Be part of, as a play
7 Isn't quite vertical
8 "S" shaker
9 Egyptian symbol of life
10 Lamebrain
11 Body of moral principles
12 British biscuit
13 Falling sounds
21 Charged particle
22 Archie's "dingbat"
25 Have rheumatic pains
26 Predigital film part
27 Bottle part that goes "pop!"
28 Voice below baritone
29 Six-legged worker
31 Cause of some urban coughs
32 "Ben-Hur" author Wallace
33 Home to more than half the world's population
34 Terse to the point of rudeness
35 Termini
37 Fish that's no longer in the sea
38 Eggs
39 Self-aggrandizing acts
43 Some '60s protests
44 Carry, slangily
45 Place for a Dr. Scholl's pad
46 Criminal burning
47 Humiliation
48 Combustible funeral structures
49 Burning
50 Cubic meter
52 Alternatives to PCs
53 Like traditional epic poetry
54 On the briny
55 Woes
56 Washington nine

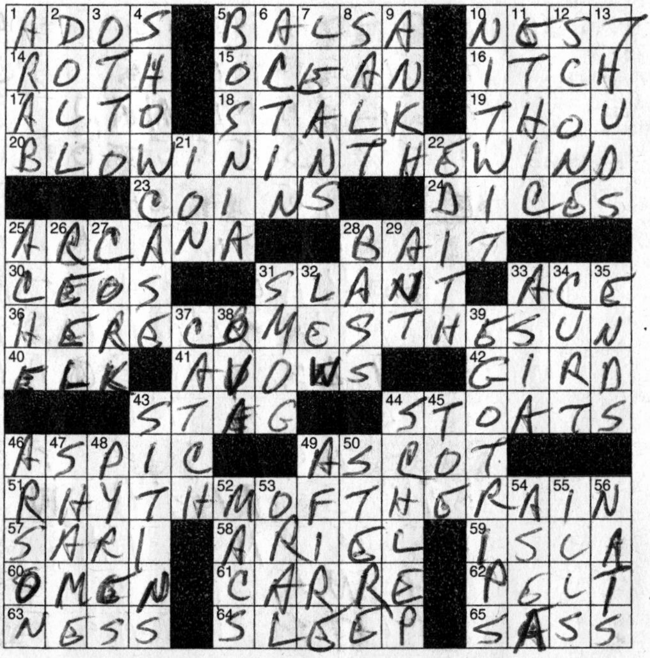

by Ronald J. and Nancy J. Byron

12

ACROSS

1 Bride's title
4 Cry of success
9 Sudden influx
14 It keeps going and going . . .
15 Express one's point of view
16 Put to rest
17 In the style of
18 Furniture within easy walking distance of the kitchen
20 Actor Mos ___
21 Takes care of
22 Jabbers
23 Give off
25 Beer ingredients
27 Start
31 Show of lowbrow taste
35 Show signs of an impending storm
39 Chevy S.U.V.
40 Pimpernel or prairie clover
41 ___ colony
43 Cheer competitor
44 Quick on one's feet
46 Headed straight down
48 Popular thesaurus
50 African heavyweight, for short
51 Throb
53 Perennial teenage feeling
57 Overly self-assured
60 Popular place
64 Consumed
65 Invitation info . . . or two alternate endings for the starts of the answers to 18-Across, 10-Down and 24-Down
67 X
68 Going gray
69 Paradise for the parched
70 Feedbag bit
71 Some tartan garments
72 Lawman Earp
73 Apt. units

DOWN

1 Union general at Gettysburg
2 Geneva-based watchmaker
3 Major muddle
4 Much-needed help
5 Early Ron Howard role
6 Fork prong
7 Alehouses
8 Canines, e.g.
9 Precollege exam
10 Popular Sony product
11 Jessica of "Fantastic Four"
12 It's cheap, proverbially
13 Ogles
19 Corner piece
24 Spy who lives dangerously
26 Peach stone
28 Soak (up)
29 Tied, as a score
30 Pavarotti, for one
32 Weapon in a gang fight
33 What a programmer writes
34 Pay attention to
35 Blacken
36 Brand of blocks
37 Not a dup.
38 Done without due consideration
42 Island garland
45 List ender
47 Procedure in a paternity suit
49 It's usually over a foot
52 Give, as a grant
54 University of Florida mascot
55 Heating choice
56 Some desert dwellings
57 Mt. Rushmore's locale: Abbr.
58 Trio in a Christmas story
59 Electric or water co.
61 Dog command
62 Site of some Galileo experiments
63 Leave out
66 Lawyers in cabinets: Abbr.

by Steven Ginzburg

ACROSS

1 Annual sleigh driver
6 Walk like an expectant dad
10 Summit
14 Martian, e.g.
15 "Yeah, right"
16 Radar sign
17 Words to a fourth runner-up
20 R.B.I. or H.R.
21 Angers
22 "Casablanca" star, informally
23 Its symbol is Sn
25 Not him
26 Words to a third runner-up
34 Latin dance
35 Push out of bed
36 Pi's follower
37 Swiss artist Paul
38 Height's companion
39 Jack who pioneered late-night talk
40 Un : France :: ___ : Germany
41 Irked
42 Alice's cake instruction
43 Words to a second runner-up
46 Finish up
47 Chicago transports
48 Norse myths, e.g.
51 Warmth
54 Gave temporarily
58 Words to a first runner-up
61 Suffix with million
62 Florence's river
63 Ahead by a point
64 Borscht vegetable
65 Lawyer Dershowitz
66 Op-Ed piece

DOWN

1 Tools with teeth
2 Disembarked
3 One of Columbus's ships
4 Science lab glassware
5 Year, in Madrid
6 Where ships dock
7 ___-bodied
8 Corp. kingpins
9 Martians, e.g., for short
10 What paper towels do
11 What paper towels do to a toilet
12 "La Bohème" soprano
13 Fencing sword
18 Skirt that exposes a lot of thigh
19 Film critic Roger
24 Boise's state: Abbr.
25 Word to a crying child
26 New Haven collegian
27 Signs for good or ill
28 Dentist's tool
29 Call in the Alps
30 Surpass
31 Poet's Muse
32 Killer whale that does tricks
33 Went 80, say
34 Distort, as data
38 Untamed
39 Salary indicators
41 Dentist's direction
42 Electric fish
44 Cups, saucers, sugar bowl, etc.
45 Presidential prerogative
48 Picket line crosser
49 "I cannot tell ___"
50 Al of "An Inconvenient Truth"
51 Throw
52 Sicilian volcano
53 Ever and ___
55 Inflated selves
56 "Peter Pan" dog
57 Deuce topper, in cards
59 Sheep's bleat
60 Actor's prompt

by Andrea Carla Michaels and Patrick Blindauer

14

ACROSS

1 Give a heads-up
5 Prefix with -syncratic
9 Valuable violin
14 Coup d'___
15 Birth place
16 French-speaking African nation
17 Hotel offering
19 Asteroid's path
20 Number of coins in the Fontana di Trevi?
21 Bow-taking occasion
23 In an obvious way
25 Early sixth-century year
26 Charisse of "Singin' in the Rain"
27 Blown away by
32 "Eso ___" (Paul Anka hit)
35 Love, Italian-style
36 Pal of Tarzan
37 Poker face
41 Mathematical proof letters
42 Novelist Zola
43 Armchair athlete's channel
44 In a calm way
46 Grier of "Jackie Brown"
48 Devoured
49 Dress store section
53 Cinema offering
58 Final: Abbr.
59 Like some committees
60 Flintlock need
62 Actress Aimée
63 Earth sci.
64 With "and" and 47-Down, Lawrence Welk's intro
65 Like ground around a tree
66 "Coffee, Tea ___?"
67 Something you can do to the starts of 17-, 21-, 37-, 53- and 60-Across

DOWN

1 Internet-on-the-tube company, formerly
2 Pong maker
3 Motel posting
4 To the ___ degree
5 "If asked, yes"
6 Bride's worldly possessions
7 "Since ___ You Baby" (1956 hit)
8 Syllables before "di" or "da" in a Beatles song
9 Has a tough time deciding
10 Friend of Peppermint Patty
11 "Waterloo" pop group
12 Slave away
13 Part of I.S.B.N.: Abbr.
18 Frozen dessert chain
22 Start of a challenge
24 Desktop graphic
27 Adequately, and then some
28 Seconds and then thirds
29 Place for a lectern
30 Each
31 Neighbor of 38-Down: Abbr.
32 Patio parties, briefly
33 General Robt. ___
34 ___ City (Baghdad district)
35 Leaf-to-branch angle
38 Home of Mammoth Cave
39 Arab chieftain: Var.
40 Teamster's rig
45 Have dinner in a restaurant
46 Us Weekly rival
47 See 64-Across
49 ___ Penh, Cambodia
50 Henry VIII's house
51 Jimmy Dorsey's "Maria ___"
52 Scatter, as seed
53 Jack who quipped "A funny thing happened to my mother one day: Me"
54 Fig. on a driver's license
55 When repeated, a train sound
56 Frozen waffle brand
57 Litigious sort
61 Roll of dough

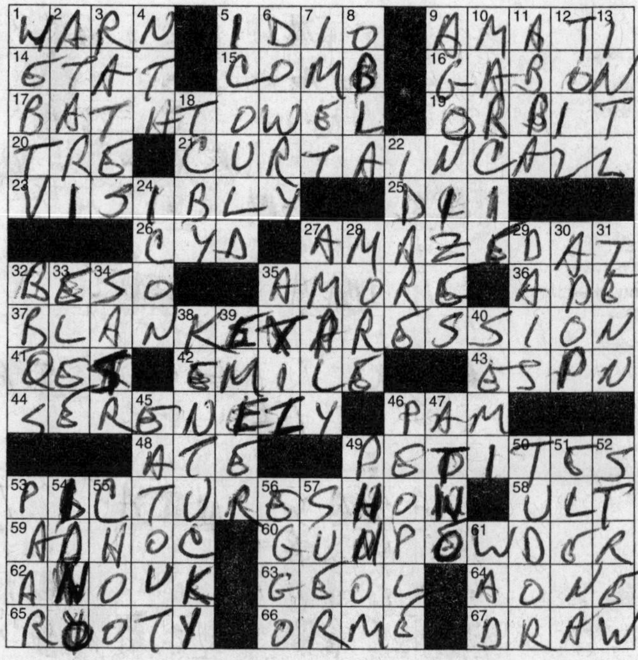

by Barry C. Silk

15

ACROSS
1 Like students in the Head Start program
5 Nonplayer's spot in the dugout
10 "Out!" or "Safe!"
14 Sharpen, as a knife
15 Meat-contaminating bacteria
16 Double Stuf cookie
17 British pop group with a repetitive name
19 This-and-that dish
20 ___ quo
21 Reagan antimissile plan, for short
23 Geller who claims paranormal ability
24 The Lord
25 Kurdistan city on the Tigris
28 Traveler's route
31 Pillages
32 ___ Francisco
33 Termination
34 Filming site
35 On-ramp
42 Gratuity
43 Nipper the dog's company
44 "Now I get it!"
45 Mark who was a swimming phenom at the 1972 Olympics
48 Lipton employee
51 Welch's soft drink
53 ___ polloi
54 Dangler on an item for sale
55 Pen point
56 Signify
59 Spanish artist Joan
61 Unexpected wallet fattener . . . and what the circled words are
64 Far from land
65 Cavaradossi's love in a Puccini opera
66 Few and far between
67 Mock
68 Tale
69 Donations for the poor

DOWN
1 Grad school achievements
2 Defeat decisively
3 Maddening
4 Buster on the silent screen
5 Mattress sites
6 Bygone French coin
7 ". . . ___ a lender be"
8 Chic
9 Worshiper of Brahma
10 Trig ratio: Abbr.
11 Conductor Toscanini
12 Regard with lust
13 Reasons for special ed
18 Like the upper half of the Venus de Milo
22 In worse health
25 Umpteen
26 Chose from the menu, say
27 Smidgen
28 Sort of: Suffix
29 Mai ___ (rum cocktail)
30 Harvest
34 Rebounds or assists
36 URL starter
37 Shrink from age
38 March Madness org.
39 Not local or state
40 Fighter with Fidel
41 Audiologist's concern
45 High-ranking noncom
46 Kudos
47 "That's my opinion, too"
48 As well
49 "Uh, excuse me"
50 Mexican state bordering Arizona
52 Looks (through), as for information
56 June 6, 1944
57 Six years, for a senator
58 Peepers
60 Crew implement
62 Support grp. for the troops
63 Big maker of checkout devices

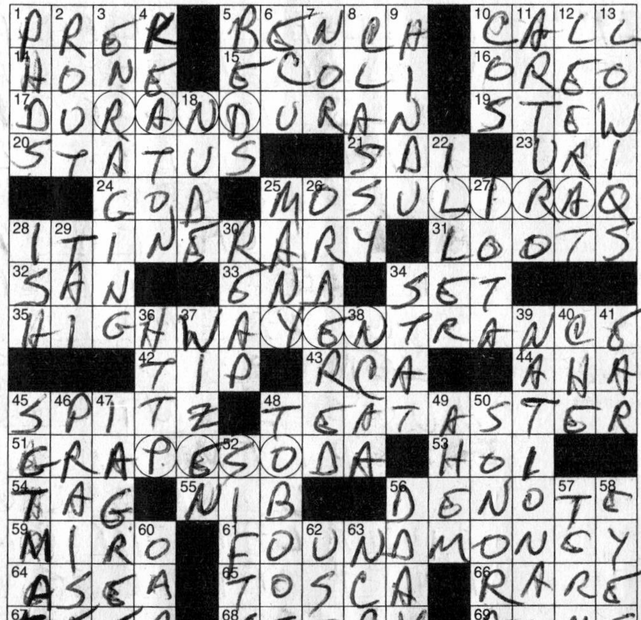

by Lynn Lempel

16

ACROSS

1 Kansas City university formerly known as College of Saint Teresa
6 Prefix with conference
10 Stds. important to the health-conscious
14 Gore who wrote "Lincoln" and "1876"
15 Eddie's character in "Beverly Hills Cop"
16 Commercial prefix with méxico
17 Retired general?
20 Surgeon's order
21 Speaker's place
22 Antlered animal
23 Part of the mailing address to Oral Roberts University
25 Field for Dem Bums
28 Was loud
31 Poetic work by Tennyson
32 Old cracker brand
35 University wall covering
36 Stringy
37 Late nobleman?
41 Grades 1–6: Abbr.
42 That: Sp.
43 "The Thin Man" terrier
44 Glass-encased item in "Beauty and the Beast"
45 Former Seattle team, for short
48 Residue locale
50 Set one's sights
55 Unit a little longer than an arm's length
56 Chest muscles, for short
58 "The Time Machine" race
59 Carillon call?
63 Groening who created "The Simpsons"
64 Together, in music
65 Egyptian peninsula
66 Sit (for)
67 Greek letters that look like pitchforks
68 Seven-year stretch

DOWN

1 "Stop!" at sea
2 Objets d'art
3 Unimprovable
4 Cobblers' forms
5 Optional hwy. route
6 1970s Japanese P.M. Kakuei ___
7 W.W. II vet, e.g.
8 A majority of August births
9 Tolkien creature
10 Horse-racing devotees, slangily
11 Dressed to the nines
12 "___ you happy now?"
13 Sisters' org.
18 Hero to many
19 Library Lovers' Mo.
24 "___ Ben Adhem" (Leigh Hunt poem)
25 Big name in ice cream
26 Impatient sort
27 Done with a wink
29 Wisconsin town where the Republican Party was born
30 "Little" Stowe character
32 Signs of goodness
33 Giant glaciers
34 Catcher's location
38 Comfy spot
39 General on Chinese menus
40 Hoeing the garden, e.g.
41 Chronology segment
46 Urges
47 Word in many Perry Mason titles
49 "___ say!"
51 Fear-inspiring
52 How hermits like to be
53 Des Moinesian or Davenporter
54 Modest dresses
56 Opium poppies have them
57 Decorative sewing kit
59 Hi-fi component
60 Kung ___ chicken
61 Access, as a resource
62 23-Across winter setting: Abbr.

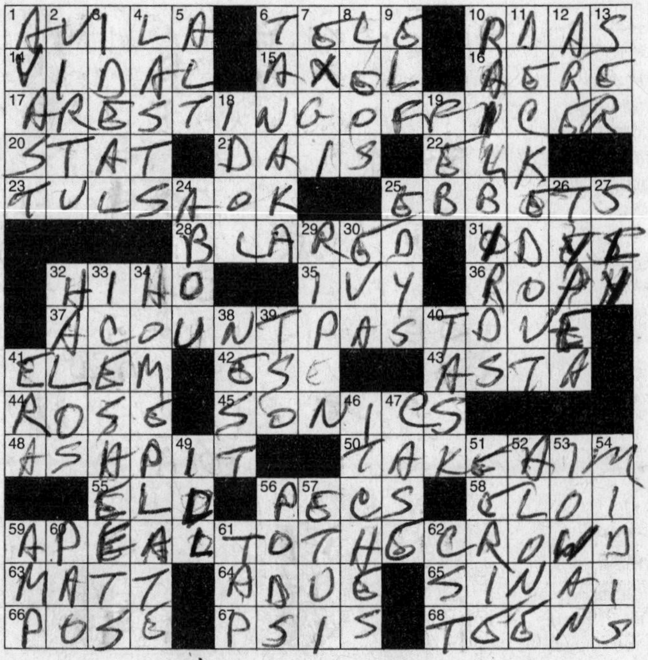

by Ken Bessette

17

ACROSS

1 Mount ___, Ten Commandments locale
6 Normandy invasion town
10 Sweat opening
14 Writer Nin
15 Cupid
16 Genesis son
17 Antiterrorism legislation of 2001
19 Gun blast
20 Proverbial saver of nine, with "a"
22 Snake or alligator
25 Playful knuckle-rub
26 Eggs ___ easy
27 Suck-up
30 Pants part
31 Kentucky's ___ College
33 Try to strike
35 "My Cousin Vinny" Oscar winner
39 Word with Asia or Ursa
40 Ultimately become
43 Necessity: Abbr.
46 "Keep it simple, ___"
49 Earthen pot
50 Bet on a one-two finish
52 Dreamlike
54 Classic battles between the Giants and Dodgers, e.g.
57 "Beetle Bailey" bulldog
58 1986 world champion American figure skater
62 Pants part
63 "The Last Tycoon" director Kazan
64 "I was at a movie theater when it happened," e.g.
65 Highlands Gaelic
66 What gears do
67 Tyson or Holyfield

DOWN

1 Maple syrup source
2 Bull ___ china shop
3 Turner who led a revolt
4 Wind tunnel wind
5 "Lord, ___?" (Last Supper query)
6 Certain sofa
7 ___ II razor
8 ___ Ness monster
9 Recurring melodic phrase
10 Green Italian sauce
11 Like angels we have heard?
12 Dormmate
13 Think the world of
18 Greasy
21 Unbranded
22 Steal from
23 December 24, e.g.
24 Salon job
28 On the ball or on the dot
29 Sch. in Cambridge, Mass.
32 Record label for the Kinks and the Grateful Dead
34 Pavarotti performance
36 Working together
37 Trivial amount
38 Not doing anything
41 Diminutive suffix
42 Buddy
43 Tranquillity
44 New Hampshire prep school
45 Airline with a kangaroo logo
47 Book after Song of Solomon
48 It'll bring a tear to your eye
51 Equivalent of 10 sawbucks
53 Place to "dry out"
55 The "T" of TV
56 Diamond stats
59 Blend
60 President Lincoln
61 Madam's partner

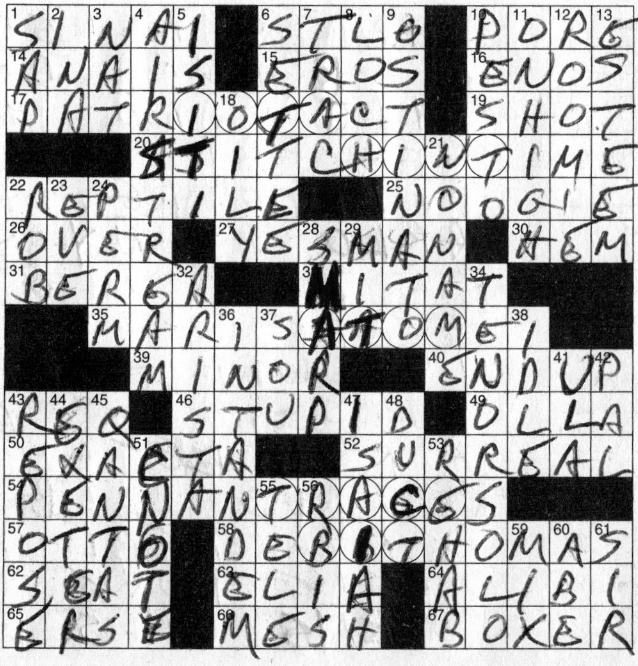

by Bob Klahn

18

ACROSS

1 Option for a H.S. dropout
4 Yaks
8 Ford misstep
13 Dispense, as milk
14 Surrounding glow
15 Throw water on
16 Big name in athletic shoes
18 Still asleep
19 Site of a tkt. booth
20 J. Edgar Hoover's org.
21 "Enough, you're killing me!"
22 Prince
28 Singer Guthrie
29 Electronics giant
30 Reader of omens
31 Supermodel Carol
34 Defendant's plea, for short
36 Neither's partner
37 End of a Napoleonic palindrome
40 Mensa figs.
42 "Wiseguy" actor Ken
43 Mediterranean, for one
44 Boring routines
46 Laments
48 Rock's Better Than ___
52 Black-and-tan purebred
56 Bush's "___ of evil"
57 Priestly vestment
58 Sgt. or cpl.
59 Three-card con
61 Carrier with a shamrock logo
64 Slang
65 Bird with an olive branch
66 Zaire's Mobutu ___ Seko
67 "Fargo" brothers
68 Singles
69 "What ___ the chances?"

DOWN

1 Possible result of iodine deficiency
2 Provider of a pass abroad
3 Basketball's Erving, familiarly
4 Greta of "Anna Christie," 1930
5 I.R.S. scares
6 Article under a blouse
7 ___ Diego
8 Mrs. Woodrow Wilson
9 Patrons of the arts, perhaps
10 Court summons
11 Chicago-to-Pittsburgh dir.
12 Commanded
13 Turkish pooh-bah
17 Frequently, to a poet
21 Modes
23 Engine sound
24 Puff the Magic Dragon's frolicking place
25 Sufficient, for Shakespeare
26 Prefix with con
27 "To ___ is human . . ."
32 Dr. Kildare player Ayres
33 Pageant toppers
35 Corrida cry
37 Alienate
38 Synagogue
39 1930s heavyweight champ Max
40 Tax planner's plan, for short
41 On the ___ vive
45 Church groundskeeper
47 Go hungry
49 Clever comeback
50 Disqualify, as a potential juror
51 Got up from sleeping
53 Removes excess poundage
54 Monthly fashion issues
55 Category in which the single-season record is 191
59 Bub
60 Gold, in Guadalupe
61 Hubbub
62 Long, long time
63 Code-crackers' org.

by Andrea Carla Michaels

19

ACROSS

1 New ___, India
6 Massachusetts vacation spot, with "the"
10 "Yeah, sure!"
14 Like the outfield walls at Wrigley Field
15 Downwind, to a sailor
16 Musical finale
17 Red Sox stadium
19 Frozen waffle brand
20 Actor Omar
21 Precious Chinese carvings
22 Look through the cross hairs
25 ". . . ___ quit!"
26 Alpha's opposite
28 New York City's ___ Island
30 Makes believe
33 Peels, as an apple
34 Copper/zinc alloy
35 Cockney's residence
36 "Anything ___?"
37 "To Autumn" poet
38 Roman poet who wrote the "Metamorphoses"
39 Fed. biomedical research agency
40 "O Come, ___ Faithful"
41 Packing string
42 Watergate and Irangate
44 Bitterness
45 Everest or Kilimanjaro
46 Diving seabird
47 College credit units: Abbr.
48 Classic Alan Ladd western
50 Lacking any guarantee of being paid
53 Score the 3 in a 4-3 game
54 Seaside community NE of Boston
58 Natural balm
59 Actress Rowlands
60 House of Henry VII and Henry VIII
61 Fairy's stick
62 Stepped (on)
63 "Tosca" or "Thaïs"

DOWN

1 "What's the ___?" ("So what?")
2 Holiday preceder
3 China's ___ Yutang
4 Cuts with an ax
5 Potatoes from the Northwest
6 Blue Grotto's island
7 Jai ___
8 Make holes in, as for ease of tearing
9 Hair-raising cry
10 Period ending about 9000 B.C.
11 Peter who directed "The Last Picture Show"
12 Periphery
13 New Mexico city or county
18 A knitter might have a ball with it
21 "Cool your ___!"
22 Forest quakers
23 Like right-slanting type
24 "The Goodbye Girl" actress
27 Cafeteria, to a soldier
29 Football kicker's aid
30 Says grace, e.g.
31 Key of Beethoven's Ninth
32 Passover meals
34 Carillon site
37 Group investigated in "Mississippi Burning"
38 Have title to
40 Together, in music
41 Likes immediately
43 "Thanks, but I'm O.K."
44 Coach Adolph in the Basketball Hall of Fame
46 Comparable to a wet hen?
48 Picnic side dish
49 Spanish greeting
51 One billionth: Prefix
52 Medium bra size
54 "___ Pepper's Lonely Hearts Club Band"
55 "To Autumn," e.g.
56 Rocky peak
57 ___ la la

by Ed Early

20

1102

ACROSS

1 Music played by Ravi Shankar at Woodstock
5 "There it is!"
10 Disconcert
14 Historic periods
15 Pianist Claudio
16 "I'll get right ___!"
17 Use of a company car, e.g.
18 Wherewithal
19 Emulates Lil' Kim or Lil Wayne
20 Fairy tale's start
23 Greeted, with "to"
24 Destination for a W-2
25 Thor Heyerdahl craft
28 That, to Tomás
29 "Exodus" author
32 "Brrrr!"
34 Grandpa's start
36 Plus
39 Adlai's opponent in '52 and '56
40 Rod's partner
41 Mom's start
46 "The Count of Monte ___"
47 Blueprint detail
48 Broadway's Hagen
51 Cooke who sang "You Send Me"
52 Indianapolis-to-New Orleans dir.
54 Like some patches
56 Legend's start
60 Balletic leap
62 Location of a starry belt
63 Cole Porter's "Well, Did You ___?"
64 Lab medium
65 Quitter's cry
66 It produces more than 20 billion bricks annually
67 Popular Microsoft product
68 Expressed disapproval
69 White blanket

DOWN

1 Period of rest
2 Gladiators' locales
3 Ice cream flavor Cherry ___
4 Made an inquiry
5 Anne Rice's Lestat, for one
6 Cookie with a floral design on it
7 Ahmadinejad's land
8 Island veranda
9 Where Schwarzenegger was born
10 W-2, e.g.
11 Bacterium that doesn't need oxygen
12 Address ending, informally
13 Some "Stargate SG-1" characters, in brief
21 Guttural refusal
22 Ideological beliefs
26 ___ vera
27 Pastoral composition
30 The G, W or B in G.W.B.
31 Followers of Guru Nanak
33 Grant in four Hitchcock films
34 Chinese cookers
35 Sob
36 Rudiments
37 Yuri's love in "Dr. Zhivago"
38 Curved saber
42 Start of a spider's description, in song
43 Barely beat
44 Condescended
45 Prefix with phobic
48 Not level
49 Trinidad's partner
50 Be that as it may
53 Gives a yellow flag
55 Law school newbies
57 Geek
58 Cafe proprietor in "Casablanca"
59 It's commonly filleted
60 Talk on and on, slangily
61 Sense of self

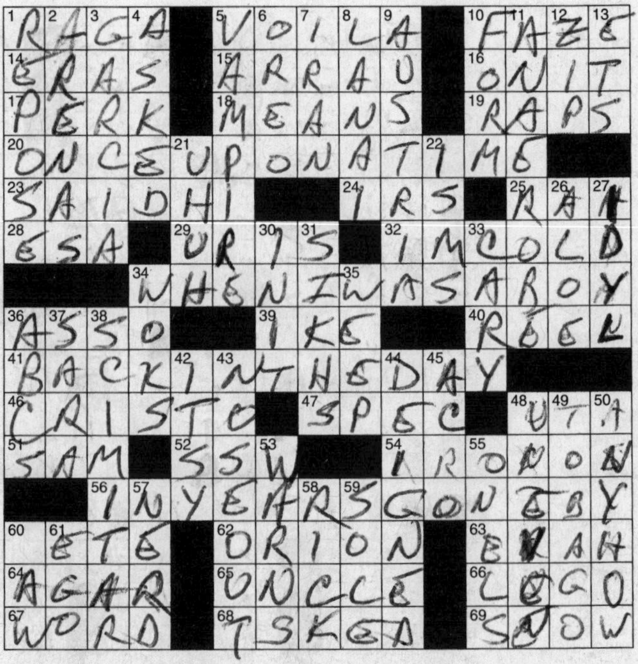

by Leonard Williams

1/18

ACROSS
1 Sword handles
6 Worker's due
10 Wood-shaping tool
14 "One for My Baby" composer Harold
15 Horse course
16 One of nine in golf
17 "Merry Christmas" to the French
19 Antique autos
20 Tipple
21 Winter melon
23 "Atlas Shrugged" author Rand
24 Shooters' grp.
26 Genie holders
29 "Merry Christmas" to Danes
33 Spar verbally
36 "I can only ___ much"
37 Sch. named for a televangelist
38 Life stories on film
40 Leak fixer
43 Toss in
44 Not e'en once
46 Inspiring sisters
47 "Merry Christmas" to Spaniards
51 "Lemon Tree" singer Lopez
52 Third after delta
53 "Pow!"
56 Federer and Nadal
59 Collected
62 Hgt.
64 "Merry Christmas" to Italians
66 Two capsules, perhaps
67 Terrier sounds
68 Animated ogre
69 Cold war superpower
70 Sectional, e.g.
71 Makeup maker Lauder

DOWN
1 Muslim pilgrim
2 Kitchen drawer?
3 Visit from the Blue Angels, maybe
4 Readying for a drive
5 Cold-shoulder
6 Hit the jackpot
7 Guacamole ingredient
8 Greek earth goddess
9 Architects' annexes
10 Car safety device
11 Prized positions
12 Menagerie
13 U.S.N.A. grad
18 TV's Warrior Princess
22 Thrilla in Manila boxer
25 It had a notable part in Exodus
27 Blender setting
28 Pronounces poorly
30 Waikiki welcome
31 Lively wit
32 Chat room chuckle
33 Sailor's behind
34 Bill tack-on
35 Piety
39 It has headquarters at N.Y.C.'s Time Warner Center
41 Thurman of "Dangerous Liaisons"
42 Spa treatments
45 Make balanced
48 "The nerve!"
49 Benzoyl peroxide target
50 "Rats!"
54 Split up
55 Knock-down-drag-out
57 Corp. recruits, often
58 Continental currency
60 Move gently
61 Apollo astronaut Slayton
62 Campus e-mail suffix
63 Acapulco article
65 Supersecretive intelligence org.

by Nancy Salomon

22

11 40
10m

ACROSS

1 Doorframe parts
6 Chinese-born American architect
11 Be a pugilist
14 Bide one's time for
15 Manicurists' concerns
16 Electrical unit
17 One who's always up for a good time
19 Coastal inlet
20 Out of bed
21 ___ Aviv
22 In the near future
23 Prefix with -lithic
24 ___ of students
26 President before D.D.E.
27 Background check for a lender
32 Jay-Z and Timbaland
35 Atop, poetically
36 ___ Speedwagon
37 Horizontally
38 Musical transitions
40 "What was ___ do?"
41 Bulls, rams and bucks
43 Goes to
44 Long, long sentence
47 "I know what you're thinking" claim
48 Mississippi's Trent
49 BlackBerry, e.g., in brief
52 Unretrievable
54 Illustration, for short
55 Husband of Isis
58 April 15 org.
59 Light hauler
61 Sgt., e.g.
62 Didn't go out for dinner
63 Gift recipient
64 Floppy rabbit feature
65 Issues an advisory
66 Edgar Bergen's Mortimer ___

DOWN

1 Where the Pokémon craze originated
2 Cognizant (of)
3 Nintendo brother
4 Kibbles 'n ___
5 Eyelid woe
6 Holiday ___
7 Drink that often comes with an umbrella
8 Olive stuffing
9 Airline to Ben-Gurion
10 Nantucket, e.g.: Abbr.
11 Bruce Springsteen's first hit
12 Akron's home
13 Marvel mutant superhero
18 Big name in fairy tales
22 Egyptian viper
25 Actor Harris and others
26 Regarding this point
27 TV's "___ Sharkey"
28 Send again
29 Place that often has picnic tables
30 Hollow-stemmed plant
31 Flip
32 Fence part
33 Play's start
34 "Nutty" role for Jerry Lewis
39 ___ Xers
42 Worker with genes or film
43 Bit of land in a river
45 Superlative suffix
46 Brenda Lee's "___ Around the Christmas Tree"
49 Trim, as branches
50 Kitchen gizmo
51 Questioned
52 Word that can follow the starts of 17-, 27-, 44- and 59-Across
53 Killer whale
54 Sandwich bread
56 Norms: Abbr.
57 Fe, to chemists
59 Furry foot
60 Little ___ (tots)

by Mark Sherwood

1152

ACROSS

1 Comment not to be taken seriously
5 ___ Marley's ghost in "A Christmas Carol"
10 Con game
14 Unwanted spots
15 Band together
16 Poi source
17 Response to a knock
19 29,035 ft., for Mt. Everest
20 Have a bawl
21 Designer label letters
22 Heap kudos on
24 "For instance . . ."
25 Empathize with
26 The important thing
31 A Chaplin
32 Sluggers' stats
33 Lhasa ___ (Tibetan dogs)
38 Doctor's query
41 Scattered about
42 Entre ___
43 Metropolitan ___
44 "Never!"
47 Some apartments
51 Uno + due
52 Apartment window sign
53 Kudrow of "Friends"
55 Mediterranean fruit
58 Both: Prefix
59 Discounter's pitch
62 Computer with an iSight camera
63 Have an ___ mystery
64 Plow pullers
65 Unit of force
66 Teammate of Snider and Hodges
67 Classic computer game set on a seemingly deserted island

DOWN

1 1975 Spielberg thriller
2 Eerie cave effect
3 One not associating with the likes of you?
4 Private eye, for short
5 Place to find auto parts
6 Have ___ with
7 Half of an E.P.A. mileage rating
8 Pony players' locale, in brief
9 Paging device
10 Incredible bargain
11 Where the San Andreas Fault is: Abbr.
12 "Ain't!" retort
13 Shaker's partner
18 Genesis patriarch
23 Convened again
24 "Can you believe this?" look
25 Come clean
26 Knocks the socks off
27 Alternative to a Twinkie
28 From the top
29 Steakhouse selections
30 Attach, in a way
34 Terrible twos, e.g.
35 Browse, as the Web
36 Sportscaster Hershiser
37 Hang around
39 Dickens's Drood
40 "Can I come out now?"
45 Armed conflict
46 Battleship shade
47 Sober
48 Rock opera with the song "Pinball Wizard"
49 Densely packed, in a way
50 Pour salt on, perhaps
53 Apollo's instrument
54 N.Y.S.E. debuts
55 Full of guile
56 Tees off
57 Fellow
60 Step on it
61 Soccer ___

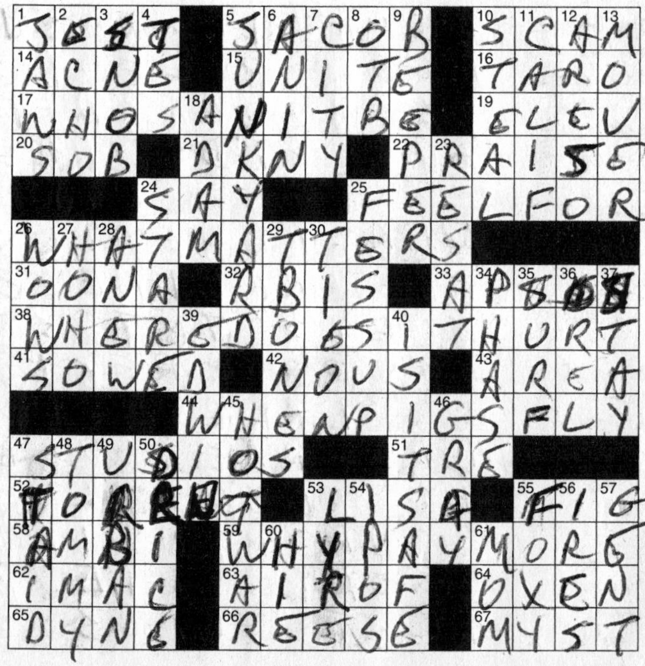

by Alan Arbesfeld

24

1152
1201

ACROSS
1 ___ mater
5 Letter-shaped structural piece
9 Lesser-played half of a 45
14 Elementary particle
15 Vex
16 Gucci alternative
17 Upstate New York city and spa
20 Remote areas
21 Imp
22 Head for
23 The boondocks
24 Honeymooners' destination
28 Alternative to .com or .edu
29 Fix, as brakes
30 Jacob's twin
34 Track events
36 Asian New Year
37 Leaves port
38 Bygone U.S. gas brand
39 Mother ___, 1979 Peace Nobelist
41 Napkin's place
42 Former president of Harvard
45 Kodak, Pentax and Nikon
48 The "L" in S.&L.
49 Is wild about
50 Mythical island that sank into the sea
54 Comic who played Robin Williams's son in "Mork & Mindy"
56 Auto route from Me. to Fla.
57 1930s migrant
58 Smell ___ (be suspicious)
59 Groups of spies
60 Fails to keep pace
61 Without: Fr.

DOWN
1 "I ___ sorry!"
2 Hawaiian cookout
3 Homeowners' burdens
4 Like clocks with hands
5 Shipment to a steel mill
6 Home of the Cowboys, familiarly
7 "Sad to say . . ."
8 ___ judicata
9 Spread out ungracefully
10 Isle of Man's locale
11 Rumba or samba
12 Mystery writer's award
13 Swiss city on the Rhine, old-style
18 Dwellers along the Volga
19 Working stiff
23 French city where Jules Verne was born
24 Alaskan city where the Iditarod ends
25 Angers
26 Raises or lowers a hem, say
27 Passionate
31 Time before talkies
32 Banned orchard spray
33 Letter carriers' grp.
35 Broad-minded
37 Pago Pago resident
39 Garbage
40 Besmirches
43 Mountain ridges
44 Powerful rays
45 Louisianan of French descent
46 Get ___ of one's own medicine
47 Pre-stereo recordings
50 Paul who sang "Put Your Head on My Shoulder"
51 Tiny branch
52 Tehran's home
53 Concordes, briefly
55 "You've got mail" co.

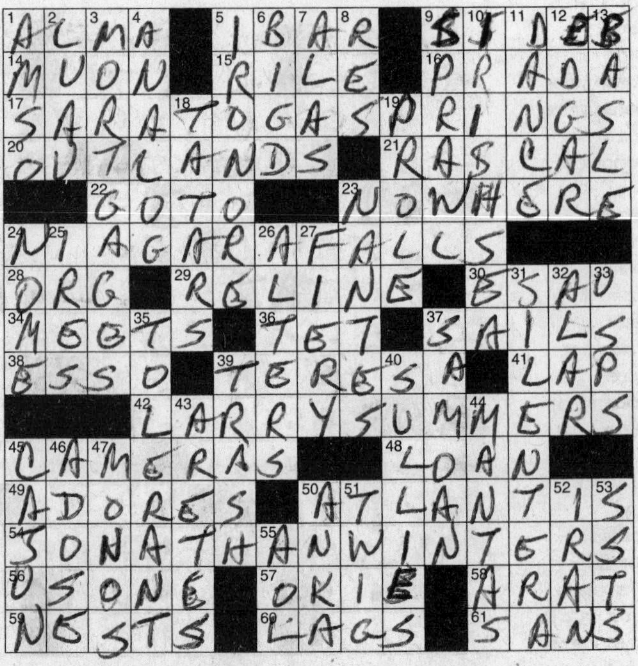

by Richard Chisholm

25

ACROSS

1 Like some petticoats
5 Own up (to)
10 Bank with significant deposits?
14 Award for "Hot L Baltimore"
15 Harness parts
16 Writer ___ Stanley Gardner
17 Teen's response to a parent's "No"
20 Somme summer
21 Greek war god
22 Novelist Joyce Carol ___
23 Blacken
24 Pumpkin pie ingredient
26 Outdated
29 Musical Count
30 "Encore!"
31 Forest in "As You Like It"
32 By way of
35 Teen's response to a parent's "No"
39&40 Change of government
41 1973 #1 hit "___ an American Band"
42 Basketball position
43 Gushed
45 Subject to legal damages
47 Like badly worn tires
48 Peter of "Casablanca"
49 "Howdy!"
50 Batman and Robin, e.g.
53 Teen's response to a parent's "No"
57 Window section
58 Power problem
59 Mideast V.I.P.
60 Narrow cut
61 Wheels for big wheels
62 Folk singer Seeger

DOWN

1 Ear or leaf feature
2 Be next to
3 Mention, as in a court opinion
4 To date
5 Couples' destination?
6 Prevent through intimidation
7 Pageant title
8 Country lodge
9 General on a Chinese menu
10 Malign
11 Steaming
12 Movie-set light
13 Plural suffix with auction or musket
18 "Aren't you the comedian?!"
19 Lugging
23 "Moonstruck" actress
24 Point from which there's nowhere to go but up
25 Depletes, with "up"
26 Meteor shooting across the sky, maybe
27 Aphrodite's domain
28 Sketched
29 Kennel club listing
31 Tennis great Agassi
32 Panorama
33 Memo phrase
34 Like some cheeses
36 "Absolutely!"
37 ___ surgeon
38 Had to hand it to?
42 January birthstone
43 What the teen wishes the parent would do instead
44 Land office map
45 Hometown-related
46 Tehran resident
47 "Ex-x-xactly!"
48 Kissers
49 Havoc
50 "It's your ___"
51 Military group
52 Nasty sort
54 Hi-speed connection
55 Non's opposite
56 With it, once

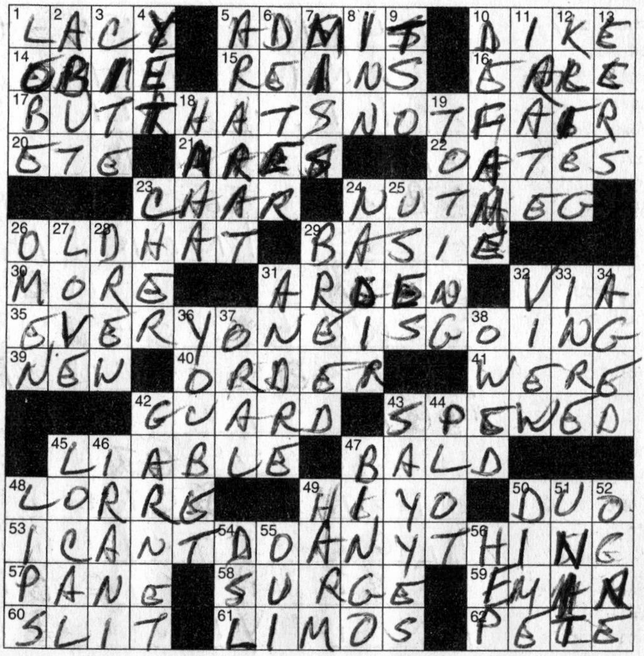

by Gail Grabowski

26

ACROSS

1 John ___, host of "America's Most Wanted"
6 "Jeopardy!" whiz Jennings
9 "Hey, you!"
13 ___ 2600 (classic video game console)
14 St. Louis landmark
15 Voice above a tenor
16 Appetizer with sweet and sour sauce
18 Gorilla watcher Fossey
19 Frightful female
20 Puccini heroine
21 Cheerful
22 Take turns
24 Dangler on a suitcase
26 Deadly long-tailed fish
28 Where you might get into hot water?
31 Schiaparelli of fashion
34 Cigarette substance
35 Interlocks
37 Bride's bounty
39 Meadow
41 Bird on birth announcement cards
42 Comes about
44 Wrigley's product
46 S.&L. conveniences
47 All U.S. senators until 1922
48 Monotonous voice
51 Birds flying in V's
53 Has confidence in
56 Beverly Sills and others
58 Young cod for dinner
60 F.D.R. job-creating measure: Abbr.
62 "Famous" cookie maker
63 Gangly guy
65 Fruit from a palm
66 "Don't hurt me!," e.g.
67 Straight up
68 Laid off, as workers
69 Wood in archery bows
70 Copenhageners, e.g.

DOWN

1 Do the laundry
2 Even, on the leaderboard
3 Slow, in symphonies
4 ___ Lanka
5 Merely suggest
6 Ray who created the McDonald's empire
7 Custardy dessert
8 Rink org.
9 City where Galileo taught
10 Goliath's undoing
11 Baseball's Musial
12 Broadway award
14 Weapons stash
17 "Oh, I see"
21 Eyelid nuisances
23 Romanov rulers
25 River blocker
27 One of the Allman Brothers
29 Straight-to-curly transformation, informally
30 Poses questions
31 Dutch city with a cheese market
32 Oral tradition
33 Make-or-break election bloc
36 Does' mates
38 Sí and oui
40 Home of the von Trapp family
43 Bro's sibling
45 Lamebrain
49 Get cozy
50 Prodded gently
52 Lessened, as pain
54 11- or 12-year-old
55 Rocket's realm
56 1920s art movement
57 Giant-screen theater
59 Backstage bunch
61 Tiny tunnelers
63 Mata Hari, for one
64 Top half of a bikini

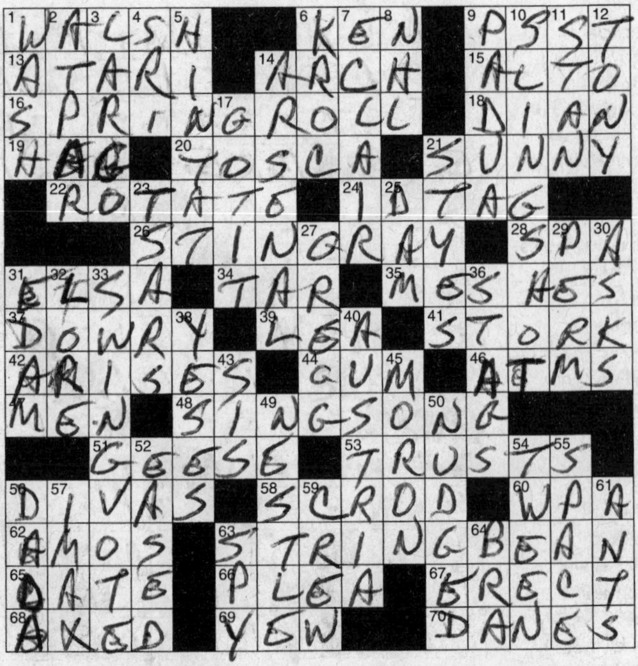

by Lynn Lempel

The answers at 17- and 51-Across and 11- and 24-Down can all be defined by the same missing three-letter word. What is it?

ACROSS

1 Keen-edged
6 Gave in
11 ___-a-cake
14 Chomping at the bit
15 Last Olds made
16 Corrida cheer
17 *See blurb*
19 Cooking spray brand
20 "When hell freezes over"
21 Grouch
23 Not exactly insightful
26 Gung-ho sort
27 Minty drinks
28 Greg's sitcom mate
30 Oklahoma Indians
31 Some earrings
32 Slugger's stat
35 Hershey confection
36 Pasta is loaded with them
37 Skier's transport
38 "I do"
39 Four-page sheet
40 An ex of the Donald
41 Martini garnishes
43 Shiny fabric
44 Regal fur
46 Brilliantly colored parrots
47 Actress Gaynor
48 Scarlett of Tara
50 "Evil Woman" band, for short
51 *See blurb*
57 Cornhusker State: Abbr.
58 Special talent
59 Fashionably old-fashioned
60 Batiking need
61 Doughboys
62 Thoroughly enjoy

DOWN

1 Trice, informally
2 "2001" computer
3 In the past
4 Counterpart of bus.
5 Engagement contracts, briefly
6 Cut up
7 "I cannot tell ___"
8 Zig or zag
9 Directional suffix
10 For whom Sandy Koufax pitched
11 *See blurb*
12 Texas shrine
13 Tantalize
18 Come clean, with "up"
22 Smash into
23 Belly button type
24 *See blurb*
25 Summer shirts
26 Nukes
27 Facetious
28 Day of "Pillow Talk"
29 Boxcar rider
31 In the pink
33 Farm bundles
34 Neighbor of Turkey
36 Place to moor
37 "Later"
39 Like a picky eater
40 Like much of Poe's work
42 Designer Claiborne
43 ___ Lee cakes
44 Make corrections to
45 Life of ___ (ease)
46 Some big trucks
48 Mideast sultanate
49 Bumpkin
52 ___ lark
53 Arthur of "The Golden Girls"
54 Hall-of-Famer Mel
55 Play about Capote
56 Toy with a string

by Alison Donald

28

12'47
56

ACROSS

1 Part of a molecule
5 Supply-and-demand subj.
9 Pepsi and RC
14 Prom night transportation
15 Furry tunneler
16 Face-to-face exams
17 Alda of "What Women Want"
18 Othello's false friend
19 White-plumed wader
20 Profanity, e.g.
23 2007 film "___ and the Real Girl"
24 "Bonanza" star Greene
25 Sit behind bars
28 Memorial designer Maya ___
29 Cowboy boot attachment
32 Madonna title role
33 Flies off the handle
35 Mail carrier's beat: Abbr.
36 1995 Woody Allen comedy
39 Number before "ignition . . . liftoff!"
40 Bank robber's job
41 Dressed to the ___
42 Arctic floater
44 Suffix with meth-
45 "No Exit" playwright
46 Becomes frayed
48 Hand protector
49 Classic "Jeopardy!" category
54 Henhouse perch
55 Earthenware jar
56 College in New Rochelle, N.Y.
57 From days of yore
58 Bring up, as children
59 Be certain about
60 Saltine brand
61 Home of the invaders in Wells's "The War of the Worlds"
62 Snaky swimmers

DOWN

1 Self-pitying cry
2 Pinball foul
3 Sharif of "Doctor Zhivago"
4 Monument carved from a single stone
5 Settler from a foreign land
6 Snowman's eyes
7 Olympic gymnast Korbut
8 Nighttime advertising sign, maybe
9 ___ de Lion, epithet for Richard I
10 Church hymn accompaniers
11 Easily read type
12 Away from the wind
13 Lander at J.F.K., once
21 Football's Broadway Joe
22 Dead duck
25 Brit's service discharge
26 Sheeplike
27 Golfer named A.P. Male Athlete of the Year four times
28 Senior moment, e.g.
30 Pure-and-simple
31 Witherspoon of "Walk the Line"
33 Cloudburst
34 Beethoven specialty
37 Have a hankering
38 Off-road two-wheeler
43 Gird oneself
45 Indian instruments
47 Prudential rival
48 Grinding tooth
49 Extremity of the earth
50 "Not guilty," for one
51 Companionless
52 Hydroxyl-carbon compound
53 Toothed tools
54 Peri Gilpin's "Frasier" role

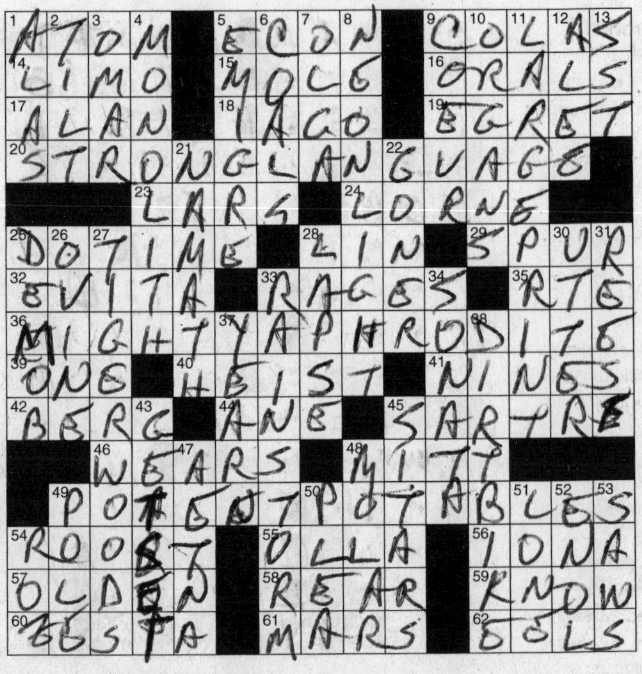

by Harvey Estes

ACROSS

1 In debt
6 Post-op locale
9 Bets build them
13 Workplace for some clowns
14 Melon exterior
16 Sign to heed
17 States confidently
18 Rice-shaped pasta
19 Late-night name
20 Number one #2?
22 Hunchbacked assistant
23 "All My ___ Live in Texas" (1987 #1 country hit)
24 Manorial worker
26 2 and 12, e.g., in dice
31 "I am such a dope!"
32 Bart's teacher, ___ Krabappel
33 Hen's home
35 Oslo is on one
39 Have-___ (poor people)
40 Traffic problem
42 Northamptonshire river
43 Yucky
45 Olympics blade
46 Toy with a cross frame
47 Dental problem calling for braces
49 Puts together hastily
51 Empty, as a stare
55 Baton Rouge sch.
56 Prefix with culture
57 Little woman?
63 Heist haul
64 Proceed slowly
65 Persian tongue
66 Cuzco native
67 Holding a grudge
68 "I surrender!"
69 Batik artist
70 In a funk
71 Manages to elude

DOWN

1 Like most folklore
2 Used a loom
3 Brainchild
4 Social misfit
5 Matthew or Mark
6 Hard porcelain
7 Magazine fig.
8 Loosen, as a parka
9 What a comedian might do before going onstage?
10 Alphabet ender
11 Carpentry joint part
12 Angry bull's sound
15 Apportioned, with "out"
21 Members of management
25 "___ Wiedersehen"
26 China's ___ Xiaoping
27 Dumpster emanation
28 Sermon preposition
29 Fish-shaped musical instrument?
30 Ivory, Coast and others
34 Made impossible
36 Alsace assents
37 Queue after Q
38 Tough to fathom
41 Most trivial
44 ___ Tomé
48 High-heel shoes
50 Really sorry
51 Not yet expired
52 Intense pain
53 Jim who sang "Time in a Bottle"
54 Missile sites
58 Ibsen's ___ Helmer
59 Hand, to Hernando
60 Rainbow shapes
61 Cruise stopover
62 Stamping tools

by Julie Ann Bowling

30

ACROSS

1 Clothing
5 It's arched above the eye
9 iPhone maker
14 Creme-filled cookie
15 Wine: Prefix
16 Burger side order
17 Bean-filled bag moved with the foot
19 Expire, as a subscription
20 Honor bestowed by Queen Eliz.
21 Farm unit
22 Bowling alley divisions
23 Postcard sentiment
25 Comedy club razzer
27 Simple
28 Electric cord's end
30 Where dirty dishes pile up
31 Say "Do this," "Do that" . . . blah, blah, blah
34 Border on
36 Prefix with classical
37 Like some hams
41 Fishing pole
42 Loads
43 Id's counterpart
44 Beverages in barrels
46 Fall
48 Statutes
52 Pop artist David
54 Bucharest's land
57 Gather, as information
58 Opposite of fall
59 Auto gizmo that talks, for short
60 Scarecrow's wish in "The Wizard of Oz"
61 2004 film "I ♥ ___"
63 ___ living
64 On the briny
65 Like a first-place ribbon
66 "What ___!" ("It's so dirty!")
67 Dakota ___ (old geog. designation)
68 Depletes, as strength

DOWN

1 "Get out of here!"
2 Where Saudis live
3 Nook
4 ___ choy (Chinese green)
5 Chocolate syrup brand
6 Stand on the hind legs, as a horse
7 "___ upon a time . . ."
8 Chinese cooking vessel
9 Insurance co. with a "spokesduck"
10 Throwing cream pies and such
11 Oil conveyor
12 Abated
13 180° from WNW
18 "That's great news!"
22 Peanut, e.g.
24 Out of ___ (not harmonizing)
25 Parts of cars with caps
26 Early MGM rival
29 ___ rest (bury)
32 Letters before an alias
33 Flax-colored
35 Dress (up)
37 3-D picture
38 "You don't say!," after "Well"
39 Actor Calhoun
40 Kind of nut
41 Stadium cry
45 Balls of yarn
47 Person comparing costs
49 Actress Lansbury
50 Use a paper towel
51 Gives some lip
53 Grandmas
55 Schindler of "Schindler's List"
56 ___ culpa
58 Subterfuge
60 Actress Arthur
61 Sombrero, e.g.
62 Kids' ammo

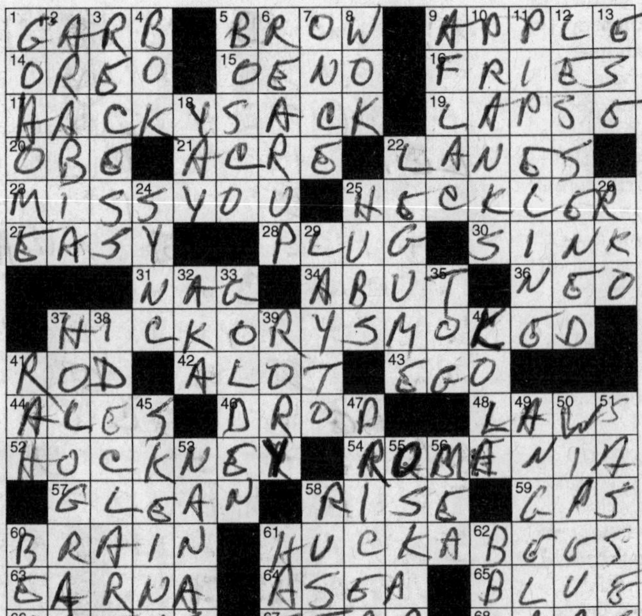

by Andrea Carla Michaels

101.5

ACROSS

1 Missing Jimmy
6 Hit the slopes
9 General feeling
14 Paula of "American Idol"
15 Chum
16 Take forcibly
17 Big spender's woe?
19 "Mule Train" singer, 1949
20 Bête ___
21 Gum arabic-yielding tree
22 Where to find the headings Books, Dolls & Bears, and Collectibles
25 Revolver toter?
27 The Ewings' soap
29 ___ Tin Tin
30 Letter-shaped support
31 Huge expanses
33 Clinic name
37 MasterCard-carrying ecclesiastic?
40 New York home of Rensselaer Polytechnic Institute
41 Give the boot to
42 Greene of "Bonanza"
43 Mark, as a ballot square
44 "Blah, blah, blah . . ."
45 Peter?
51 Deck wood
52 Country singer Milsap
53 Quick Pick game
55 Worse than bad
56 Where this puzzle's theme pairs would like to meet
60 Chain unit
61 Reproductive cells
62 Condor's nest
63 Tender spots
64 Prickly husk
65 Pasta sauce brand

DOWN

1 Witchy woman
2 Sapporo sash
3 Rx watchdog
4 1975 Barbra Streisand sequel
5 Chorus voice
6 Richard's first vice president
7 Superman's birth name
8 Under the weather
9 Spock, on his father's side
10 Asimov of sci-fi
11 LaCrosse carmaker
12 Bert's Muppet pal
13 Pickle portion
18 Some ballpoints
21 Imitative in a silly way
22 Papal bull, e.g.
23 Kiddie lit elephant
24 Olds discontinued in 2004
26 Developer's plot
28 "___ Blue"
31 Spa feature
32 Overhead trains
33 Reggie Jackson nickname
34 Think alike
35 Buttinsky
36 Vacuum maker
38 Library no-no
39 Supermodel Carol
43 "Trust No One" TV series, with "The"
44 Sermon ending?
45 Lacking couth
46 Self-help category
47 Due to get, as punishment
48 Toughen
49 Romantic message, in shorthand
50 Without face value
54 Pipe section
56 Cry out loud
57 Seam material
58 Rug, of a sort
59 Zodiac beast

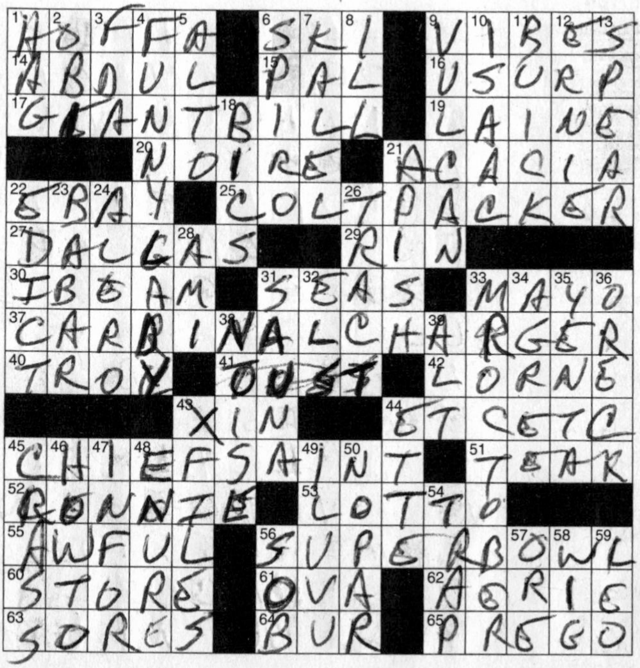

by Larry Shearer

32

1059

ACROSS

1 Bit of smoke
5 "Jeepers!"
11 Burton who produced "The Nightmare Before Christmas"
14 Popular plant gel
15 Native name for Mount McKinley
16 Long-distance number starter
17 Subversive group
19 Buddy
20 Four: Prefix
21 QB Manning
22 Repulsive
23 Soap or lotion, say
27 Searched
29 Gardner of Hollywood
30 Debtor's promise
31 Wise ones
34 Suspect's excuse
38 ___ Ness monster
40 Where you may find the ends of 17-, 23-, 52- and 63-Across
42 Social slight
43 Actor Hawke
45 Sirius or XM medium
47 Three: Prefix
48 No ___, ands or buts
50 Furry burrowers
52 Notorious stigma
57 Umpteen
58 Fish eggs
59 Mullah's teaching
62 Traveler's stopover
63 Coveted film honor
66 Stocking's tip
67 Hardly hip
68 Drooling dog in "Garfield"
69 Evil spell
70 Freshman's topper
71 Spiffy

DOWN

1 Blow gently
2 Tennis champ Nastase
3 One who'll easily lend money for a hard-luck story
4 Fuel by the litre
5 U.S. health promoter: Abbr.
6 Auto last made in the 1930s
7 Shoreline opening
8 Newswoman Zahn
9 New York city where Mark Twain is buried
10 What it is "to tell a lie"
11 Subject of discussion
12 With everything counted
13 Fracas
18 Flags down, as a taxi
22 Pharmacy containers
24 Vault
25 Ventriloquist Bergen
26 Big electrical project inits.
27 Mah-jongg piece
28 Underlying cause
32 Fed. air quality monitor
33 Marsh plant
35 Period between
36 Jefferson's first vice president
37 Curve-billed wader
39 Hirsute
41 Real sidesplitter
44 Org. for Colts and Broncos
46 Eye-related
49 Calm
51 Charlton of "The Ten Commandments"
52 Suffix with black or silver
53 It gets a paddling
54 Building add-on
55 Puccini opera
56 Pretend
60 Met highlight
61 Assemble
63 Fella
64 Hawaiian dish
65 ___ du Diable

by Lynn Lempel

1114

ACROSS

1 Prefix with sphere
5 Assigned stars to
10 Thriving time
14 Jewish ritual
15 Visibly stunned
16 Humorist Bombeck
17 Ornery sort
18 Cutoffs fabric
19 Yemeni port
20 Striptease business?
23 Drive-thru convenience, perhaps
24 Having lunch, say
25 "___ to say this, but . . ."
26 Some auto deals
28 Stereotypical sandwich board diner
31 Young 'un
32 Younger brother, say
33 Knight's attendant
35 Wrestling business?
39 Former "Dateline NBC" co-host Jane
40 Beanery sign
43 Cockpit abbr.
46 Carefully arranged
47 Portugal's place
49 The March King
51 ___-Caps (Nestlé candy)
52 Row C abbr., maybe
53 Comb business?
58 Volcano known to locals as Mongibello
59 Dweller along the Arabian Sea
60 "Darn!"
62 Goatee site
63 Mullally of "Will & Grace"
64 ZZ Top, e.g.
65 Look after
66 Dummy Mortimer
67 Thanksgiving side dish

DOWN

1 "Dancing With the Stars" airer
2 One on a board
3 Jumble
4 ___ buco
5 Figure that's squared in a common formula
6 Go-between
7 Zesty flavor
8 Cast-of-thousands film
9 Floor model
10 Place for an umbrella
11 Tough time
12 Mafia code of silence
13 Unlike drone aircraft
21 Reason to cry "Alas!"
22 Some Japanese-Americans
23 Jungfrau or Eiger
27 Metro map feature
28 A singing Jackson
29 Bacchanalian revelry
30 Polar drudge
33 TV handyman Bob
34 Kind of diagram
36 The Pineapple Island
37 Expected in
38 Sauce for some seafood
41 Cratchit boy
42 Bummed out
43 Appearance
44 Not be able to stomach
45 Submit, as homework
47 Under consideration
48 Dizzy Gillespie's genre
50 Witness's place
51 School locator?
54 Pierre, François, etc.
55 Hood fighters
56 Parakeet keeper
57 Pseudo-cultured
61 Brillo alternative

by Fred Piscop

34

1137

ACROSS

1 Pear variety
5 Filthy place
11 Mardi ___
15 Paul who sang "Puppy Love"
16 Win over
17 Bringing up the rear
18 "Floral" film that was the Best Picture of 1989
21 Ran into
22 Some ales
23 Wilderness photographer Adams
24 Quit, with "out"
25 Glossy alternative
26 "Again!"
27 Gave utterance to
29 Customers
30 Celtic dialect
31 Regional dialect
34 "Floral" film of 2006 with Josh Hartnett and Scarlett Johansson
40 Cowboy contests
41 "SportsCenter" channel
43 Feudal workers
47 Traveling group of actors
49 Motown's Franklin
50 Newspapers, TV, radio, etc.
53 Teacher's favorite
54 "Get lost!"
55 System of government
56 La ___, Bolivia
57 "Floral" film of 1986 based on an Umberto Eco novel
60 Swedish soprano Jenny
61 Like some inspections
62 ___-friendly
63 "For" votes
64 Shorthand takers
65 Fictional detective Wolfe

DOWN

1 "You'll regret that!"
2 Written up, as to a superior
3 Easily startled
4 Cleveland cager, for short
5 Group of five
6 Bar of gold
7 Entire range
8 Slug, old-style
9 ___ and turn
10 1812, 2001, etc.: Abbr.
11 Quick look
12 ___ d'être
13 State with conviction
14 Shag, beehive, updo, etc.
19 "Woe ___!"
20 From Copenhagen, e.g.
26 Kazan who directed "On the Waterfront"
28 Grade between bee and dee
29 Atlantic swimmers
31 Cushions
32 Hole in one
33 W.B.A. decision
35 The Creator, to Hindus
36 Name repeated in "Whatever ___ wants, ___ gets"
37 Virgo's predecessor
38 Noncommittal agreement
39 One who's making nice
42 EarthLink alternative
43 To a huge degree
44 Jughead's pal
45 One of tennis's Williams sisters
46 Bleachers
47 Gives 10% to the church
48 Funnywoman Martha
50 Bullwinkle, e.g.
51 Spritelike
52 "Me, too"
55 Shut (up)
58 Calendar pgs.
59 Hurry

by Harvey Estes

1151

ACROSS

1 Home in an old warehouse district
5 Virus named for a river
10 Trans-Siberian Railroad stop
14 Peculiar: Prefix
15 U.S./Canada early warning syst.
16 City bond, for short
17 Eisenhower was one
20 Move unsteadily
21 Delon of "Purple Noon"
22 Cedar Rapids college
23 2:30, aboard ship
27 Dele undoers
29 Something new
30 Ho Chi Minh's capital
31 Boris Godunov, for one
32 Rove, with "about"
35 Full range
37 It's off the tip of Italy
40 Bad-mouth
41 ___ war syndrome
45 ___ plume
46 Chiang Kai-shek's capital
48 Mountain cats
49 Rests for a bit
52 Singleton
53 "Waiting for Lefty" playwright
54 Like Dickens's Dodger
57 Shortly after quitting time, for many
62 Forearm bone
63 Shul V.I.P.
64 Pizzeria fixture
65 Hot times in France
66 Befuddled
67 Try for a role

DOWN

1 Brit's elevator
2 Garfield's foil
3 Nickel
4 Slugging it out
5 ___'acte
6 Feathery wrap
7 Bobby of the Bruins
8 Dillydally
9 Fruity quencher
10 Brunch dish
11 Wall art
12 Symbol of slowness
13 Ceramists' baking chambers
18 Welcomes, as a guest at one's home
19 Catches red-handed
23 Jack Sprat's taboo
24 Hypotheticals
25 Rome's ___ Veneto
26 Blunders
27 Outbuilding
28 Vehicle with a medallion
32 Request for a congratulatory slap
33 Pierce player
34 Gray concealers
36 End-of-workweek cry
38 At a cruise stop
39 Be worth
42 A.P. competitor
43 "My Name Is Asher ___"
44 "For shame!"
46 Colorful fishes
47 Helper: Abbr.
49 Brimless cap
50 At least 21
51 "The Family Circus" cartoonist Bil
54 Home to most Turks
55 Iris's place
56 Libraries do it
58 Big Band ___
59 Turn state's evidence
60 "Sesame Street" channel
61 Honest ___

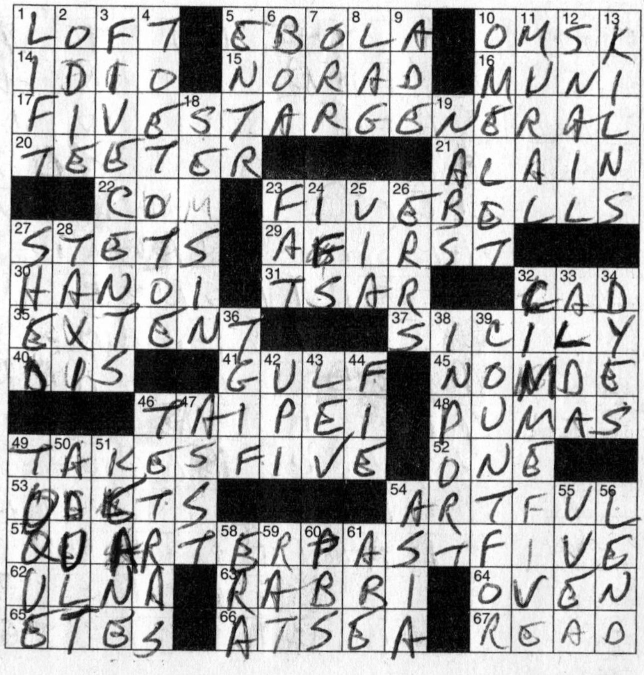

by John Underwood

36

ACROSS

1 "Lady Marmalade" singer ___ LaBelle
6 Musical phrase
10 On the briny
14 Birdlike
15 Poet ___ Khayyám
16 Butter slices
17 T. S. Eliot title character who measures out his life with coffee spoons
20 Not just recent
21 Muck
22 "The Simpsons" bartender
23 Light throw
26 Studio sign
29 Actress MacDowell of "Groundhog Day"
32 Really impressed
34 Geller with a spoon-bending act
35 Light golden lager
38 ___ Bator, Mongolia
39 Editor out to smear Spider-Man
42 Parti-colored
43 Dance class outfit
44 Quantity: Abbr.
45 Sheep cries
46 Rapids transits
50 A goose egg
52 Phobia
55 Unfortunate sound when you bend over
56 Hay storage locale
58 Saw-toothed
61 Vice president who once famously mashed "potato"
65 Come to shore
66 Baby bassoon?
67 War horse
68 Lyric poems
69 Puppy bites
70 Sexy nightwear

DOWN

1 ___ party (sleepover)
2 Frankie of "Beach Blanket Bingo"
3 Cultivated the soil
4 President who later served as chief justice
5 Initials on a cross
6 Where you might hear "Ride 'em, cowboy!"
7 Little devil
8 Distant
9 Lively '60s dance
10 Kitchen spill catcher
11 Brazil's largest city
12 And so on: Abbr.
13 "___ and ye shall receive"
18 CPR pro
19 Grocery offering
24 California city in a 1968 Dionne Warwick hit
25 Accumulation on the brow
27 Persia, today
28 ___ Tin Tin
30 Its first ad touted "1,000 songs in your pocket"
31 German article
33 Humorist Bombeck
36 Singsong syllables
37 Grain bundle
38 Beef quality graders: Abbr.
39 Guitarist Hendrix
40 747, e.g.
41 Be mistaken
42 La ___, Bolivia
45 Hit, as on the noggin
47 Worn at the edges
48 Like the Marquis de Sade or the Duke of Earl
49 Rapid
51 Unilever skin cream brand
53 Fireplace remnants
54 Necessary: Abbr.
57 Roger Rabbit or Donald Duck
59 Corrosion sign
60 Appraise
61 Female singer's 2001 album that debuted at #1
62 "Dear old" guy
63 Slugger's stat
64 Blouse or shirt

by Jeremy Horwitz

1219

ACROSS

1 Peak
5 Chattered incessantly
10 TV horse introduced in 1955 . . . or a Plymouth model introduced in 1956
14 Partiality
15 Seeing red
16 Prime draft status
17 Drug-yielding plant
18 Opposite of serenity
19 Cartoonist Al
20 Scary sound from the ocean?
23 Park, e.g., in N.Y.C.
25 "Sting like a bee" athlete
26 Having seniority
28 Scary sound from a war zone?
33 Juillet's season
34 Kodiak native
35 Physics unit
36 Theory's start
37 Scary sound from a cornfield?
41 Splinter group
44 Motel-discount grp.
45 Sales slips: Abbr.
49 Galley implement
50 Scary sound from a steeple?
53 Tedious
55 Boot part
56 "Whew!"
57 Misspells, say, as a ghost might at 20-, 28-, 37- and 50- Across?
62 Abominate
63 African antelope
64 Hot rod's rod
67 ___ Lackawanna Railroad
68 Countryish
69 Boot part
70 Card game for three
71 Walk leisurely
72 Stealth bomber org.

DOWN

1 Charles Gibson's network
2 A.F.L.-___
3 Cane cutter
4 Biblical son who sold his birthright
5 Wavelet
6 Language whose alphabet starts alif, ba, ta, tha . . .
7 Child's caretaker
8 Suffix with hypn-
9 Part of a bottle or a guitar
10 Kind of point
11 Helpless?
12 Filled to the gills
13 Big fat mouth
21 Country just south of Sicily
22 Moo goo gai pan pan
23 Lawyers' org.
24 Kilmer of "The Doors"
27 ___ Irvin, classic artist for The New Yorker
29 Cowlick, e.g.
30 Fit for a king
31 Blunder
32 "Long ___ and far away . . ."
36 Creep (along)
38 Name that's an anagram of 27-Down
39 ___ de mer
40 Egyptian dry measure equal to about five-and-a-half bushels
41 Soak (up)
42 Tag for a particular purpose
43 Neighbor of Slovenia
46 Co. addresses, often
47 A duo
48 Crafty
50 Tournament pass
51 Like some music
52 Musically improvise
54 Sport utilizing a clay disk
58 Hospital shipments
59 Styptic agent
60 Part of a fishhook
61 Island with Waimea Bay
62 Gentlemen
65 Meadow
66 Shoemaker's helper, in a fairy tale

by Gary Steinmehl

38

1245

ACROSS

1 Started a cigarette
6 Sail supporter
10 Rooters
14 Left one's seat
15 Gumbo vegetable
16 Track shape
17 Allotment of heredity units?
19 Parks who pioneered in civil rights
20 Our language: Abbr.
21 Took the blue ribbon
22 Room to maneuver
24 Nuclear power apparatus
27 Top 10 tunes
28 Hole-punching tool
29 Slender cigar
33 Prefix with -hedron
36 Is false to the world
37 Get from ___ (progress slightly)
38 Battle of the ___ (men vs. women)
39 Stadium section
40 Studied primarily, at college
42 Holder of 88 keys
43 Caveman's era
44 Vintage automotive inits.
45 Tennis great Arthur
46 Mediums' meetings
50 Stewed to the gills
53 King Kong, e.g.
54 Lacto-___-vegetarian
55 Sitarist Shankar
56 Preacher's sky-high feeling?
60 Twistable cookie
61 Turn at roulette
62 Decaf brand
63 Give an alert
64 Direction of sunup
65 Sticky problem

DOWN

1 Hearty brew
2 Jim Carrey comedy "Me, Myself & ___"
3 Kingdom east of Fiji
4 Milk for all its worth
5 Pay-___-view
6 Travel by car
7 Closely related (to)
8 Sign at a sellout
9 Bikini wearers' markings
10 TV channel for golfers?
11 State frankly
12 Shuttle-launching org.
13 Murder
18 Delinquent G.I.
23 Greek H's
25 Pasta-and-potato-loving country?
26 Former rival of Pan Am
27 Safe place
29 Mischievous sprite
30 Director Kazan
31 Claim on property
32 Prefix with dynamic
33 Scots' caps
34 Coup d'___
35 Japanese P.M. during W.W. II
36 Mantel
38 Equine-looking fish
41 Take a siesta
42 Split ___ soup
44 Fishing line winder
46 Paid out
47 Nickels and dimes
48 Call to mind
49 Sunken ship finder
50 Furrowed part of the head
51 Dr. Zhivago's love
52 1964 Dave Clark Five song "Glad All ___"
53 Hertz rival
57 Mileage rating org.
58 Cleopatra's biter
59 Eastern "way"

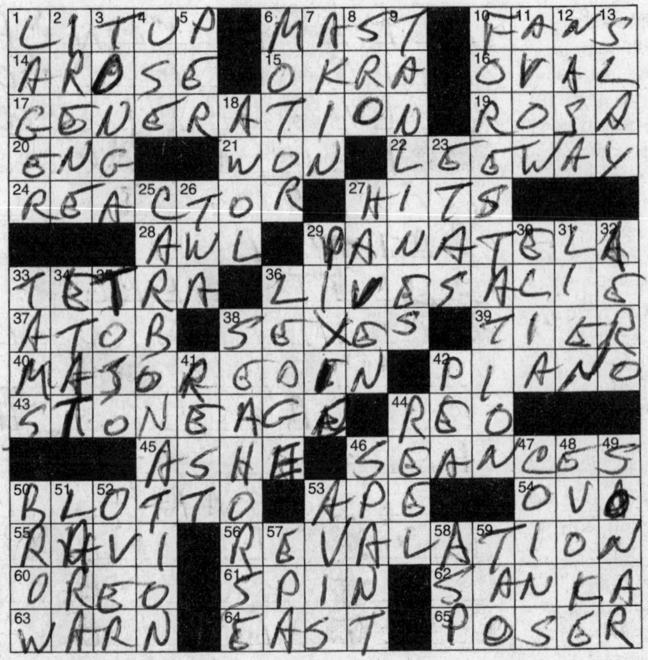

by Fred Piscop

39

1059
19

ACROSS

1 Play place
6 Ballroom dance
11 Chart-topper
14 Sign of spring
15 Mountaineer's tool
16 E.T.'s ride
17 Play follower, usually
19 Unruly do
20 Amateurish
21 "___ economy is always beauty": Henry James
23 Buggy rider
26 Loofah, e.g.
30 108-card game
31 Start the pot
32 Pest control brand
33 Spoil
35 Bibliophile's suffix
36 Tipplers
37 Circulatory system flow
41 Singer ___ P. Morgan
43 Early 11th-century year
44 Back at sea?
47 Actress Chase of "Now, Voyager"
48 For dieters
51 Smidgen
52 Shoot-'em-up figure
54 Harmony, briefly
55 Clobber, biblically
56 Computer that uses OS X
58 Director Lee
59 What the starts of 17-, 26-, 37- and 52-Across are
66 Crib cry
67 Burger topper, maybe
68 Site of Ali's Rumble in the Jungle
69 Salon job
70 Cuts and pastes
71 TV awards

DOWN

1 Amniotic ___
2 Play about Capote
3 Put on TV
4 Manage, barely
5 Jacob's twin
6 G.I.'s helmet, slangily
7 Duke's sports org.
8 "Read Across America" grp.
9 Guy's partner
10 Primrose family member
11 Saroyan novel, with "The"
12 "It slipped my mind!"
13 Letterman lists
18 ID on a dust jacket
22 Acknowledges nonverbally
23 PC glitch
24 "Wheel of Fortune" buy
25 Hoops coach with the most N.C.A.A. Division I wins
27 Playful mockery
28 Rural event on horseback
29 Work out in the ring
31 Commotion
34 Red Sox div.
38 Old Dodge
39 Singer of the 1962 hit "The Wanderer"
40 Guinness Book suffix
41 Tools for making twisty cuts
42 Barnard grads
45 Bled, like dyes
46 "Deal or No Deal" network
49 Fakes, as an injury
50 Weaponry
53 Leave alone
54 "Beat it!"
57 Wood-shaping tool
60 Suffered from
61 Here, in Paris
62 "I'm kidding!"
63 Deadeye's asset
64 Dryly amusing
65 Nintendo's Super ___

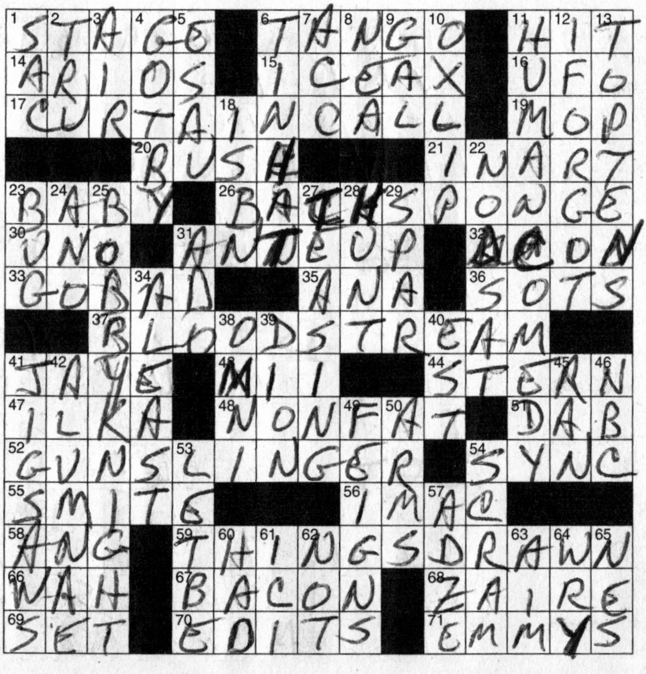

by Alan Arbesfeld

40

ACROSS

1 Does sums
5 Pillow filler
9 Flapper hairdos
13 Scuttlebutt
14 Like a manly man
15 Escapade
16 Part of the eye that holds the iris
17 ___ and pains
18 What "thumbs up" means
19 Bandleader in the Polka Music Hall of Fame
22 Explosive initials
23 Pinocchio, famously
24 Mock
28 Dance with a wiggle
30 Lord
31 Card that's taken only by a trump
32 Mail carriers' assignments: Abbr.
34 Creamy soup
38 City where van Gogh painted sunflowers
40 Suffix with sucr- and lact-
41 Pacific republic
42 Substantial portion
45 Pile
46 Component of bronze
47 Permit
48 Washington's Capitol ___
50 Precipitates at about 32°F
52 Left hurriedly
54 New Deal program inits.
57 One who lost what's hidden in 19-, 34- and 42-Across
60 Hawaiian isle
63 More than perturbed
64 "Unfortunately . . ."
65 Give a hard time
66 Nobodies
67 Small field size
68 Branch of Islam
69 Plow pullers
70 Jean who wrote "Wide Sargasso Sea"

DOWN

1 No longer a minor
2 Couch
3 Made a stand and would go no further
4 Polaris, e.g.
5 Bangladesh's capital, old-style
6 Color of fall leaves
7 "Thank goodness!"
8 Rhinoplasty
9 Chap
10 Tree loved by squirrels
11 Maidenform product
12 Cloud's site
14 Psycho
20 90° turn
21 Ushered
25 "Fantastic Voyage" actress
26 Honda division
27 Get ready to drive, in golf
29 ___-friendly
30 Agents under J. Edgar Hoover, informally
32 Balsa transports
33 Path
35 Booty
36 Tempe sch.
37 Comedian Mort
39 1972 U.S./U.S.S.R. missile pact
43 Latin American with mixed ancestry
44 Oedipus' realm
49 Wedding vow
51 Doolittle of "My Fair Lady"
52 Distress signal shot into the air
53 Divulge
55 Explorer who proved that Greenland is an island
56 Basilica recesses
58 Fearsome dino
59 Jack of early late-night TV
60 ___ Butterworth's
61 What a doctor might ask you to say
62 Israeli gun

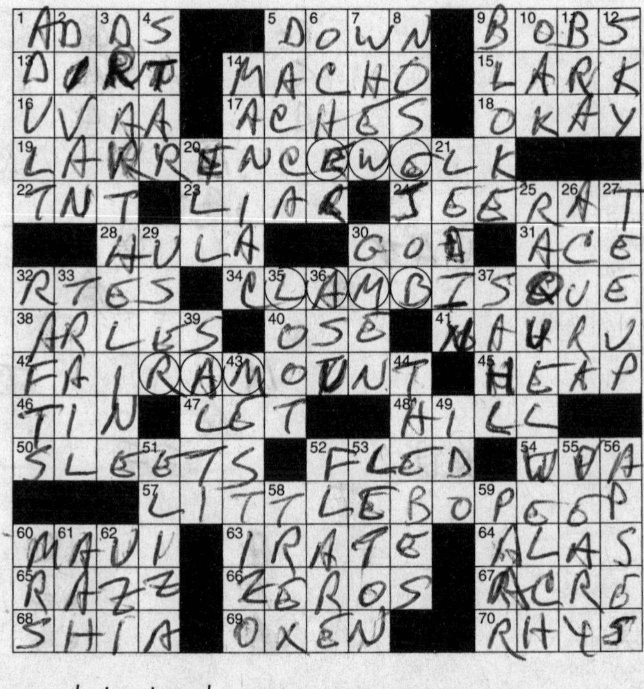

by Lynn Lempel

1137

ACROSS

1 Show anger
5 Round before the final
9 Washroom tub
14 Ph.D. awarder
15 Gave the boot
16 Blessing-inducing sound
17 Flank
18 Gimlet garnish
19 Crockpot concoctions
20 Relax during a drill
23 Temp's work unit
24 Polite affirmation
25 Brazilian dance
27 Big Apple awards
30 Like hair, usually, after combing
33 Post-O.R. stop
36 Craps natural
38 Impoverished
39 Sgt. Friday's org.
41 Calendar units hidden in 20- and 61-Across and 11- and 35-Down
43 Worker's pay
44 Like a brainiac
46 Fire remnants
48 The "R" in Roy G. Biv
49 Trojan War hero
51 Popular snack chip
53 Surveyor Jeremiah, for whom a famous line is partly named
55 Beatle, endearingly
59 Meadow sound
61 Sunshine State school
64 Minute Maid Park player
66 Baylor's city
67 Sp. girl
68 Rodeo animal
69 From the top
70 Ticks off
71 TV shout-out from the team bench
72 It's sold in skeins
73 "Great" kid-lit detective

DOWN

1 Hard to please
2 Bring together
3 Greedy monarch
4 "Nevertheless . . ."
5 On the payroll
6 Lighted sign in a theater
7 Hand-waver's cry
8 They may be bright
9 One in the infield
10 Follow direction?
11 Show sadness
12 Political caucus state
13 Like a yenta
21 "That's mine!"
22 Deplete, as energy
26 Cold one
28 FEMA recommendation, briefly
29 Play by a different ___ rules
31 Upper hand
32 Like batik fabrics
33 Ingrid's role in "Casablanca"
34 Showed up
35 "Time to rise, sleepyhead!"
37 Within earshot
40 Zwei follower
42 Lose the spare tire
45 Schedule B or C, e.g.
47 Ancient Greek colonnade
50 La preceder
52 Chooses to participate
54 "Impossible!"
56 ___ firma
57 Largish combo
58 Terrible twos, e.g.
59 Bad-mouth
60 Sparkling wine city
62 ___ deficit (lost money)
63 Pastry prettifier
65 Vintage auto

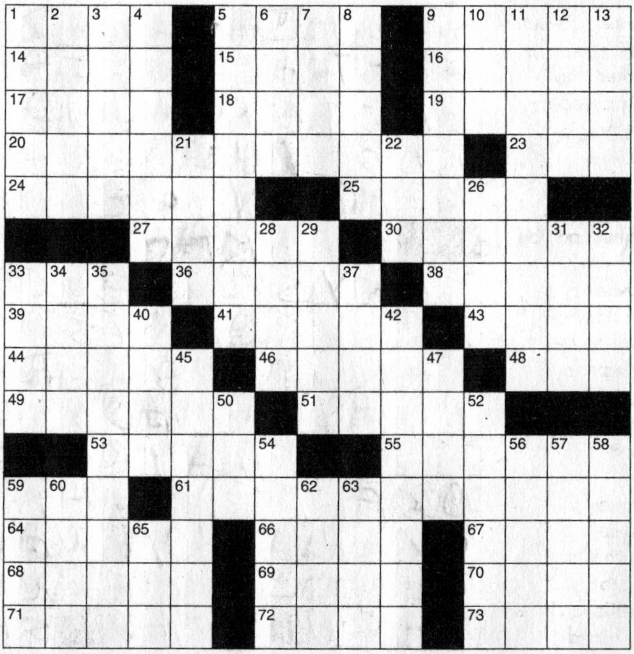

by Michael Kaplan

42

ACROSS
1 Indifferent to pleasure or pain
6 Close
10 Jacket
14 Toyota rival
15 Impulse
16 ___ of office
17 Taking back one's words in humiliation
19 "Oh, that's what you mean"
20 Excitement
21 ___-de-sac
22 Receiver of a legal transfer
24 Actress Zellweger
26 Anger
27 Negotiating in a no-nonsense way
32 Baby kangaroos
34 Joel who directed "Raising Arizona"
35 "These ___ the times that . . ."
36 One-named Art Deco designer
37 Vehicles in airplane aisles
39 "Love ___ the air"
40 Big elephant feature
41 Theater award
42 Prayers' ends
43 Pretending to be dead
47 The "et" of et cetera
48 Lock of hair
49 Rip off
53 Moo goo ___ pan
54 Ewe's call
57 Supervising
58 Raising a false alarm
61 Roman statesman ___ the Elder
62 Daylight saving, e.g.
63 ___ Rae (Sally Field title role)
64 Didn't just guess
65 Locales of mineral waters
66 Say with one's hand on the Bible

DOWN
1 Former New York stadium
2 Relative of a frog
3 Seeing through the deception of
4 Dictator Amin
5 Calls off
6 Cell centers
7 Misplay, e.g.
8 Slack-jawed
9 Edits
10 Neologist
11 Kiln
12 Suit to ___
13 Biblical pronoun
18 Sticky matter
23 Give ___ for one's money
24 Comedic actress Martha
25 Put into cipher
27 Four: Prefix
28 "___ Milk?"
29 Casey with a radio countdown
30 Land o' blarney
31 Achings
32 Army transport
33 Spoken
37 Leads, as an orchestra
38 "Hulk" director Lee
39 Don with a big mouth
41 One of the Sinatras
42 Hands out, as duties
44 Peter of Peter, Paul & Mary
45 Unrestrained revelries
46 Actor Penn
49 Marina fixture
50 "___ Almighty," 2007 film
51 Honor with a roast, say
52 What icicles do
54 Drill
55 ___ mater
56 Many miles away
59 Singer Sumac
60 "Man alive!"

by Andrea Carla Michaels

ACROSS

1 Speaks, informally
4 Speak
9 Smokey Robinson's music genre, for short
14 ___ de France
15 End of a hangman's rope
16 Love to bits
17 BORE
20 Have ___ in one's head
21 ___ and outs
22 The "I" in T.G.I.F.
23 BOAR
28 Nap
29 "Golden" song
32 Ad-lib, musically
35 Sign before Virgo
36 Person performing an exorcism
37 Gives a stage cue
40 Honeybunch or cutie pie
41 Glowing remnants of a fire
42 Abbr. after many a general's name
43 Meyerbeer's "___ Huguenots"
44 Painting surface
45 Publisher of Cosmopolitan and Good Housekeeping
48 BOER
53 Before, in poetry
55 Baseballer Mel
56 "Maria ___," Jimmy Dorsey #1 hit
57 BOHR
62 Actress Garbo
63 "Er . . . um . . ."
64 Old tennis racket string material
65 Stand for a portrait
66 Taboos
67 Cry before "Get your hands off!"

DOWN

1 Have a chair by, as a table
2 ___ Yale, for whom Yale University is named
3 Six in 1,000,000
4 Out of sight
5 Also
6 ___ Sawyer
7 Reverse of WNW
8 Fix the electrical connections of
9 Didn't have enough supplies
10 Problem in focusing, for short
11 "Don't worry about it"
12 "Phooey!"
13 Panhandles
18 Club with a lodge
19 Bankbook abbr.
24 Knuckleheads
25 Tribulations
26 ___ dye
27 Lena or Ken of film
30 "This ___ . . . Then" (Jennifer Lopez album)
31 French summers
32 Computer image file format
33 French weapon
34 Sights at after-Christmas sales
36 Lab's ___ dish
38 Mini-plateau
39 "Will you marry me?," e.g.
40 Brandy fruit
42 Hoops official
45 Sticker through a lady's headgear
46 Coils of yarn
47 Soft powder
49 Biblical suffix
50 Stable sound
51 Come afterward
52 Wretched
53 Scoring advantage
54 ___ avis
58 Suffix with Israel
59 Dr. provider
60 Japanese moolah
61 ___ Paulo, Brazil

by Timothy Powell

44

ACROSS

1 Witty sorts
5 Make sense
10 Choice word
14 Think tank nugget
15 On the lam
16 Gerund, e.g.
17 Bond villain
19 Saw red?
20 Ph.D. thesis: Abbr.
21 Gets corroded
22 Bemoan
25 "Beats me" gesture
28 Rub out
29 Certain trout
33 Basis of a suit
34 Endless, poetically
35 Fraternity P
36 "Survivor" shelter
37 Some red wines
38 Obey the coxswain
39 Cheroot residue
40 Wings it
41 Place for a hoedown
42 Classic blues musician
44 Intuit
45 The "35" in John 11:35
46 Prodded
47 Woods or Irons
50 Flair
51 Laugh heartily
52 Patriarchal gorilla
58 Pond organism
59 Primp
60 Natural soother
61 Lounge in the sun
62 Feel nostalgia, e.g.
63 Crips or Bloods

DOWN

1 Faux 'fro?
2 Brouhaha
3 Goo in a do
4 Most mournful
5 Most-wanted group for a party
6 Puts on
7 Follow everywhere
8 Put to work
9 Part of r.p.m.
10 "Stop!"
11 Wall Street minimums
12 Fatty treat for birds
13 Pulls the plug on
18 Ticket cost?
21 Game sheet
22 Deadly
23 Work up
24 First first lady
25 Germ-free
26 As a result of this
27 Patronizes U-Haul, e.g.
29 Plays for time
30 Gofer's job
31 When repeated, cry by Shakespeare's Richard III
32 Consumed heartily
34 Octogenarian, for one
37 Pole tossed by Scots
41 Nontraditional chair style
43 Czech composer Antonín
44 Go up, up, up
46 Filmdom's Close
47 Omani, e.g.
48 Fast-food drink
49 Makes "it"
50 ". . . ___ after"
52 U-2 pilot, e.g.
53 Ill temper
54 Grazing ground
55 Carte start
56 Bamboozle
57 Fraternity party setup

by Steve Kahn

45

ACROSS

1 "Do you like green eggs and ham?" speaker
7 In the style of
10 Lao-tzu's way
13 Meeting handout
14 Broke from the band, maybe
17 Cosmopolitan staple
19 Date
20 Uncertainties
21 It can be silly
22 Spot en el mar
24 W.W. I German admiral
26 N.F.L. star
32 Slip
33 Conquistador's quest
34 Actress Turner
36 Opposite of WSW
37 Period of human benightedness
41 Stroke
42 Overall feel
44 Coquettish
45 Relative of a mole
47 Colorful bed cover
51 Corrida cheers
52 Pageant adornment
53 Highest peak of Crete
56 Egg: Prefix
57 Wide shoe spec
60 "Behave!" . . . and a hint to this puzzle's theme
65 Representative
66 Tie, as a score
67 Cry between "ready" and "go!"
68 "Kid-tested" breakfast cereal
69 Keep

DOWN

1 Fools
2 Author James
3 Slight
4 Special connections
5 Bustle
6 Port seized by Adm. Dewey, 1898
7 Poking tools
8 Luau offering
9 Queen of the hill?
10 Ballyhoo
11 Dismounted
12 Like mud
15 Easygoing
16 Sound at a greased pig contest
18 In the distance
22 Figs. clustered around 100
23 Like a malfeasant, often
24 Fluids in bags
25 Bull Moose party: Abbr.
26 Appeal
27 Incurred, as charges
28 "La Traviata," e.g.
29 Site of the first Asian Olympics
30 Kind of pants
31 Prepare to propose
35 1, for hydrogen: Abbr.
38 What a massage may ease
39 Theater seating
40 Titles for attys.
43 In disagreement
46 "Say what?"
48 Pottery materials
49 Reply, briefly
50 Onetime German leader
53 Mlles. after marriage
54 Red-bordered magazine
55 The "W" in Geo. W. Bush, e.g.
56 Straight-horned African animal
57 Author Ferber
58 Prefix with distant
59 "SportsCenter" channel
61 Yellow ribbon holder, in song
62 Geller with a psychic act
63 St. crosser
64 Bring home

by Oliver Hill

46

ACROSS

1 Wager
4 Gush
10 Willie of the 1950s-'60s Giants
14 Israeli submachine gun
15 Last words of the Pledge of Allegiance
16 ___ vera
17 Atomic energy org.
18 *Popular Sunshine State vacation destination
20 Prepare to shoot
22 Docs
23 Stop for the night, as soldiers
25 Daughter's counterpart
26 Dartboard, for one
28 The "I" of I.M.F.: Abbr.
30 Austrian affirmatives
33 "The Thin Man" pooch
34 Rim
36 Put (down), as money
38 Theater focal point
40 Select, with "for"
41 Language akin to Urdu
42 Serious drinker
43 Arnaz of "I Love Lucy"
45 Depression-era migrant
46 "But I heard him exclaim, ___ he drove . . ."
47 Take too much of, briefly
49 Objected to
51 Brouhaha
52 Keep just below a boil
54 Not deceitful
58 Deck covering to keep out moisture
61 *Like players below the B team
63 "This means ___!"
64 Sets of points, in math
65 "Relax, soldier!"
66 U.K. record label
67 Newspaper essay
68 Mascara goes on them
69 King, in old Rome

DOWN

1 Part of a suicide squeeze
2 Poet Pound
3 *Material for an old-fashioned parade
4 Wipe off
5 Decorate with leaves
6 Erich who wrote "The Art of Loving"
7 Bygone Mideast inits.
8 Slender
9 Firstborn
10 "___ Whoopee!" (1920s hit)
11 One of the Baldwin brothers
12 Toy that might go "around the world"
13 Period in Cong.
19 Coach Rupp of college basketball
21 Take on
24 *Sties
26 One of the five senses
27 Fur trader John Jacob ___
29 Basketball rim attachments
30 Location for the ends of the answers to the four starred clues
31 Actress MacDowell
32 Schussed, e.g.
35 Dumbbell
37 Hampton of jazz fame
39 Wore away
44 Really, really big
48 ___ fin
50 Representations
51 Pungent
53 Former N.B.A. coach Thomas
54 Normandy town
55 Breakfast restaurant letters
56 "Good shot!"
57 Kett of old comics
59 Designate
60 Cereal whose ads feature a "silly rabbit"
62 ___ ipsa loquitur

by Allan E. Parrish

ACROSS

1 President before Jefferson
6 Couch
10 "Picnic" Pulitzer winner William
14 Performing poorly in
15 Knocks for a loop
16 Gas in advertising lights
17 With 59-Across, lyric from "America, the Beautiful"
20 Bro's counterpart
21 U.N. working-conditions agcy.
22 Molecule part
23 Guinness suffix
24 Dict. info
26 For adults, as films
30 Lyric from "The Star-Spangled Banner"
33 Numbskull
34 Perlman of "Cheers"
35 Society newcomer
36 These break the silence of the lambs
39 Derisive laugh
40 Huff and puff
41 Prints, pastels and such
42 Hollywood's Ken or Lena
44 Nasdaq debut: Abbr.
46 Lyric from "America"
51 Lunatic
52 Japanese wrestling
53 Smallish batteries
55 Thick slice
57 Band booking
58 Air conditioner meas.
59 See 17-Across
64 "Garfield" dog
65 Talk wildly
66 Etc. and ibid., e.g.
67 Magician's stick
68 Jazz singer James
69 Unlike a rolling stone?

DOWN

1 Humiliate
2 Breakfast roll
3 Extends
4 Apple computer, for short
5 Large steps
6 Took to the airport, say
7 Confess, with "up"
8 Greek salad cheese
9 Wood source for a baseball bat
10 Director Bergman
11 Newcomer, briefly
12 Moo ___ gai pan
13 Finish up
18 Bread spreads
19 ___ Linda, Calif.
25 Leaves in the lurch
27 "Look what I did!"
28 Fifty-fifty
29 Borrower's burden
31 Apron wearers, traditionally
32 L.B.J.'s veep
36 Soothing ointment
37 Neck of the woods
38 Env. notation
39 Get a move on, quaintly
40 Luau paste
42 Toothbrush brand
43 Spy novelist John
44 Shooting marble
45 Write computer instructions
47 Dropped a line in the water
48 Should, informally
49 Bigwigs
50 Swamp swimmers
54 Like dishwater
56 Dinghy or dory
59 "I'm impressed!"
60 Rhoda's TV mom
61 10th-anniversary metal
62 Blasting stuff
63 "The Sopranos" network

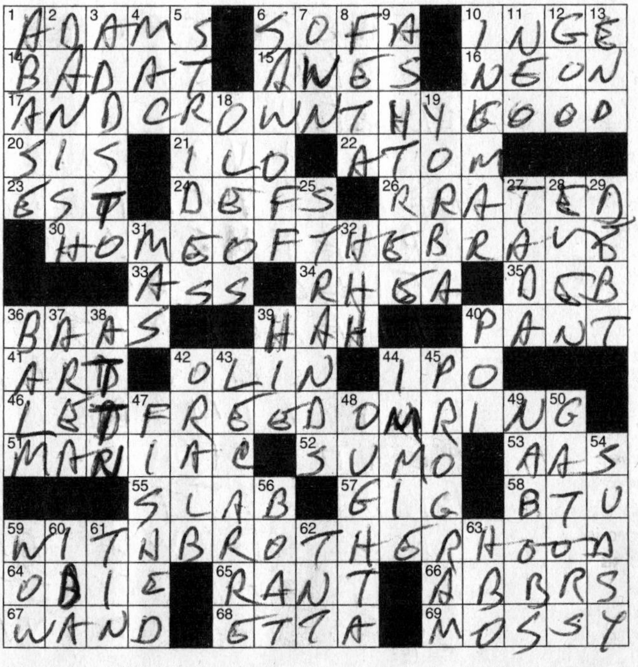

by Nancy Salomon

48

38 | 51

ACROSS

1 Tough trips
6 Poster holder
10 Shi'ites, e.g.
14 Two under, on the links
15 Double-reeded woodwind
16 Pertaining to
17 Tee off
18 Elbow/hand connector
19 Marked, as a box on a test
20 Noted actor's writing implements?
23 "Nope"
25 Actress Hatcher
26 Candidate's concern
27 Instruction to a woman in labor
30 Get-up-and-go
32 Danger signal
33 Yo-Yo Ma's instrument
34 Rodeo wear, often
36 Noted actor's sons?
41 Farmer's spring purchase
42 Orderly grouping
44 Dear old ___
47 Headlight setting
48 Public face
50 "Wheel of Fortune" purchases
52 Huge-screen film format
54 Church perch
55 Noted actor's underarms?
59 Shopper stopper
60 Fiddle sticks
61 California/Nevada lake
64 Keep ___ (persist)
65 A couple of chips in the pot, maybe
66 Tempest
67 Perfect Olympic scores
68 Makes calls
69 "Breaking Away" director Peter

DOWN

1 Lipton product
2 Made haste
3 Shade of white
4 Swiss artist Paul
5 Word repeated after "Que" in song
6 Rug with nothing swept under it?
7 More competent
8 Plotted
9 9/11 commission chairman Thomas
10 Rush-hour hr.
11 Win over
12 Shrink in fear
13 Made tight, as muscles
21 Highest degree
22 Analogous
23 "The West Wing" network
24 Plane measure
28 Resigned remark
29 Cut down on the flab
31 Electees
34 Dentist's deg.
35 Neighbor of Earth
37 Floral necklace
38 Movie ticket mandate
39 Finesse stroke in tennis
40 With it, mentally
43 Not fly absolutely straight
44 Blots lightly
45 Supply with oxygen
46 Join a teleconference
48 Written permissions
49 Abbr. before a date on a pkg.
51 "Golden Boy" playwright
53 Workweek letters
56 Construction beam
57 Wee
58 "See ya!"
62 Miner's find
63 German spa

by Beth Hinshaw

49

38

ACROSS
1 Swiss peaks
5 Bit of dust
10 It holds a bunch
14 Blood fluids
15 Cather who wrote "My Ántonia"
16 Personal flair
17 Greeting for Julius
19 In position, as a cornerstone
20 One who proffers an arm
21 Destructive beetles
23 Dictation taker
24 Number of zodiac signs
26 Words to live by
28 Rand McNally product
32 24-hour conveniences, for short
36 Fund for old age: Abbr.
37 One under one
38 Bit of bridal attire
39 Giant
41 Catch ___ (start to understand)
42 Rationalization
44 Humble home
45 Struggle for air
46 Cash in a cache, e.g.
47 Fruit whose seeds are spit out
49 Sand trap, for one
51 Following
56 Oscar winner for "Kramer vs. Kramer"
59 Star, in Paris
60 Org. that defends individual rights
61 Title song of a Prince film
64 Baseball's Musial
65 Duos
66 Gait between walk and canter
67 Duck's home
68 "Tiny Alice" playwright Edward
69 Diner sign

DOWN
1 Fireplace remnants
2 "That's the ___ I can do"
3 Three for a dollar, e.g.
4 Hairdresser's shop
5 Big baseball hit
6 Cobbler
7 Raised railways
8 Mauled, as by a bear
9 Capek who wrote "R.U.R."
10 Mel Tormé's sobriquet, with "the"
11 Jai ___
12 Mast item
13 Means justifiers, some say
18 Relative of a gator
22 Hoosier senator Bayh
24 Actress Garr
25 This puzzle's theme
27 Ceremony
29 Actress Turner
30 Kitchen pests
31 Cease
32 Madison and Fifth, in N.Y.C.
33 What's read
34 Isinglass
35 Illicit reserve
37 Mad about
40 "___ Lang Syne"
43 Fraud
47 Alternative to automatic
48 Archibald of the N.B.A.
50 Frank of the Mothers of Invention
52 Strong point
53 Queen's headgear
54 Author T. S. ___
55 Income for Fred and Ethel Mertz
56 Trunk closer
57 Eight: Prefix
58 Sweet Spanish dessert
59 Otherwise
62 Kid
63 Before: Prefix

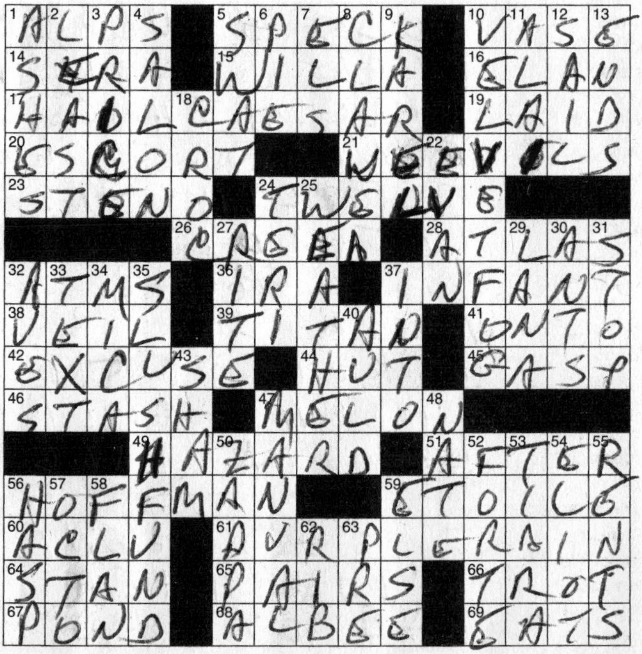

by Janice M. Putney

50

54/10

ACROSS
1 Nurses' workmates
5 Leave clueless
10 Headliner
14 Russia's ___ Mountains
15 Lack of laxness
16 Kent State's state
17 "I'm game"
19 On guard
20 Jane of "Klute"
21 Had in mind
23 "Telephone Line" rock grp.
24 Pretend to sing
28 Star Wars mil. project
31 "I'm game"
33 One of the Twin Cities
35 Cold-relief brand
37 "Love Story" author Erich
38 Drop anchor
41 Hedge former
43 D.C. bigwigs
44 Out of kilter
46 Letter lines
48 "Tommy" rockers
50 "I'm game"
54 Stable diet?
55 Fashionable
57 Soccer standout Hamm
58 Plug
60 They leave marks on the road
62 New Mexico resort town
64 "I'm game"
68 Like a G.I. peeling spuds
69 Susan Lucci's Emmy role
70 Don Juan, for one
71 Sight seers
72 Got up
73 Cultural doings

DOWN
1 ___ bag (camper's tote)
2 Baltimore ballplayer
3 Defeatist's word
4 Musher's transport
5 Hindu honorific
6 Small songbird
7 "Gross!"
8 Daddy's counterpart
9 Fixes feathers
10 Scattered, as seed
11 "I'm game"
12 Go public with
13 "Crying" singer Orbison
18 Hider in kids' books
22 Does something
25 Electrified particles
26 Cores
27 Ogle
29 Twofold
30 Sorry situations
32 You may make its head turn
34 Coke competitor
36 One of the Three Stooges
38 Trig, e.g.
39 Govt. workplace watchdog
40 "I'm game"
42 One, for one
45 Passing fancy
47 Mouthing off
49 Unwelcome obligations
51 Key with two flats
52 Lay low
53 Has a bite
56 Brief burst
59 Cairo cobras
61 Actress Sedgwick
62 Bunion's place
63 Whatever
65 Brazilian hot spot, briefly
66 System starter?
67 Roll of dough

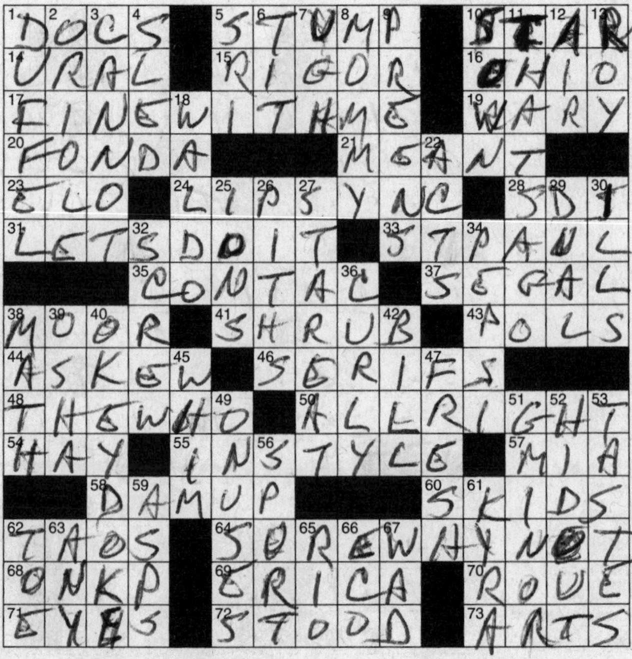

by Nancy Salomon

51

50/60

ACROSS

1 Swine
5 "Money ___ everything"
9 Northern Scandinavians
14 Toward shelter, nautically
15 Burn the surface of
16 Devoured quickly
17 Soft light
18 Give new decor
19 Desmond of "Sunset Blvd."
20 Lungful
21 1976 Hoffman/Olivier film
23 Music from Jamaica
25 Dover fish
26 Coward's color
29 Portugal's capital
33 It may be acute or obtuse
35 Master hand
37 The woman of Lennon's "Woman"
38 Dik Browne's "Hi and ___"
39 Strikingly bright
40 Habeas corpus, e.g.
41 Make a boo-boo
42 2005 Christo display in New York City, with "the"
43 Social class
44 Got quiet, with "down"
46 Take back, as one's story
48 Draft status
50 Hold back
53 Character who debuted in All Star Comics, December 1941
58 August 1 sign
59 April 1 sign
60 Word said before opening the eyes
61 Cain's victim
62&63 First two names of Guy de Maupassant
64 Inlet
65 Advances of money
66 Conclusions
67 Looks at

DOWN

1 Dik Browne's "___ the Horrible"
2 Stan's partner in old comedy
3 Title song of a 1966 hit movie
4 Darn, as socks
5 Tel Aviv's land
6 Prophet
7 Nothin'
8 Brings (out)
9 Lipstick ingredient
10 Makes up (for)
11 Salon job, informally
12 Cougar
13 Bridge
21 Stag party attender
22 ___ up (hid out)
24 Hair goops
27 Fail to mention
28 Be unsteady
30 Brendan Behan book
31 Step ___ (hurry)
32 Observe
33 Actor Guinness
34 Nick Charles's wife
36 Workshop gripper
39 Darth ___ of "Star Wars"
40 Kind of ad
42 Book before Exodus
43 Normandy city
45 One of the M's in MoMA
47 Construction site machines
49 Cognizant
51 Christopher of "Superman"
52 Bob and Elizabeth of politics
53 Actor Ken of TV's "Wiseguy"
54 Creme cookie
55 Ship of Columbus
56 What a prophet reads
57 Darn, as socks
61 High card

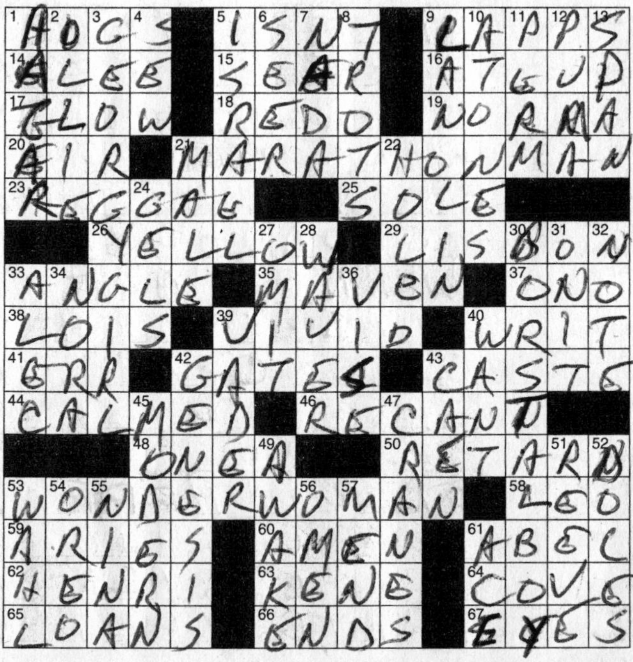

by Randy Sowell

52

ACROSS

1 Observe Yom Kippur
5 Small snack
9 Foxhole, basically
14 Darth Vader's son
15 Immunity item on "Survivor"
16 ___ Gay (W.W. II plane)
17 God who rode an eight-legged horse
18 Latch (onto)
19 Disastrous
20 "Everything can't work out perfectly"
23 Actress Lupino
24 Binary digit
25 Tactic during police questioning
32 The Amish raise them
33 Figure-skating division
34 Judo setting
36 401(k) alternatives
37 Moves a muscle
38 Word processor command
39 Giants outfielder Mel
40 What a bloodhound tracks
41 Wing, perhaps
42 It's one's word against the other
45 Pound sound
46 Pear-shaped fruit
47 Not continuous
56 Place with a "vacancy" sign
57 Folk singer Guthrie
58 "The Joy of Cooking" author Rombauer
59 Like the Vikings
60 Boxer Max
61 Without ice
62 Hopping mad
63 Part of a venetian blind
64 Othello, e.g.

DOWN

1 Move like lava
2 Carmaker from Bavaria
3 Tattoo artist's "canvas"
4 Causes of stress
5 Whopper rival
6 Just chilling
7 Hammer or hoe
8 "Tickle me" guy
9 Keeps safe
10 "Very soon"
11 The Wizard of Oz's exposer
12 Littleneck, e.g.
13 Robust
21 Part of a sweepstakes's fine print
22 Flies high
25 "Wayne's World" sidekick
26 Speak at length
27 Was decisive
28 Minor nuisances
29 Blessed event
30 Citizen of Muscat
31 Put asphalt on
32 Story of one's life
35 Country singer Ritter
37 Heinlein's genre
38 Laying hold of
40 Frozen dessert brand
41 Where Tibet is
43 Most like a swami
44 Attempt
47 Magazine that had a "UFO Update"
48 Jordan's Queen ___
49 Gillette brand
50 Catches in the act
51 Spoken
52 Small circus performer
53 Square footage
54 Islamic holy man
55 "Six Feet Under" character

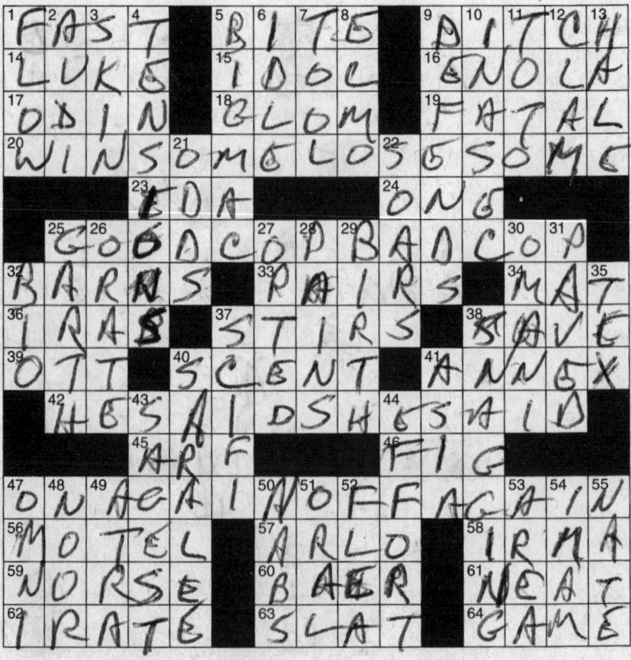

by Trip Payne

53

21 36

ACROSS

1 Be in harmony
5 Lewis with Lamb Chop
10 ___ out (barely made)
14 Functions
15 Poison
16 Editor's strikeout
17 Removed as with a wave of the hand
19 Altar area
20 Asian New Year's festival
21 Forever and a day
22 Bother
24 Upstream swimmer
26 Chicken of the Sea product
27 Popular sandwich cookie
28 Gung-ho
32 Backward-looking
35 Field of flowers?
37 Jong who wrote "Fear of Flying"
38 Downs' opposite
41 Coach's encouraging words
43 Nicotine's partner
44 R & B singer LaBelle
46 Tough time
48 Santa ___, Calif.
49 Santa ___, Calif.
50 Every one
54 Fly catcher?
56 Baby's noisemaker
58 Robert ___ . . . believe him, or not!
60 Tailless cat
62 Wee bit
63 Savvy about
64 Mom-and-pop event . . . and a hint to the insides of 17- and 41-Across and 11- and 40-Down
67 Blow one's horn
68 Champing at the bit
69 Hankering
70 Alluring
71 Twirls
72 First lady before Mamie

DOWN

1 Precisely
2 "Honest!"
3 Classic Volkswagen
4 Psychic ability, for short
5 Remain in a rut
6 Hydrant attachment
7 Base line on a graph
8 Free (of)
9 All thumbs
10 Mary Tyler Moore co-star
11 Persisted
12 Otherwise
13 Does and bucks
18 Confucian path
23 "I got it!"
25 Mafia
29 Water in the air
30 Foreword
31 Twosomes
33 Major TV maker
34 Boat mover
36 Narcotic
38 It's scanned at checkout: Abbr.
39 Chum
40 Major irritant for American colonists
42 Students
45 Three-part work
47 Tennis umpire's cry
51 Garb
52 Gong sounds
53 Bushes between yards
55 Varieties
57 Tree feller
58 Burglarizes
59 Regarding
60 Visitors to Jesus
61 "___, brother!"
65 Listening-in device
66 Where you may get a soaking

by Lynn Lempel

54

51

ACROSS

1 Electronic journals
6 Stretchy candy
11 The elder Geo. Bush once headed it
14 Lover boy
15 Trixie's best friend, on TV
16 Some rush-hour periods: Abbr.
17 Pair of socks?
19 Sch. in Troy, N.Y.
20 Comes out on top
21 Funny Conway
22 Called strikes and balls
24 It turns the tide
26 Frog-to-be
28 Spears
31 Architect Jones
32 Stiller's comedy partner
33 Stat for Ali
34 Science class feature
37 Pair of sneakers?
42 Lorne Michaels show, for short
43 Neckline shape
44 Took to the station house
45 Confessed, with "up"
48 Caught, as with a tree limb
50 "March!" opener
52 Time's partner, in brief
53 Means to solving a sudoku puzzle
54 I love, in Mexico
55 "Tosca" number
59 Britney Spears's "___ Slave 4 U"
60 Pair of pants?
64 Engine speed, for short
65 Lustful looker
66 Dutch pottery
67 It's definite
68 Ostentatious
69 Low cards

DOWN

1 Knitted body part
2 Actress Anderson
3 Divine sign
4 Wise up
5 Piglet's mother
6 Gimme putts
7 Homecoming guest
8 Swimming aid
9 Obscenity watcher: Abbr.
10 Violinist Menuhin
11 Fuel-saving strategy
12 Motivate
13 Stage mutter
18 Plains tribe
23 Driver's stat.
25 Pearl Buck heroine
26 Polynesian pendant
27 See 38-Down
28 Bratty types
29 Nasty
30 Charades, e.g.
33 Philosopher Lao-___
35 French gal pal
36 Give a bit
38 ___ and 27-Down (for all time)
39 Comic Foxx
40 Burn the midnight oil, student-style
41 Linen pulp product
46 It ended at 11:00 on 11/11
47 Crispy snacks
48 Beatified mother
49 Dodge model
50 Coquette
51 Get-up-and-go
54 Not many
56 Be a monarch
57 In doubt
58 Backs of boats
61 "Ick!"
62 Andy Capp's wife
63 Banned insecticide

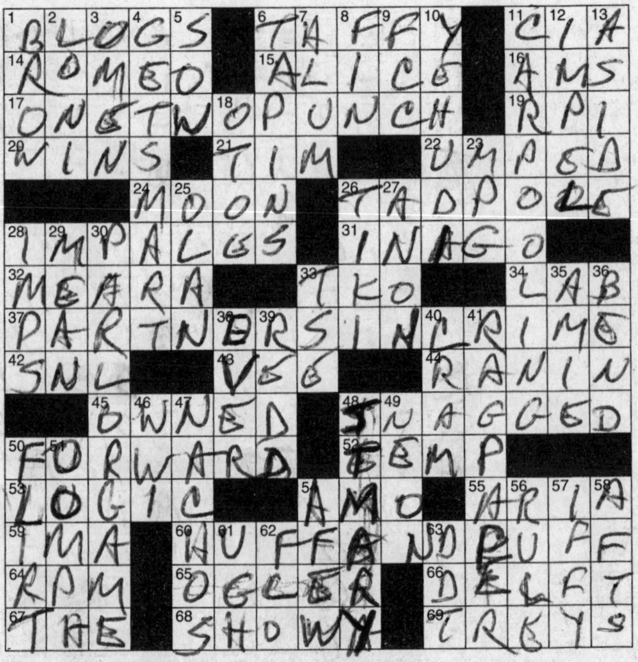

by Lee Glickstein and Nancy Salomon

55

36/80

ACROSS

1 Dennis the Menace-type kids
6 Luxuriates
11 "Just ___ thought!"
14 Love to pieces
15 Maine college town
16 Stanley Cup org.
17 Start a negotiation
19 Dover's state: Abbr.
20 Minor setback
21 Raises canines?
23 Body parts with claws
26 Pizzas
28 Mrs. Chaplin
29 Miner's discovery
30 Give a little, take a little
33 Euripides drama
35 "___ a gun!"
36 Late, as a payment
39 Incited
43 Street-smart
45 Spine-tingling
46 Agree
51 SSE's opposite
52 "This won't hurt ___"
53 Seen once in a blue moon
54 Korean soldiers
55 To the point
58 Nick and Nora's dog of story and film
60 ___-tac-toe
61 Shake on it
66 Put into service
67 Jazz great Shaw
68 ___ cum laude
69 Basic version: Abbr.
70 Atwitter, with "up"
71 Fork feature

DOWN

1 "Kapow!"
2 Nutritional inits.
3 "All systems go"
4 Lock of hair
5 Actor Connery
6 Dance energetically
7 Terrier's sound
8 Tap dancing without taps
9 Patella's place
10 Achy
11 "You said a mouthful!"
12 Singer Easton
13 "Amen!"
18 Back of the neck
22 Chewy candy
23 Ceremonial splendor
24 Square footage
25 Ties the knot
27 UFO occupants
30 Angry with
31 "The Ice Storm" director ___ Lee
32 Theater seats
34 ". . . yadda, yadda, yadda"
37 One, in Madrid
38 Petition
40 First 007 film
41 Pigpen cry
42 Front page fill
44 Nay's opposite
46 It has points in Arizona
47 Double-reed woodwind player
48 Chopped into small pieces, as food
49 Not suitable for kids, as a movie
50 Go well together
54 Speeder spotter
56 "Out of Africa" author Dinesen
57 Parched
59 Office worker just for the day
62 Commit perjury
63 Sense of self
64 Raggedy doll
65 Fall behind

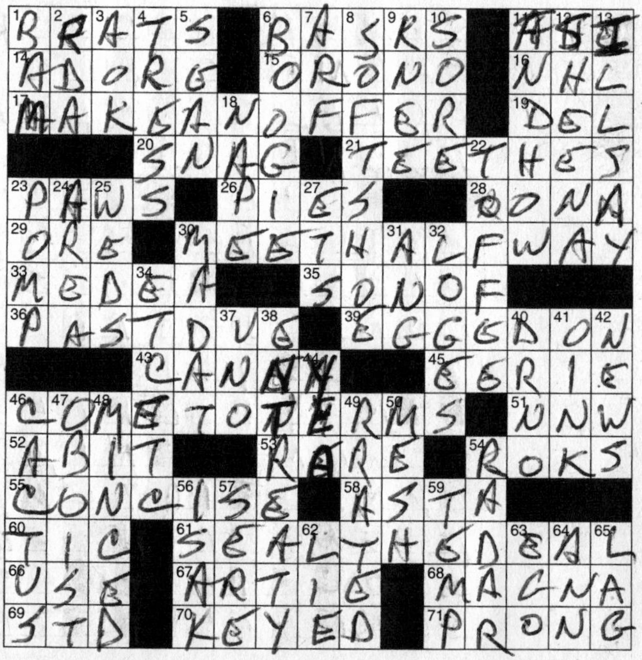

by Kendall Twigg

56

32/48

ACROSS

1 Sandal part
6 Hamlet, by nationality
10 Cabbagelike plant
14 Motif
15 Test that's hard to cheat on
16 ___ of Evil
17 Sharon of Israel
18 One of the Spice Girls
19 Emcee
20 Easy-to-manage financial record
23 Early second-century year
24 Writer Fleming
25 Feature of some apartments
34 Flax fabric
35 Homer's hangout on "The Simpsons"
36 Co. with a triangular logo
37 Unwanted spots
38 Got wind of
40 Centers of activity
41 Winter driving hazard
42 ___ Valley, Calif.
43 Where Pago Pago is
44 One who might take bribes for favors
48 O.R. workers
49 Vardalos of "My Big Fat Greek Wedding"
50 Sandra Bullock film of 1998
58 Large diving bird
59 Noted garden site
60 "My Fair Lady" character
61 Allied group
62 It may be put on after a bath
63 Mister, in Madrid
64 Word that may follow the start of 20-, 25-, 44- or 50-Across
65 Speak indistinctly
66 "Yikes!"

DOWN

1 Headliner
2 Drive-___
3 Horse controller
4 Word of agreement
5 It might present you with a big bill
6 ___ bag
7 Territory
8 Bust maker
9 Drew forth
10 V.I.P.
11 Neural transmitter
12 Aid to Santa
13 Superlative ending
21 Annual b-ball shootout
22 Scullers' needs
25 Tartan design
26 Perfume maker Nina ___
27 ___ tube
28 Flying geese formation
29 Paperless communication
30 Negative conjunction
31 Judd who wrote and sang "Change of Heart"
32 Hot drink
33 Cuban boy in 1999–2000 news
38 Beatniks
39 Funny Philips
40 Fond du ___
42 In ___ (together)
43 Blue-eyed cat
45 Hypnotic state
46 Sillier
47 Up to, briefly
50 Sport with horses
51 Corner piece
52 Hero
53 Philippine island
54 "Break ___!"
55 Actress Gershon
56 Shirt label name
57 Mercury and Saturn, but not Uranus
58 J.F.K.'s successor

by Nancy Kavanaugh

57

ACROSS

1 Gentlemen tipped theirs to ladies, once
5 Home improvement pro Bob
9 Boxing ring boundaries
14 1970s tennis champ Nastase
15 Figure skater's jump
16 God, in the Koran
17 F.D.R.'s dog
18 Irritated state
19 "Silly" birds
20 "Do tell!"
23 Sailor's affirmative
24 With competence
25 Greets with gales of laughter
27 Be that as it may
30 Irish accent
31 Hits a golf ball to the side, e.g.
32 Burn on the outside
33 Sunnyside up servings
36 "The Simpsons" storekeeper
37 Roster of enemies
40 Granola bit
41 Four-poster and others
43 Window ledge
44 Hooch
46 How cough syrup is taken
48 Shakespearean verse
49 Barely enough
51 Warrior princess of TV
52 Buffalo's summer hrs.
53 "Do tell!"
58 Snooped, with "around"
60 Gershwin's "___ Plenty o' Nuttin'"
61 Active sort
62 Knocks dead
63 Ball hit out of bounds
64 Top draft level
65 Up to the present
66 Noted Art Deco illustrator
67 Not, in dialect

DOWN

1 Old 45 player
2 "Too bad!"
3 Pinball play ender
4 Seattle football player
5 To a huge degree
6 Slangy no
7 Mariner ___ Ericson
8 Bar in the front of a church
9 Motley, as an army
10 Bullring cheer
11 "Do tell!"
12 High mark with low effort
13 Ghost costume, basically
21 Bring shame to
22 Beer from Golden, Colo.
26 Regret
27 "Moby-Dick" captain
28 Yep's opposite
29 "Do tell!"
30 Word before dance or laugh
32 Painting of a fruit bowl, e.g.
34 Long look
35 Leave in, as text
38 Religion of the Koran
39 New York strip alternative
42 ___ Lanka
45 Interminably
47 In the thick of
48 Agree out of court
49 High-I.Q. club
50 Fanzine profilees
51 Strikes through
54 Composer Stravinsky
55 College in New Rochelle, N.Y.
56 ___-do-well
57 Confederate uniform color
59 Hurricane hub

by Harvey Estes

58

49

ACROSS

1 Nonsensical talk
5 Film repair
11 Lighter brand
14 Quick approval: Abbr.
15 Family support group
16 "___ Beso" (Paul Anka hit)
17 Place for rolls
19 U.S.P.S. delivery
20 Congressional periods
21 Mary Lou of gymnastics
23 Range units: Abbr.
24 Do a pre-op chore
25 Washes with detergent
29 Tranquil state
32 Artery problems
33 Stubble remover
34 "Silent" prez
35 Haloed one, in France
36 Naturally belong
37 Kind of milk
38 Family dog, for short
39 Stiff hairs
40 Model wood
41 Ward denizen
43 Anne who married Henry VIII
44 Socks
45 Part of a jazz combo
46 Summarizes
48 "Watch out now"
53 ___ de toilette
54 Numbskull
56 Hosp. picture
57 Household helper
58 Impulse
59 Choose, with "to"
60 Comedian Russell
61 Faucet brand

DOWN

1 Sails on sloops
2 Memo starter
3 Goes (for)
4 H H H, to Greeks
5 Wooden shoes
6 Floor sketches
7 Girl
8 Octopus's defense
9 Force
10 One matriculating
11 A cowboy might have a big one
12 Middle of a ratio
13 Word that can precede the start of 17- or 54-Across or 11- or 27-Down
18 March of ___
22 When repeated, a reproach
24 "The World of ___ Wong" (1960 movie)
25 Resell illegally
26 Of an arm bone
27 Treat for a trick
28 ___ Jeanne d'Arc
29 Persian Gulf state
30 Part of a simple bouquet
31 Violinist Mischa
33 Marriage and others
36 Literally, "wind and water"
37 Mule of song
39 Noted Warhol subject
40 Pug, e.g.
42 Hearst kidnap grp.
43 Business that makes a lot of dough
45 ___ Hawkins Day
46 San ___, Italy
47 O.K. Corral lawman
48 "Jabberwocky" start
49 Buddy
50 Prefix with nautical
51 Craze
52 Genesis home
55 Facing: Abbr.

by Victor Fleming

ACROSS

1 Kuwaiti ruler
5 Computer/phone line link
10 The late Peter Jennings's network
13 Tightwad
15 Atop
16 Likewise
17 Not laughing or crying
19 Cut (off)
20 R-rated
21 River's curve
22 Labyrinth
23 Cancún cash
25 Van Gogh subjects
27 Volcanic coating
30 Curtain holder
31 Affirm
32 "Every good boy does fine" and others
38 Doll's cry
39 "Wow!"
40 Diva's solo
41 Best time to act
46 Deli loaves
47 Administered
48 Itsy-bitsy
49 Landmark near the pyramids of Giza
52 Excited, with "up"
54 Gets rid of weeds
55 Sigma's follower
57 Cherished
61 Letters before an alias
62 2003 animated film . . . with a hint to 17-, 32- and 41-Across
64 Sunset hue
65 Singer at Diana's funeral
66 1978 jazz musical
67 Snoop
68 Ehrich ___, Houdini's real name
69 Makes a doily

DOWN

1 Outback birds
2 Item on a hotel pillow
3 "Aha"
4 Chart anew
5 ___ tai (drink)
6 Slender woodwinds
7 Mafia chiefs
8 Shifty
9 Brooks of "The Producers"
10 Oversized reference book
11 Rotgut, e.g.
12 Makes do
14 Cesar ___, classic player of the Joker
18 Boxer Mike
22 Singer Makeba
24 Loathsome
26 M.L.K. Jr., for one
27 Buckshot and such
28 Rice Krispies sound
29 Rope fiber
31 Stick (to)
33 Native New Zealanders
34 Voting "nay"
35 Pilot and flight attendants
36 "___ kleine Nachtmusik"
37 Fill to capacity
42 Rembrandt van ___
43 Fabric
44 Like some Central American pyramids
45 Jittery
49 Opposite of mild, in cheeses
50 Texas hold 'em, e.g.
51 Intoxicating
52 "Great job!"
53 Krispy Kreme product
56 Voting "nay"
58 Country crooner McEntire
59 Give off
60 John and Jane, in case titles
62 Handful
63 Those with clout

by Lynn Lempel

60

ACROSS

1 Oktoberfest band instrument
5 Retirement spots?
9 Singer Cline
14 Caspian Sea feeder
15 Saudi Arabia neighbor
16 Toulouse ta-ta
17 Main point
18 Scarlett's home
19 Aerodynamic
20 Drummer Ringo, taking pictures?
23 Off one's feed
24 Jackie's O
25 Rare hit for a slow runner
29 A ton of
31 Family nickname
34 Like "Goosebumps" stories
35 Hostilities ender
36 Spewer of 2002
37 Educator Horace, acting like a barbarian?
40 Renaissance family name
41 Post-it
42 Broadcast
43 L.P.G.A. supporter?
44 Throws in
45 Takes in or out
46 "-ite" compound, often
47 Gardner of film
48 Actor Jack, circling the globe?
55 Obliging spirit
56 A mothball may have one
57 Colorado skiing mecca
59 Playwright Chekhov
60 Weightlifter's count, informally
61 Old Harper's Bazaar illustrator
62 Mango's center
63 Actress Winslet
64 Call for

DOWN

1 Harbor craft
2 "The Haj" author
3 Wild party
4 Deep-voiced, for a woman
5 Bit of skid row litter
6 Letters on screens
7 "Rats!"
8 Fly in the ointment
9 Danish, e.g.
10 Loser to Dwight, twice
11 Amphitheater section
12 Palmist, e.g.
13 Big laugh
21 Drunk as a skunk
22 Seasonal temp position
25 Basic principle
26 Witherspoon of "Legally Blonde"
27 Boiling mad
28 Bench material
29 Dillon and Damon
30 Need Advil, say
31 Pre-fight psych job
32 City or child preceder
33 ___ of time
35 Poke
36 Send out
38 Wound up
39 1980s–'90s courtroom drama
44 "What's My Line?" panelist Francis
45 Disinclined
46 Heavenly hunter
47 Take on
48 Exploded, with "off"
49 Savvy about
50 Task
51 Think tank nugget
52 20-20, e.g.
53 Expose
54 Dentist's concern
55 Interstate sign
58 Had an edge

by Randall J. Hartman

ACROSS

1 Frank ___, leader of the Mothers of Invention
6 High Ottoman official
11 Boeing 747, e.g.
14 Hawke of Hollywood
15 Speck in the sea
16 Lode deposit
17 Keep cool
19 Break a Commandment
20 Fraternity hopeful
21 Twisted in pain
23 Gorillas and such
24 "The most trusted name in electronics" sloganeer, once
27 Three: Prefix
28 Conclude negotiations
33 Large feather
37 Knights
38 Unadorned
39 Second chance for viewers
40 Scheduling abbr.
41 Ambulance sound
42 Egg-shaped
43 Smelting waste
44 Rand McNally product
45 Be just what's needed
48 "So there!"
49 11-pointer, in blackjack
50 Slugger Willie
54 Woolen blankets
58 "In" group
60 (The) bug
61 Be a lulu
64 B-ball official
65 Amazed
66 Shady retreat
67 Bumbler
68 Overfull
69 Horses of a certain color

DOWN

1 Zoo equine
2 Consumed eagerly
3 Developmental stage
4 Trajectories
5 Gambler's stake
6 Word with cutie or sweetie
7 ___ Wednesday
8 Whole bunch
9 Cozy spots by the fire
10 Get-up
11 Tease
12 Lake near Niagara Falls
13 Watch over
18 ___ and now
22 Morsel
25 Fairy tale dwelling
26 "Arabian Nights" hero
28 Upper house member: Abbr.
29 Heartbreaking
30 British nobleman
31 Zone
32 Optical device
33 Grad student's mentor
34 Big name in denim
35 Eurasia's ___ Mountains
36 Islamic leader
41 Actor Mineo
43 Doo-wop group that sang in "Grease"
46 In other words
47 Polish Nobelist Walesa
50 Small: Prefix
51 Mideast's Gulf of ___
52 1890s gold rush destination
53 Prophets
54 Place to stick a comb, once
55 Pet's tiny tormentor
56 Back talk
57 Trick-taking game with 32 cards
59 Mad king of the stage
62 Female sheep
63 Newsman Koppel

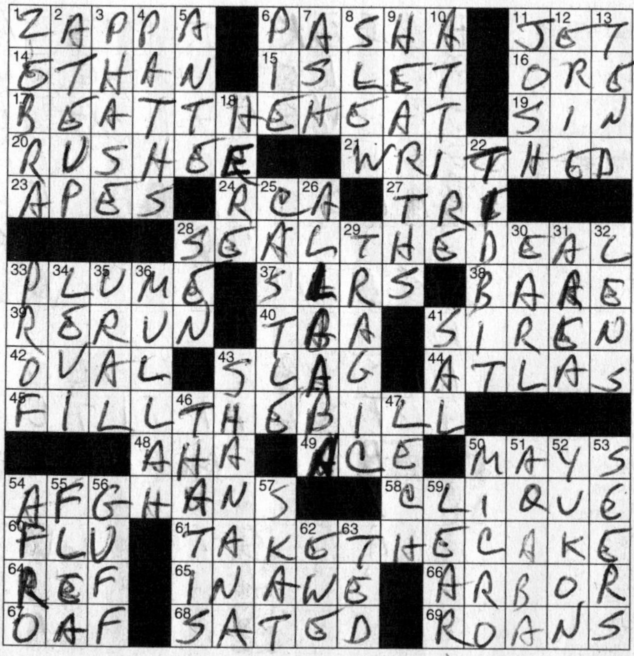

by Lynn Lempel

62

19/32

ACROSS

1 Bit of dandruff
6 Drivers' aids
10 Captain of the Pequod
14 Debussy contemporary Erik
15 Cart part
16 "Damn Yankees" vamp
17 Document shown at border patrol
19 Writer Harte
20 Prefix with duct
21 Yeats or Keats
22 Cape Canaveral event
24 California observatory
26 Salon jobs
27 Fixation indication
31 Meager
33 Served up a whopper
34 Magic org.
35 Feathery scarves
36 Very humble home
38 Score for a 34-Across player
39 Satisfied sighs
40 1952 Hope/Crosby "Road" destination
41 Pool part?
42 Rubbernecker at the Ritz, perhaps
46 Fuss with feathers
47 Zilch
51 Celestial Seasonings alternative
53 Gin flavorer
54 "So there you ___!"
55 Long stretches
56 Part of a suit of armor
59 Derby
60 "I smell ___!"
61 Perfect places
62 Took it on the lam
63 Candied tubers
64 Like Vikings

DOWN

1 Shutterbug's setting
2 Caterpillar, for one
3 Internet commerce
4 Opposite of military: Abbr.
5 Button one's lips
6 Pub
7 Off-ramp
8 Raised railroads
9 Denver is way above it
10 Philatelists' books
11 Interrupts
12 Knighted Guinness
13 The Wife of ___ (Chaucer story teller)
18 Credit union offering
23 Like the Kalahari
25 Elevator pioneer Elisha
26 Ballerina's bend
28 The King (subject of four "sightings" elsewhere in this puzzle)
29 Cousin of an English horn
30 Catch a few Z's
31 Arty Manhattan district
32 The cellar
35 "Balderdash!"
36 Participate in decision-making
37 Lena of "Chocolat"
38 Sister and wife of Zeus
40 Ran in the wash
41 Settled a score
43 Rubbed out or off
44 Estuaries
45 Labor saver
48 More despicable
49 Steam items
50 Abrupt
51 Lowly laborer
52 Asia's fast-shrinking ___ Sea
53 Ore deposit
57 ___-la-la
58 Words of commitment

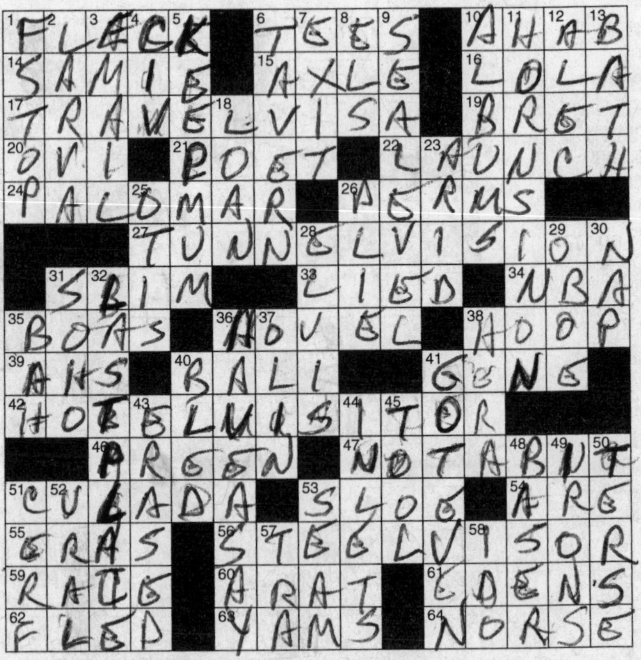

by Holden Baker and Nancy Salomon

ACROSS

1 The "C" of U.S.M.C.
6 Opinion tester
10 "That's enough!"
14 France's Joan ___
15 Samoa's capital
16 Spy Mata ___
17 City chief
18 Lady's escort
20 Bit of encouragement
22 Bent over
25 Frankie of the Four Seasons
26 Stephen King novel
30 Wide shoe width
31 "Farewell"
32 The WB rival
33 Old draft letters
34 Casino supervisor
38 Cambridge sch.
41 Stocking's end
42 "___ hooks" (box warning)
44 CPR giver
47 Antes
50 "Me, too"
52 Pixies
53 Hoodwink
57 On the way
58 Wrinkled citrus fruits
62 Barbara of "I Dream of Jeannie"
63 Cries of surprise
64 Poor
65 Georgia and Lithuania, once: Abbr.
66 Corduroy feature
67 One with a dish towel

DOWN

1 Dot follower
2 Son ___ gun
3 Bit of sunshine
4 Request a hand?
5 Barely gather together, as funds
6 Chinese temple
7 Dentist's request
8 ___ remover
9 Plaster backing
10 Queen of ___, biblical V.I.P.
11 Mexican dish
12 Soothsayer
13 Little finger
19 Impose, as a tax
21 President pro ___
22 Restful resorts
23 Kennedy and Turner
24 "Miss ___ Regrets"
27 Centers of Christmas wrapping paper
28 G.I.'s address
29 M.D.'s associates
35 Skater Midori
36 Wee one
37 Envelop
38 Competition with shot putters and hurdlers
39 As to, in legal memos
40 Use a Frisbee
43 Bee or wasp
44 Catches sight of
45 Piles
46 Rag
47 ___ colada
48 Infectious fly
49 Kind of financing, for short
51 Daybreaks
54 Plenty, to a poet
55 Fed. workplace watchdog
56 Six-stringed instrument
59 Hula hoop?
60 Suffix with chlor- or sulf-
61 Damascus' land: Abbr.

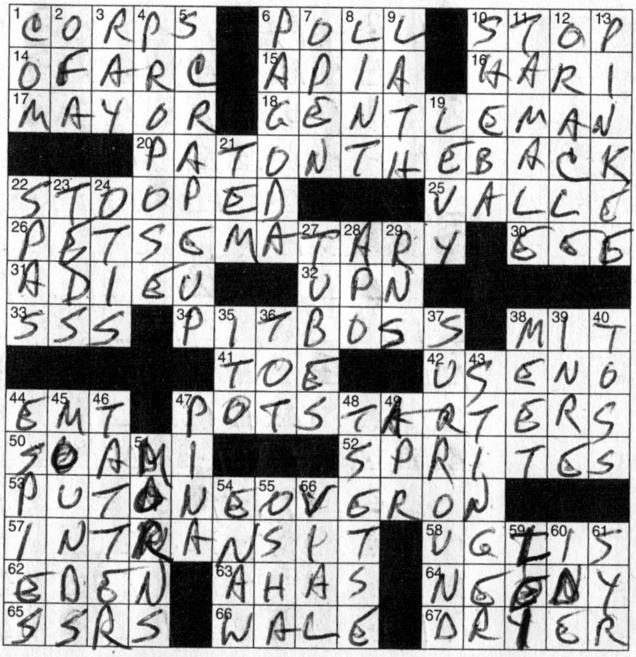

by Sarah Keller

64

1145/04

ACROSS

1 Congregation leader
6 Noted movie terrier
10 Excellent, in slang
14 Columnist Goodman
15 Very top
16 Prefix in the airplane industry
17 Large antelope
18 Numbers game
19 A bit blue
20 False rumor about seafood?
23 Needle part
24 Whistle blower
25 "Delta of Venus" author
26 Barnyard sound
29 40¢ per fifth of a mile, in New York City?
32 Greek earth goddess: Var.
35 New Deal program, for short
36 C. S. Lewis's "The Chronicles of ___"
37 It's trapped indoors
38 Finis
40 Polish border river
41 Protozoan
44 Preschooler
46 Guernsey, e.g., in the English Channel
47 Holy chicken?
50 Disco ___, "The Simpsons" character
51 A Perón
52 Timberwolves' org.
53 Onetime United rival
56 Chic scavenger?
60 Usually unopened mail
62 Eisenhower's Korean counterpart
63 George Burns movie
64 St. ___, spring break mecca
65 Evening on Mt. Etna
66 MapQuest offering
67 Parrots
68 Mince words?
69 "Fabulous!"

DOWN

1 Witherspoon of "Vanity Fair"
2 Put to rest, as fears
3 Proclaim loudly
4 Not stay rigid
5 A Gandhi
6 Rest awhile
7 Oil price-setting grp.
8 Lessee
9 Tony Blair, collegiately
10 Catherine who wed Henry VIII
11 Sweat absorbers
12 Parabola, essentially
13 Play (with)
21 Queue cue
22 Kournikova of tennis
27 Sharon of Israel
28 On ___ (how pranks may be done)
29 Spud
30 ___ Domingo
31 C-3PO, e.g., for short
32 Lens
33 Shoot for
34 Immunize
39 Conductor's cue, maybe
42 Shade of red
43 Unfavorable
45 Forbidden: Var.
48 Redeemed, as a check
49 Stubble removers
53 Advice to a base runner before leaving base
54 Penned
55 Viper
57 Iowa college town
58 Actress Garr
59 Mao colleague
60 Bathroom installation
61 Get-up-and-go

by Leonard Williams

ACROSS

1 N.B.A.'s O'Neal, informally
5 Armada parts
10 Shoots the breeze
14 Andean land
15 1992 and '96 third party candidate
16 Milky white gem
17 A couple of chips in the pot, say
18 Knight in shining ___
19 Waiter's offering
20 California senator
23 Lucy's best friend
26 Water pitcher
27 Singer at Woodstock
31 Pharmacy weights
35 Historical period
36 Comet feature
37 Exactly right
38 Humorist Bennett who co-founded Random House
40 Long-billed marsh bird
42 Abhor
43 One-on-one teachers
45 Pitts of Hollywood
47 "Oh, my!"
48 Johanna ___, author of "Heidi"
49 1972 Olympic swimming sensation
51 '60s civil rights org.
53 Came about
54 Comment when things are tough . . . or a title for this puzzle
60 Bulletin board fastener
61 Middle of a sink
62 Baby carriage
66 Tip-off
67 Slugger with 755 home runs
68 Prince Charles's sport
69 ___ and haws
70 Tchaikovsky ballet roles
71 Puppy's cry

DOWN

1 Healthful retreat
2 Rooster's mate
3 Paintings and such
4 Where Montreal is
5 Wrangle
6 Parsley or bay leaf
7 "___ la Douce," 1963 film
8 More in need
9 Old mattress stuffing
10 Sin city of Genesis
11 Pinnacle
12 Cause of distress
13 "Dirty, rotten scoundrel," e.g.
21 Oodles
22 George Eliot's "Adam ___"
23 Kicks out
24 Shredded
25 Robust
28 Mama of the Mamas and the Papas
29 Cousins, e.g.
30 Henry's fair lady
32 Slow symphonic movement
33 Sacred songs
34 "Bless you" preceder
37 Kneehole site
39 Abandons
41 What a golfer might shoot
44 Peel
46 Grp. with F-16's
49 Country singer Tim
50 Ivy League-ish
52 Musical endings
54 Measles symptom
55 Chronicle
56 Lowlife
57 ___ Lee cakes
58 One guarding the steps of the New York Public Library
59 Rustic lodgings
63 Fish-to-be
64 Completely
65 Floor cleaner

by Lynn Lempel

66

04/21

ACROSS

1 Cavalier or Impala
6 N.B.A. star in the '96 film "Kazaam"
10 Predicament
14 Eagle's home
15 Hot-and-sour soup ingredient
16 Get misty-eyed
17 Fifth Amendment issue
20 Boat in "Jaws"
21 Guesstimate phrase
22 Church recesses
23 City on the Rhone
25 Gung-ho
26 Ulterior motive
31 To no ___ (fruitlessly)
32 Biblical flood insurance?
33 ___ vu
37 Congressional declaration
38 "Mr. Jock, TV quiz Ph.D., bags few lynx," for example
42 Wrigley Field player
43 Where pants may have a hole
45 Director Howard
46 Lyric poem
48 Australia was the first country to implement it
52 Billiard shots
55 Longtime host of "Scientific American Frontiers"
56 Cover story?
57 Bantu language
59 ___ Toys, maker of the Magic 8-Ball
63 Intelligence endeavor
66 Pirouette points
67 Like most graffiti: Abbr.
68 Flower part
69 "Provided that is the case . . ."
70 Man with a top hat and cane
71 College chief

DOWN

1 Mafia bigwig
2 Frau's partner
3 Rocker Clapton
4 "The Four Seasons" composer
5 Roll-call vote
6 Breastbones
7 Brewer's need
8 A young Michael Jackson had one
9 Quid pro ___
10 Acquired family member
11 Intrinsically
12 Like some cereals
13 Rendezvous
18 Tom or Jerry of "Tom and Jerry"
19 Cowpoke's bud
24 Canine plaint
25 44-Down singer
26 Peddle
27 Pavlov of Pavlov's dogs fame
28 "How ___ you?!"
29 Eric ___, 2004 Dodger All-Star pitcher
30 Blunder
34 E.P.A. concern: Abbr.
35 Unarmed combat
36 Help in a heist
39 Circle segments
40 Neither here ___ there
41 Lake ___, reservoir on the Colorado
44 1962 hit subtitled "That Kiss!"
47 45, e.g.
49 Qatari leader
50 "American Idol" display
51 Fuzzy image
52 Desert bloomers
53 Reserved
54 Tears apart
57 Basketball defense
58 Stratford-___-Avon
60 "Holy cow!"
61 Try to persuade
62 Exclusive
64 Put out, as a base runner
65 Egyptian snake

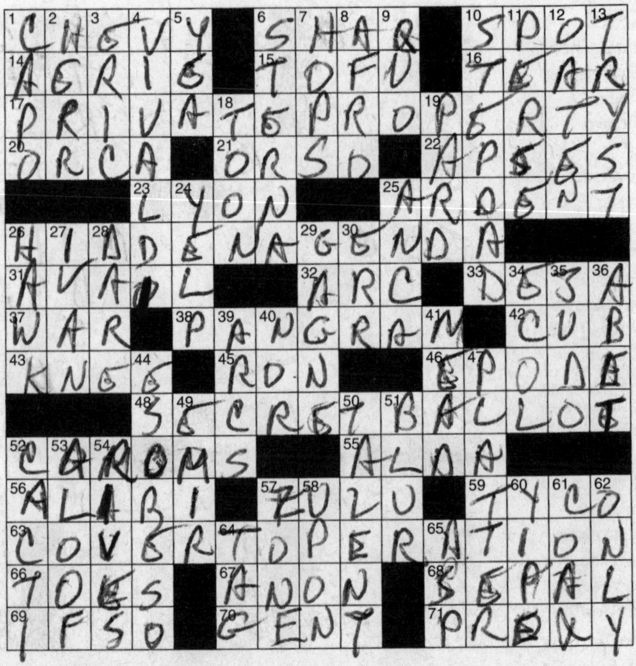

by Barry C. Silk

67

ACROSS

1 British rule in India
4 Eject, as lava
8 Multigenerational tales
13 Cowboy boot feature
15 Read (over)
16 Trashy sort
17 Lowland
18 First-rate
19 With 67-Across, a whisker cutter
20 Dollar amount indicated on 55-Across
23 Sunshine State city
24 "That hurts!"
25 Gathers leaves
28 Mailing label words
33 "Stop yelling ___!"
36 Jazzy Fitzgerald
38 Lend ___ (listen)
39 Niceties following 29-Downs
42 Instant
43 Opposite of "ja"
44 Canadian gas brand
45 "Seriously, don't bother"
47 Mythical being with horns
49 Playing card dot
51 Gives the gas
55 Forms filled out for potential employers
61 Smell
62 Ignoring modern sensibilities, for short
63 Island of Napoleon's exile
64 Hysterical
65 Yards rushed, e.g.
66 "Hold it!"
67 See 19-Across
68 Nozzle site
69 Hwys.

DOWN

1 Replies to an invitation, briefly
2 Separately
3 Minty drink
4 Backup means for gaining entrance
5 Impoverished
6 Sea eagle
7 Full of dandelions, say
8 Summer headwear
9 ___ Sea, which is really a lake
10 Strip in the Mideast
11 Love god
12 Surprisingly lively
14 Letter often accompanying 55-Across
21 Flight board abbr.
22 Call for help
26 North Carolina's ___ University
27 Swings around
29 Helpful step for an employment seeker
30 Preceders of cues, alphabetically
31 Blackens
32 Approximately
33 Memo heading abbr.
34 "Comin' ___ the Rye"
35 Common street name
37 Inter ___
40 Not fall behind
41 Theater intermission
46 Plunge
48 "Is it soup ___?"
50 Luxurious
52 ___-powered
53 Ignored, as a bridge suit
54 Hurdles for H.S. juniors
55 Doorpost
56 Face-to-face exam
57 ___ fide
58 In the thick of
59 Wild about
60 Book auditors, for short

by Michael Shteyman

68

ACROSS

1 With the bow, in music
5 Dutch pottery city
10 Disney clownfish
14 Satirical Mort
15 Writer Zola
16 Plow team
17 Author Silverstein
18 Like some panels
19 Diamond complement
20 1994 Ethan Hawke movie
23 D.C. baseballer
24 Choler
25 Singers James and Jones
28 Nougat candies introduced in 1922
33 Milo of "Ulysses"
34 Luau strings
35 Run without moving
36 Like tumblers
40 Use an old phone
43 Ram's ma'am
44 Capital at 12,000 feet
48 "Monty Python" birds
52 Gaynor of "South Pacific"
53 Airline's home base
54 Teachers' org.
55 Some e-mailed news reports
60 Leopold's 1920s co-defendant
62 Cook in a wok, perhaps
63 Sweep's schmutz
65 Book after Proverbs: Abbr.
66 Tree with catkins
67 Heavy reading?
68 Siouan speaker
69 Rebellious years, often
70 Snick-or-___

DOWN

1 Chucklehead
2 Cheering section cheers
3 Fastest land animal
4 Spicy stew, or its pot
5 Hanker for
6 Is histrionic
7 Pad producer
8 Spare tire, so to speak
9 Dustin's "Tootsie" co-star
10 Hardly aboveboard
11 Used to be
12 Game pieces
13 Calorie count of some diet drinks
21 Purplish
22 Gumshoe
23 Sgt. or cpl.
26 Shoemaker's tool
27 Chicago-to-Miami dir.
29 Within reach, as a goal
30 Down the ___
31 River to the Volga
32 Tightrope walker's need
37 Stephen of "The Crying Game"
38 Have in hand
39 "Well, ___!"
40 Hoover, e.g.
41 "See ___ care!"
42 Erté forte
45 Seaplane float
46 "Totally cool!"
47 When doubled, sister of Eva
49 Early second-century year
50 Make less dingy
51 Boring tools
56 Aspiring J.D.'s exam
57 Where the Clintons met
58 Fellow, slangily
59 J.F.K. landers, once
60 Late July baby
61 When the Supreme Court reconvenes: Abbr.
64 Ball raiser

by Stella Daily and Bruce Venzke

40

ACROSS

1 "Whew! The workweek's almost over!"
5 Ready for picking
9 Adjust
14 Indian princess
15 Disney's "___ and the Detectives"
16 Nonsocial type
17 Memo-heading abbr.
18 Alan Alda series
19 Weak and thin, as a voice
20 Chinese main dish
23 Veer sharply
24 Hymn-playing instruments
28 Actress ___ Dawn Chong
29 Slight downturn
31 Trade
32 Wading bird
35 Unyielding
37 Santa ___ winds
38 Reagan's tax policy, to detractors
41 Astern
42 Less polite
43 Emblem on an Indian pole
44 Dire prophecy
46 Frisbee or Slinky
47 Big mfr. of A.T.M.'s
48 Mailing a letter or picking up a quart of milk, e.g.
50 Hype
53 Holler upon walking in the front door
57 State bordering Canada for 45 miles
60 Japanese sashes
61 Wife of Osiris
62 Carries
63 Solomonlike
64 Pics from which to make more pics
65 "You should be embarrassed!"
66 Reply to "Shall we?"
67 Suffix with switch

DOWN

1 Streetcar
2 Los ___, Calif.
3 Like a trailer behind a car
4 ID'd
5 Erase
6 Icon
7 Leaning tower site
8 1-to-12, gradewise
9 Place to exchange vows
10 Events
11 Raggedy ___
12 Bic or Schaefer
13 Attempt
21 Rhetorician
22 Make a surprise visit
25 Expect
26 1930s vice president John ___ Garner
27 Twitch
29 Rather risky
30 Composer Stravinsky
32 Escape, as detection
33 Attempt to get
34 Helicopter feature
35 Make over
36 E-business
39 Surpass
40 Narcotic pain reliever
45 Havoc
47 Squeak and squeal
49 Condemned's neckwear?
50 Raise
51 Doofus
52 Friend in a sombrero
54 Wolf's sound
55 Theater award
56 Bygone U.S. gasoline
57 The "I" in the answer to 1-Across
58 Dumbbell's cry
59 See ___ glance

by Timothy Powell

70

ACROSS

1 Eller of "Oklahoma!," for one
5 Striped swimmer
9 Signs of boredom
14 Dagger of old
15 Folkie Guthrie
16 Cultural values
17 Mouth, slangily
18 Pastry finisher
19 Piece of the action
20 Peace offering #1: "___"
23 Normand of the silents
24 Mini-dog
25 Grounded speedsters
27 Hayworth husband ___ Khan
28 Satisfied sounds
31 Fly catcher
33 Sister
34 Plant firmly
36 Last Olds ever made
38 Peace offering #2: "___"
42 Plumber's gadget
43 Ill-tempered
44 Haifa's land: Abbr.
45 Heed the coxswain
48 Bleat
49 Great Society initiator's inits.
52 Toupees, slangily
54 "Hogwash!"
56 Cathedral topper
58 Peace offering #3: "___"
62 Laces into
63 Have the nerve
64 Trident-shaped letters
65 "Who's there?" reply
66 Blue-pencil
67 Alternative digest magazine
68 Flows slowly
69 Wall Street inits.
70 The "P" of PX

DOWN

1 Inhaler target
2 "Can you believe it?!"
3 Just around the corner
4 Home on the range
5 Can of worms, maybe
6 St. Louis landmark
7 Winter hazard
8 Blue feeling
9 Polite reply from a ranch hand
10 Dumas swordsman
11 "How's tricks?"
12 Like some soda bottles
13 157.5° from N
21 Hoosegow
22 Needle feature
26 ___-cone
29 SHO alternative
30 Do some quilting
32 Ship stabilizer
34 Caribou kin
35 Sot's symptoms, for short
37 ___ of the land
38 Wrap in fiberglass
39 Generous gifts
40 Center of activity
41 Division of history
42 Round Table title
46 Web address ending
47 Like some dummies
49 Deceives
50 Gray matter
51 Trendy travelers
53 Snail mail attachment
55 Apple-polisher
57 Toaster type
59 Fr. holy women
60 "Trinity" author
61 Where to put un chapeau
62 Towel stitching

by Harriet Clifton

71

41/55

ACROSS

1 Top stories of barns
6 With 26-Across, Massachusetts resort area
10 Toot one's horn
14 Onetime Dutch fad item
15 " 'Potpourri' for a thousand, ___"
16 Mother of Apollo and Artemis
17 Theater school study
18 ___ Ness monster
19 Natural soother
20 Any of the Stones or the Who, e.g.
23 Multichanneled
25 It may have screwdrivers on it
26 See 6-Across
27 Moving jerkily
31 English cathedral site
32 Bettors' promises, e.g.
34 Cave
36 White-collar crime investigators follow them
40 Patronize, as a restaurant
41 Barbie or Ken
44 Cumberland ___
47 Default modes
50 Vote in favor
51 Start of a cry by Juliet
53 Didn't talk smoothly
55 Sidestroke features
59 Hourglass fill
60 See 2-Down
61 Loathes
64 Look ___ (study)
65 Author Wiesel
66 Les ___-Unis
67 Shells out
68 Indoor arena feature
69 Not saying much

DOWN

1 Inc., abroad
2 With 60-Across, Thornton Wilder play
3 Recurred, as an ailment
4 East ___ (U.N. member since 2002)
5 They may be wide open
6 Tranquility
7 Outfielder Moises
8 Chest muscles, briefly
9 Most damning evidence, maybe
10 "The ___ Witch Project"
11 Tell
12 Lacking a key, in music
13 Is called
21 Keystone ___ (old comedy figure)
22 Spiny plants
23 Physics, for one: Abbr.
24 Overly
28 What "I" and "am" do
29 Niñas: Abbr.
30 Rich dessert
33 Unhappy
35 The "O" in G.O.P.
37 Church organ features
38 Deep-seated
39 Susan Lucci, notably
42 Strong alkaline
43 Batted first, with "off"
44 Grapevine contents
45 Obscure matters
46 Like the tops of dunce caps
48 Prefix with state
49 Fragrant pouch
52 Windows predecessor
54 Play ice hockey
56 Caramel candy brand
57 Sink's alternative
58 Elbow's lower counterpart
62 Aliens, for short
63 Reverse of NNW

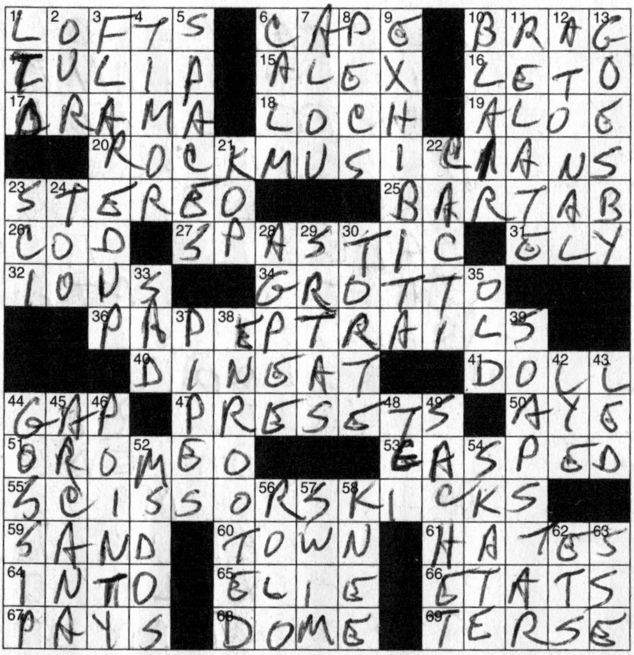

by Ethan Cooper

72

ACROSS

1 Big maker of metal products
6 "The Fox and the Grapes" author
11 The "it" in "Step on it!"
14 Imam's declaration
15 Shelley's "Cheers" role
16 Prov. on Niagara Falls
17 Egg-shaped
18 E
20 London's Big ___
21 "Do the Right Thing" pizzeria
23 Actor Bruce
24 Good-for-nothing
26 Some Baltic residents
29 Jazz's Fitzgerald
30 Equals
33 Rodeo rope
34 "Must be something ___"
35 M
42 Massage deeply
43 Hotmail alternative
44 C
50 Classmate
51 Challenged
52 Get an ___ (ace)
53 Prenatal test, for short
55 Halloween wear
57 Morse Tony-winning role
59 Squared
62 Like a game in which batters bat .000
64 6 on a phone
65 Many an ex-dictator
66 Not just fat
67 Elton John, e.g.
68 Flip out
69 Michelins or Pirellis

DOWN

1 "This is ___ for Superman!"
2 Worms or grubs
3 Setting of the movie "Eight Crazy Nights"
4 Stable bit?
5 Drinks stirred in pitchers
6 Title subject of a 1975 Truffaut film
7 $E=mc^2$ (first presented 9/27/1905)
8 Mediterranean isl.
9 Yoko ___
10 One of the Ivys
11 Modern means of search
12 "Measure for Measure" villain
13 Minnesota college
19 Place
22 PC key
25 "Get ___ the Church on Time"
27 30-second spot, e.g.
28 Exam with a perfect score of 2400
30 Part of a chorus line?
31 Lizard: Prefix
32 Actress Lotte
36 Auctioneer's shout
37 Italian sports car, briefly
38 ___ avis
39 "Nuts!"
40 Event on the horizon
41 Ages and ages
44 Jerks
45 Sana'a native
46 Yoda, to Luke Skywalker
47 Elton John, e.g.
48 Collected
49 Nonvinyl records, briefly
54 Designer Cassini
56 Granny ___
58 Salt Lake City collegians
60 Prefix with skeleton
61 Darken
63 Formal Japanese wear

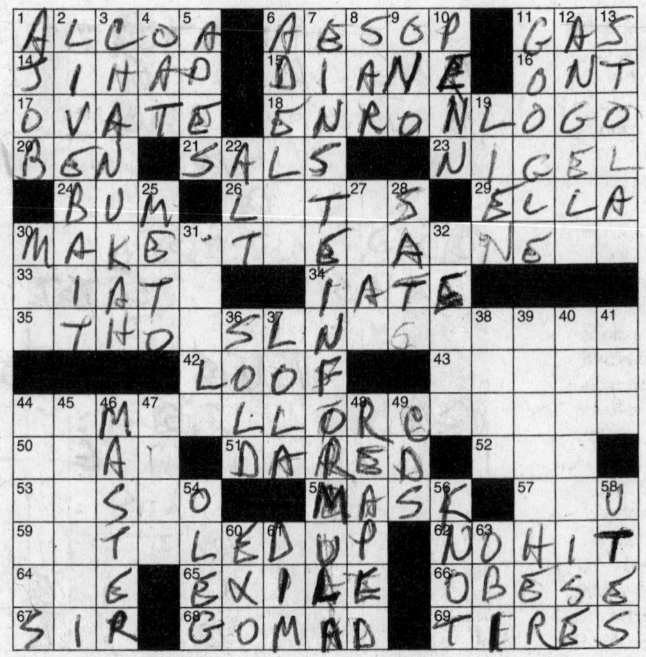

by Kevan Choset

ACROSS

1 Top
5 ___ Lingus
8 Sleeping sickness transmitter
14 Film ___ (movie genre)
15 Multiplatinum album with the 2002 hit "Ain't It Funny"
16 Met productions
17 Star of 64-Across
19 Dancer Ginger
20 2004 World Series "curse" beaters
21 Exchange blows
23 Summer drink
24 Henry Ford's son
25 Number of 17-Across in 64-Across
27 Putdown
29 Shakespeare's "___ Like It"
30 Explosive
33 "___, meeny, miney, mo"
35 Sand
38 Catchphrase of 25-Across
43 Out of kilter
44 "___ Lisa"
45 Bread with seeds
46 Paint palette accompanier
50 Artist Bonheur
52 Gadget for 25-Across
55 Check for odors
59 ___ Mahal
60 Part of an interstate
61 Quite the party
62 Small garage capacity
64 Campy 1960s hit sitcom
66 Spin
67 "Xanadu" band, for short
68 "Don't look ___!"
69 Fellow
70 Ex-G.I.'s grp.
71 Gifts at Honolulu International Airport

DOWN

1 Tennis's Agassi
2 Murmured
3 Watches, as a store
4 Wipes clean
5 Comet competitor
6 Nightmarish street, in film
7 Martini & ___ vermouth
8 Hebrew scrolls
9 Like Corvettes and Mustangs
10 Brain scan, for short
11 Money manager
12 Famed New York restaurateur
13 Elizabethan earl
18 Dressed (up)
22 Links org.
25 Rubik who invented Rubik's Cube
26 Bear or Berra
28 180° turn, slangily
30 Bygone carrier
31 "This instant!"
32 Some airplanes
34 "Tasty!"
36 Old-fashioned Christmas trim
37 Summer shirt
39 Ancient Greek instrument
40 Yawn inducer
41 British musician Brian
42 Ropes in
47 Still awake at 1 a.m., say
48 Generous one
49 Darlin'
51 20 Questions category
52 Tempest
53 Vietnam's capital
54 Israeli desert
56 Angered
57 Physicist Enrico
58 Honors in style
61 Pack away
63 Cool dude, in jazz
65 Keebler baker, supposedly

by Roy Leban

74

ACROSS

1 Mongrel dogs
5 Color of honey
10 On the road
14 Meltable food item
15 One of the Flintstones
16 Salad cheese
17 Keyboard key
19 Go smoothly
20 No Mr. Nice Guy
21 Joint with a cap
22 View in northern Italy
23 Cantankerous
25 Throw off track
27 Dates
29 16-Across is preserved in it
32 "Surely you ___!"
35 Geronimo, e.g.
39 Powder holder
40 Que. neighbor
41 Theme of this puzzle
42 Fraction of a joule
43 The year 56
44 Toughen, as glass
45 O.T.B. postings
46 First president to marry while in office
48 Dovetail
50 Memory gaps
54 "Enough!"
58 Clubmates
60 "Quickly!"
62 Imam's faith
63 Door sign
64 Where thunderstorms may occur
66 Teeming
67 Iraq's ___ Triangle
68 Mary Kay rival
69 Manipulative one
70 Bakery supply
71 Make (one's way)

DOWN

1 Hearst magazine, familiarly
2 Gastric woe
3 Played over
4 Most quickly
5 Saddler's tool
6 Do some work on a dairy farm
7 Strawberry ___
8 Toaster, or roaster
9 Autumn toiler
10 Fling
11 Popular
12 On
13 Swerves at sea
18 Cousin of a harp
24 Long (for)
26 Genesis son
28 Board game turn
30 Encyclopedia reader from A to Z, say
31 Caviar, essentially
32 Bump hard
33 It's a sin
34 Painting of flowers, e.g.
36 Barbary beast
37 Secretive sort
38 Lady of Troy
41 Stadium rollout
45 Electrical principle
47 Parade day
49 Make dirty
51 Fresh-mouthed
52 Suffix with Roman
53 Spot for sweaters
55 Oil source
56 Wouldn't stop
57 Touch up
58 Lima's land
59 W.W. II enemy
61 Gives zero stars to
65 Torched

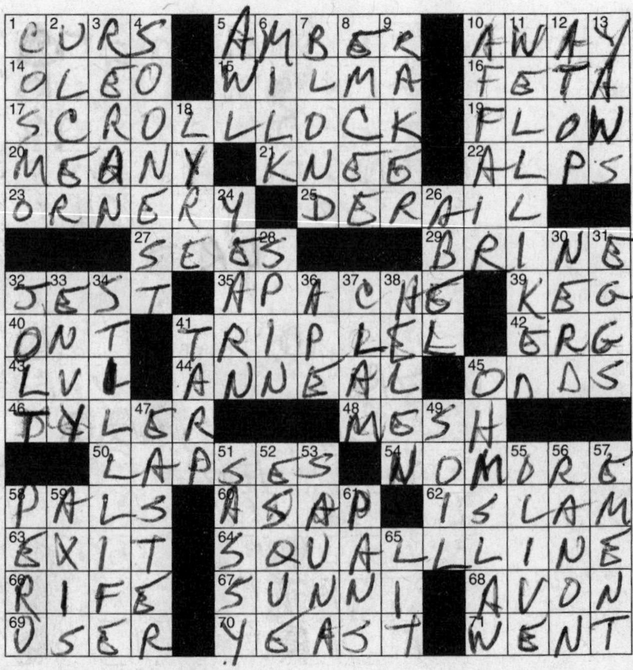

by Barry C. Silk

ACROSS

1 Swimming units
5 Not tight
10 Possess
14 Geometry calculation
15 City on the Missouri
16 Asia's ___ Sea
17 Laurel or Musial
18 VCR button
19 Pastrami purveyor
20 Actor Quaid transgressed
23 Giant Hall-of-Famer
26 Not as much
27 Condoleezza Rice's department
28 Bongos
30 Two-striper in the Army: Abbr.
32 Draft org.
33 Frontiersman Boone did some carpentry
38 Bridge
39 St. Nick
40 Capital on a fjord
44 Actor Hickman showed boredom
47 Fuel economy stat.
50 Non-earthlings, for short
51 Asinine
52 Move on all fours
54 Hydrofluoric ___
57 Exxon product
58 President Ford stared fiercely
62 As a czar, he was terrible
63 Home of the University of Maine
64 ___ Romeo (sports car)
68 Olympic sled
69 Assign to, as blame
70 Potting material
71 Popular jeans
72 Fencing weapons
73 Very large

DOWN

1 ___ Cruces, N.M.
2 "But is it ___?"
3 Vegetable that rolls
4 Hourglass contents
5 Greene of "Bonanza"
6 Black cats, to the superstitious
7 Caravan's stop
8 "___ a Lady" (Tom Jones hit)
9 Diner sign
10 Lacked, briefly
11 Sporting venues
12 Gentlemen's gentlemen
13 Omits, in pronunciation
21 Ultimatum ender
22 Man or Wight
23 ___ and ends
24 Links hazard
25 Albacore or yellowfin
29 Intellect
30 Hit with a ticket
31 Thespian production
34 Future D.A.'s exam
35 Ayes' opposite
36 Cape ___, Mass.
37 Low in spirits
41 Hose problem
42 ___ the Hyena
43 Praiseful poems
45 Place to make a wish
46 Assistant
47 Montreal university
48 Advance look, informally
49 It may have a remote-activated door
53 Declines
54 "Home ___," Macaulay Culkin movie
55 Tippy craft
56 Numbered clubs
59 Latest news, slangily
60 Stagehand
61 Sprinter's event
65 Singer Rawls
66 Tiniest amount to care
67 "Cakes and ___" (Maugham novel)

by Holden Baker

76

ACROSS

1 Mrs. Loopner player
7 Tells a bedtime story
14 Free drinks set-up
16 Mr. Blues player
17 Tickler of the ivories
18 Figured out, as secret writing
19 Show that debuted 10/11/1975, for short
20 Buffet table heater
22 Hail Mary, e.g.
23 King, in Cádiz
24 Bard's nightfall
25 Wearies
28 Syr. neighbor
29 Weekend Update anchor
34 Les États-___
35 Literary piece
36 Wretched
37 Longstanding 19-Across opener
40 Kuwaiti leaders: Var.
41 Take a swing
42 Old Venetian official
43 Announcer for 19-Across
44 Org. for Mariners
45 Lachesis and Clotho, in myth
46 Ground breaker
47 Ottoman ruler
48 University mil. group
52 Terrible trial
54 Network of 19-Across
57 Mistakenly
59 New York's ___ Bridge
61 Samurai tailor player
62 Medal giver
63 Naps, for señores
64 Ms. Conehead player

DOWN

1 Police
2 ___ arms
3 Genuine
4 Old cable TV inits.
5 Nile birds
6 Foul
7 Ms. Roseanne Roseannadanna player
8 Keep an ___ (watch)
9 Dog breeder's assn.
10 Withdraw from, as a case
11 Kind of water
12 Sailing ropes
13 Bookie's figure
15 Hwy.
21 Looked like
23 Tend to, as a barren lawn
25 Kentucky Derby drink
26 True inner self
27 Springboard performer
28 Phrase of commitment
29 Intimidate
30 The best of times
31 Under way
32 Power glitch
33 Actress Sommer and others
35 Surgeon's locales, quickly
36 Dripping
38 To and ___
39 Collar
44 Mr. Escuela player
45 Catlike
46 Big to-do
47 Von Richthofen's title
48 Barbecue fare
49 R.E.M.'s "The ___ Love"
50 Prefix with conference
51 Vineyards of high quality
53 Biblical suffix
54 Benchmark
55 La ___ Tar Pits
56 Foot ailment
58 String after Q
60 Close a show

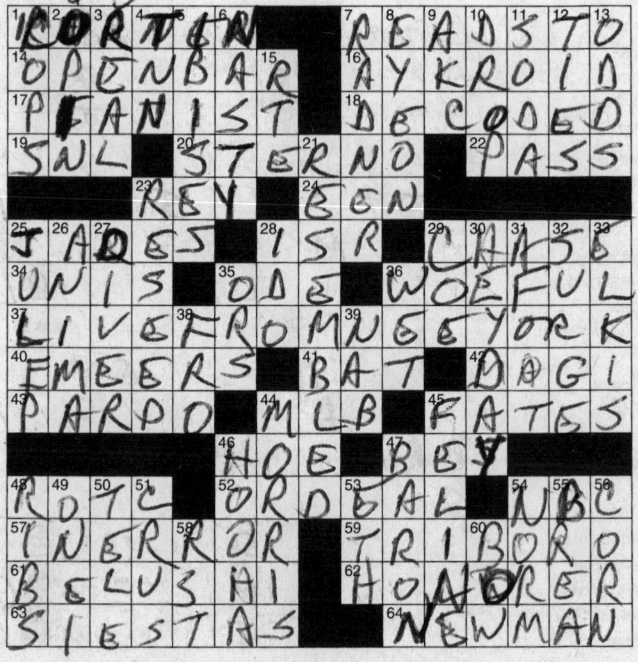

by Mike Torch

ACROSS

1 Unravel, as a cord
5 Hand support
9 Fissures
14 Christmas season
15 To be, in Toulon
16 Messages via MSN.com, e.g.
17 "___ small world!"
18 Extended family
19 Backside
20 Old-fashioned
23 Nonverbal O.K.'s
24 Author Harper ___
25 Amer. soldiers
28 Result of a hung jury, maybe
31 Fit ___ fiddle
34 Fess up (to)
36 Driver's lic. and such
37 +
38 Fundamental
42 ___ liquor
43 Two halves
44 "All in the Family" spinoff
45 The whole ball of wax
46 Mt. Rushmore material
49 "Law & Order" fig.
50 Shipwreck signal
51 Instrument hit with a hammer
53 Petty
59 Lethal snake
60 Yankee nickname starting 2004
61 Workbench attachment
63 "Doe, ___, a female . . ."
64 Sagan or Sandburg
65 Glimpse
66 It might be 18 oz. on a cereal box
67 Safe sword
68 ___ the wiser

DOWN

1 Memo letters
2 Justice ___ Bader Ginsburg
3 By the same token
4 Long (for)
5 Ebb
6 "Finally!"
7 Tehran's land
8 What usurers do
9 Gas up again
10 Spitting ___
11 Weapon of 59-Across
12 Wee
13 Underhanded
21 After a fashion, informally
22 Really good time
25 Alpha, beta, ___ . . .
26 Perfect
27 Wee
29 Turn red, as a strawberry
30 Wedding vow
31 Not silently
32 Luxury leather
33 Liability's opposite
35 Cousin ___ of "The Addams Family"
37 School fund-raising grp.
39 Like the Vikings
40 Genetic stuff
41 Change, as the Constitution
46 Fun park car
47 Tune out
48 Walk like a little 'un
50 Carpenter's fastener
52 First, as a name
53 Lymph bump
54 "Yeah, sure"
55 Open fabric
56 Amount not to care
57 Soybean paste
58 Armchair athlete's channel
59 Pop-top's place
62 Storm's center

by Gregory E. Paul

78

ACROSS

1 ___ Brockovich, Julia Roberts title role
5 Mex. misses
10 Tom, Dick or Harry
14 1998 N.L. M.V.P. from Chicago
15 Sports hiree
16 Sen. Bayh of Indiana
17 See 35-Across
20 Ladies of Lisbon
21 Crowbar, e.g.
22 "I've Got ___ in Kalamazoo"
23 Soccer ___
25 See 35-Across
30 Geniuses' group
31 12/24 or 12/31
32 Golfer Ballesteros
34 Samuel's teacher
35 This puzzle's theme, succinctly
39 Gen-___ (boomer's kid)
40 Shakespeare's stream
42 Hood's gun
43 Rhone tributary
45 See 35-Across
49 Cold war inits.
50 "___ No Mountain High Enough" (1970 #1 hit)
51 Underground Railroad user
54 Least drunk
58 See 35-Across
61 Follower of inter or et
62 "Marat/Sade" playwright
63 Statement to a judge
64 Chicken cordon ___
65 Cosmetician Lauder
66 Teamster's rig

DOWN

1 A.B.A. members' titles
2 Lecherous sort
3 "Beauty ___ the eye . . ."
4 Famous name in hot dogs
5 Japanese beetle, e.g.
6 Isle ___ National Park
7 Small amounts
8 90° from down: Abbr.
9 Any ship
10 Unbeatable foe
11 Tel ___, Israel
12 Luxuriant locks
13 M.I.T. grad., often
18 Bowser's identification
19 Diva Gluck
23 "Outta my way!"
24 Prime S.S.S. classification
25 Probe, with "into"
26 Bagel choice
27 Major mattress maker
28 Nettled
29 Each's companion
30 "___ culpa"
33 Bard's before
36 Soufflé needs
37 Asian goat
38 Holder of claimed property
41 ___ riche
44 Persian governors
46 Hand-me-down
47 Supposed founder of Taoism
48 Nucleic acid sugar
51 Strike defier
52 Vegetate
53 Gallic girlfriend
54 Fit of pique
55 Creator of Perry and Della
56 Goblet feature
57 Bangkok native
59 Have a tab
60 Jazz's Montgomery

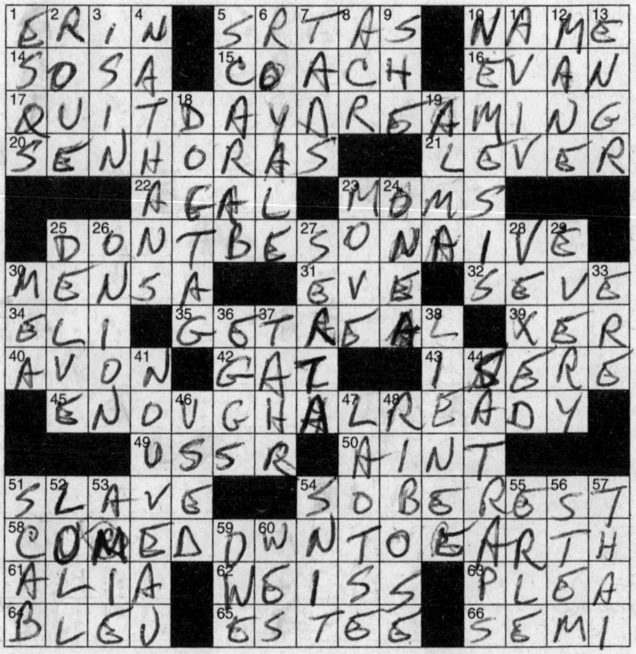

by Jay Leatherman

ACROSS

1 Wood for Woods
5 Where to set books
10 Community service group
14 Queue
15 Four-bagger
16 Pipe problem
17 Writer Wiesel
18 Breathing
19 Unnerve
20 Hopping mad
23 Mother hog
24 Chafes
25 Tear-jerking sentiment
27 In good spirits
30 Obliterate
32 Wrestling maneuvers
33 Lose-weight-fast plan
37 Antipollution org.
38 About half of crossword clues
39 "Gotcha!"
40 Step just before publishing an article
43 Outranking
45 Sheets, tablecloths, etc.
46 Annual event at 43-Down Stadium
47 Frugality
50 Fed. watchdog since 1971
51 Motorists' org.
52 Change defeat into victory
58 Egyptian pyramids locale
60 Itinerary
61 One with a duster
62 Hawaiian strings
63 Tribal leader
64 Like good wine
65 Urge on
66 Visionaries
67 Prying

DOWN

1 Musical symbol
2 1953 Leslie Caron film
3 The "U" in I.C.U.
4 Visibly embarrassed
5 "Not too ___"
6 The 18 in a round of 18
7 Send out
8 ___ Strauss & Co.
9 Complimentary ticket
10 Santa's little helper
11 Tether
12 Musical instrument for the nonmusical
13 Distorts
21 Owned jointly by you and me
22 Sprint
26 One of the Kennedys
27 Person who's often sent compliments
28 Indian tribe with kachina dolls
29 Spirit
30 W.W. II German general Rommel
31 Sound off
33 Morse ___
34 Denny's alternative
35 Roof overhang
36 Next
38 They may sit in a glass at night
41 He could "float like a butterfly, sting like a bee"
42 Boost
43 See 46-Across
44 Ferry operator
46 Wedding helpers
47 Get ready to run, in baseball
48 Three-line poem
49 Demolishes
50 Bewhiskered swimmer
53 Film part
54 In the raw
55 Shakespearean villain
56 Fizzles out
57 Whirlpool
59 Cigar waste

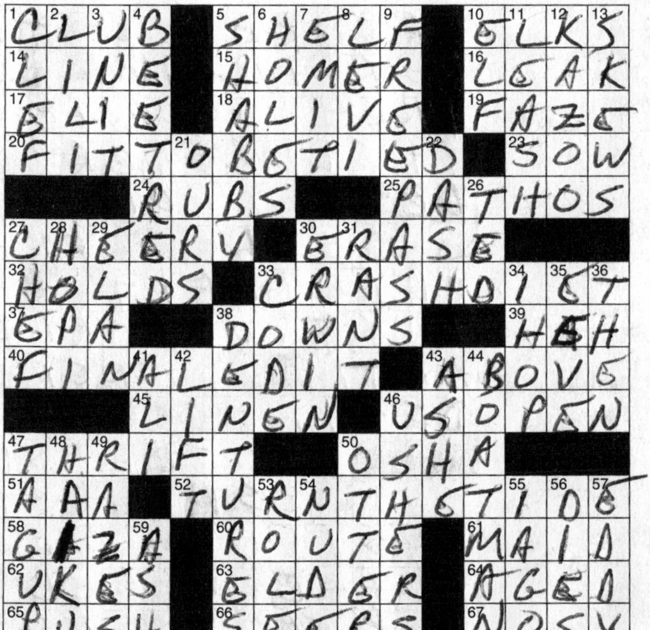

by Lynn Lempel

80

24

ACROSS

1 Held a session
4 Crustaceans eaten by whales
9 Arcade flubs
14 Each
15 Kind of ink
16 Former TWA honcho Carl
17 Ill temper
18 2003 Tom Cruise movie, with "The"
20 Children's song refrain
22 Mint or chive
23 Mound dweller
24 In memoriam phrase
28 "Quién ___?" ("Who knows?"): Sp.
29 Creamsicle color
33 When doubled, a dance
36 Blue eyes or curly hair, say
39 Like many college dorms, now
40 Lean right, at sea
44 Diva's delivery
45 Copier need
46 "You, there!"
47 Hanker for
50 Greek consonants
52 What Bo-Peep did
58 RR stop
61 Workers' welfare overseer: Abbr.
62 Looie's underling
63 Van Gogh biography
67 Refinable rock
68 Put down
69 Atelier prop
70 Pa. neighbor
71 Alternative to plastic
72 Colorado's ___ Park
73 Otherworldly visitors, for short

DOWN

1 Pitchman's pitch
2 Hilltop home
3 Shoe stiffeners
4 Electrical power unit
5 Genetic letters
6 Cards with photos, for short
7 Certain print, briefly
8 Surgical beam
9 Lumberjack's call
10 Hosp. area
11 Tomb raider of film, ___ Croft
12 Comparison connector
13 Foul mood
19 Cornstarch brand
21 "___ been real!"
25 River of Aragón
26 Eat like a king
27 Snack in a shell
30 Wyle of "ER"
31 Richard of "Chicago"
32 Whirling water
33 Decked out
34 Take on
35 Sales tag words
37 "Am ___ believe . . . ?"
38 Oncle's wife
41 Follow closely
42 Paddler's target
43 NATO headquarters site
48 Housetop laborer
49 Gas brand in Canada
51 ___ Na Na
53 Birdie score, often
54 N.F.L. coach called "Papa Bear"
55 Wear down
56 "Snowy" bird
57 Suffers from sunburn
58 Retaliation for a pinch
59 Hefty horn
60 Quickly, in memos
64 China's Lao-___
65 Adherent's suffix
66 Agent's due

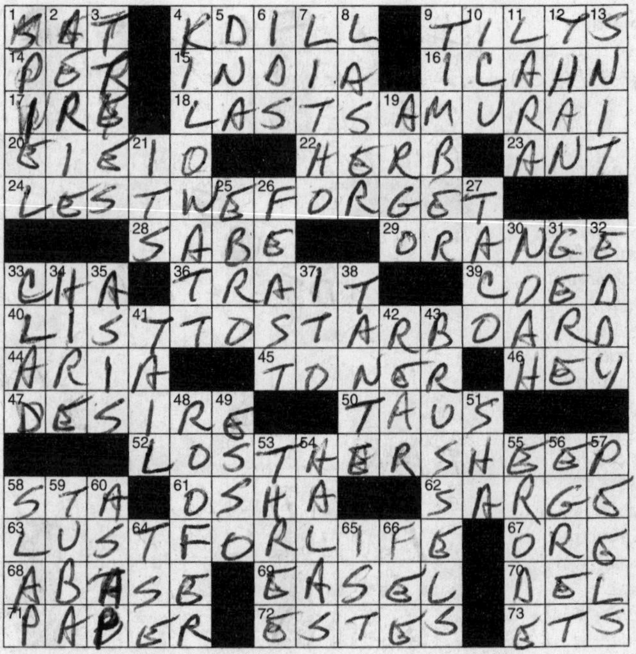

by Kurt Mengel and Jan-Michele Gianette

38/53

ACROSS

1 Put up, as a picture
5 ___ salts
10 Restaurant acronym
14 Fit for drafting
15 Mamma's mate
16 Shore bird
17 Headliner
18 Strand, as during a blizzard
19 Give a nudge, so to speak
20 "Take a chill pill"
23 CD predecessors
24 Conservative pundit Alan
25 Old copy machine, briefly
28 Pea's place
29 Exams for future attys.
33 Female in a flock
34 Whistle-blower on a court
35 Error
36 Out of it, as a boxer
40 Embedded
41 Witch
42 Stephen of "The Crying Game"
43 When some news airs
44 Like hearts and diamonds
45 Great time
47 Treated a lawn, perhaps
49 Winning tic-tac-toe row
50 Finally accept
57 Gave the boot
58 Pep up
59 Wax-coated cheese
60 Big rig
61 Singer Lopez
62 El ___ (Pacific Ocean phenomenon)
63 Ship's speed unit
64 Tennis champ Monica
65 Recipients of the cries seen at the starts of 20-, 36- and 50-Across and 7-Down

DOWN

1 "Bonanza" son
2 Opposed to
3 In order
4 Scramble, as a signal
5 Grand stories
6 Small indentation
7 "We were just talking about you"
8 Voiced a view
9 1975 Barry Manilow #1 hit
10 "Sure, why not"
11 Toss
12 Gymnast Korbut
13 Common movie house name ending
21 G.I.'s address
22 Excavation find
25 TV, radio, etc.
26 Words of refusal
27 Whimpers
28 Word before capita or annum
30 Integra maker
31 Adjusts, as a piano
32 Went after
34 Reel's partner
35 Ryan of "When Harry Met Sally"
37 Performed a routine perfectly
38 Mr. ___
39 Ate
44 Stop working at 65, say
45 Baseball's Jackson and others
46 Bargain-basement
48 Drops feathers
49 Old Dodges
50 Wine holder
51 Field team
52 Quick note
53 Philosopher Descartes
54 Peculiar: Prefix
55 Powdered drink mix
56 Med. care choices

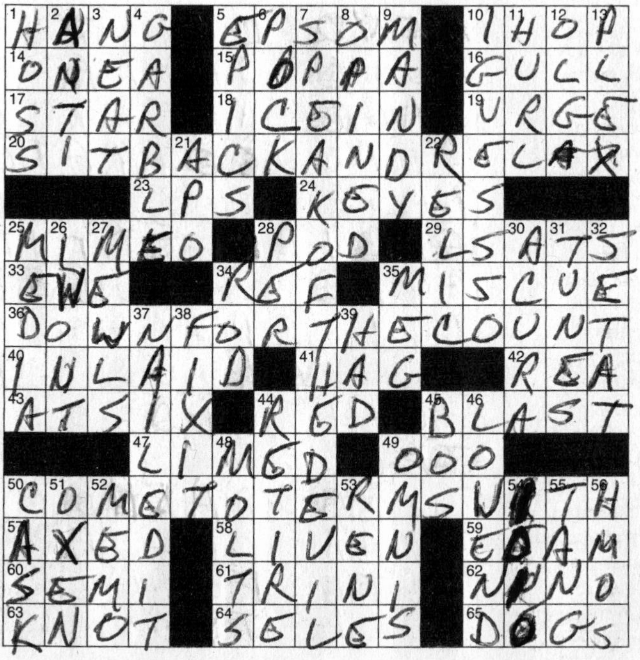

by Jim Hyres

82

ACROSS

1 "Jaywalker" of late-night TV
5 C sharp equivalent
10 ___ Spumante
14 Worse than bad
15 Something coffee has
16 Golda of Israel
17 Leaves for cooking
18 About 39 inches
19 Scottish hillside
20 Coming attractions shot at a mobile home park?
23 It may be passed on the Hill
25 ___ Speedwagon
26 ___ work (road sign)
27 Full-length films shot at a day spa?
32 To any extent
33 Chafes
34 Lariat
35 Late civil rights pioneer Rosa
37 Gillette razor
41 "___ on Down the Road"
42 Throat malady
43 Film segments shot at an arsenal?
48 Ice cream sundae, e.g.
49 Eggs
50 Anka's "___ Beso"
51 Documentaries shot at a vacation paradise?
56 Did laps, say
57 Modern reading material
58 "Sorry about that!"
61 Fountain of jazz
62 Water ride
63 Expert
64 Iditarod entry
65 Like most manuscripts
66 On

DOWN

1 French article
2 "Deliver Us From ___," 2003 film
3 Nip before a tuck?
4 Table spread
5 Interest of a knight in shining armor
6 Without
7 Trent of the Senate
8 From the U.S.
9 Skater Lipinski
10 English novelist Eric
11 Unruffled
12 Jeweled coronets
13 "___ my case"
21 River to the Caspian
22 Don of morning radio
23 Many miles away
24 Roman statesman and writer
28 Spot of land in the Seine
29 Goofed
30 Diving bird
31 Superstation letters
35 Scorecard number
36 "___ was saying . . ."
37 U.S./Eur. divider
38 Auditions
39 Counts in the gym
40 Lhasa ___ (dog)
41 Words to Brutus
42 Surgery reminder
43 Embroidery yarn
44 Make fizzy
45 Rear-ended, e.g.
46 "Beat it!"
47 Brought forth
48 Kitchen measures: Abbr.
52 Skillful
53 Skillfully
54 Egg drop, e.g.
55 "Animal House" attire
59 For
60 "How's it hangin', bro?"

by Sarah Keller

12/24

ACROSS

1 Tiff
5 Go out on the ocean
9 Bogged down
14 Letter before kappa
15 Longest river of Spain
16 "___ fired" (Trump catchphrase)
17 Classic holiday entertainment
20 In whatever way
21 Swing that rips the leather off the ball
22 "Waking ___ Devine" (1998 film)
23 Co. photo badges, e.g.
24 W.W. II female
26 Expectorate
28 Houston major-leaguer
30 Crouches
34 Amo, amas, ___ . . .
37 Morays
39 Dickens's ___ Heep
40 Shock
43 Three to one, e.g.
44 Nick and ___ Charles of "The Thin Man"
45. 44-Across's dog
46 Lagoons' surroundings
48 Sleek fabric
50 "Too bad!"
52 Mos. and mos.
53 Clemson competes in it: Abbr.
56 Fit ___ fiddle
59 Horse feed
61 20 Questions category
63 "The Thin Man," for one
66 Bygone airline
67 Corner chesspiece
68 Sacked out
69 Sound made while sacked out
70 I's
71 Chess ending

DOWN

1 Biblical mount
2 Hit with a hammer
3 Lawyers: Abbr.
4 Dashboard dial, for short
5 Brine
6 Network of "Lost"
7 Nettles
8 Many movie houses
9 Magical aura
10 Letters of debt
11 Undo
12 Art Deco master
13 Monopoly card
18 Has the oars
19 Emulates Eminem
25 King of Thebes, in myth
27 Headdress that's wound
28 Head of the Huns
29 Actor Edward James ___
31 Is under the weather
32 Stretched tight
33 Former Queens stadium
34 Magician's opening
35 Castle protector
36 Choir voice
38 Leave the straight and narrow
41 Leader's cry, said with a wave
42 Where to hang derbies and fedoras
47 Volvo rival
49 "But there ___ joy in Mudville . . ."
51 Look steadily
53 Itsy-bitsy creature
54 West Pointer
55 Bonnie's partner in crime
56 Nile slitherers
57 Good, close look
58 Florence's river
60 Walk with difficulty
62 Mosque V.I.P.
64 Hearing aid
65 British john

by Jay Livingston

84

25

ACROSS

1 Poisonous plants
7 Letters for Letterman
10 "Right now!"
14 Discordant
15 Cry heard in a bullring
16 Small jet maker
17 Place to test aerodynamics
19 Isaac's eldest
20 Bakery gizmo
21 One of the Lennons
22 Broadway background
23 Hoopster Archibald
24 Kukla or Ollie, e.g.
28 Give it a go
30 Employ more employees
31 Glass marble
34 Clutch
37 Chinese author ___ Yutang
38 Placing (and a hint to the first words of 17-, 24-, 47- and 60-Across)
41 Stool pigeon
42 Out of style
43 Dull drills
44 2,000 pounds
46 Telepathic letters
47 Skinny Minnie
51 Funnyman Sandler
55 Offbeat
56 Some shortening
57 Brazilian soccer legend
58 Amorphous mass
60 Author's success
62 "La Bohème" heroine
63 Bit of sunshine
64 Practical
65 Direction wagon trains headed
66 Alias
67 Nebraska river

DOWN

1 Greeted, as the New Year
2 Central New York city
3 "Water Lilies" painter
4 Mario of the Indianapolis 500
5 Hipster
6 Like half-melted snow
7 Arthur ___ Doyle
8 It's not 100% this or that
9 French seasoning
10 Is in dreamland
11 Aviator in search of bugs
12 Battery size
13 Robert Morse Tony-winning role
18 PBS benefactor
22 Potluck get-togethers
25 Face, slangily
26 Some cyber-reading
27 Looks after
29 Give an answer
31 '60s–'70s dos
32 Goliath
33 Vestibules
34 Dogfaces
35 Hosp. staffers
36 Count of candles on a cake
39 "___ in there!"
40 Come to terms for less jail time, say
45 Gossip unit
46 Ultimately becomes
48 Dickens's "___ House"
49 Cushy course
50 Know-how
52 Blue-and-white earthenware
53 Alaskan native
54 Singer Haggard
58 Upscale auto initials
59 Practice tact, perhaps
60 Playtex offering
61 Immigrant's subj.

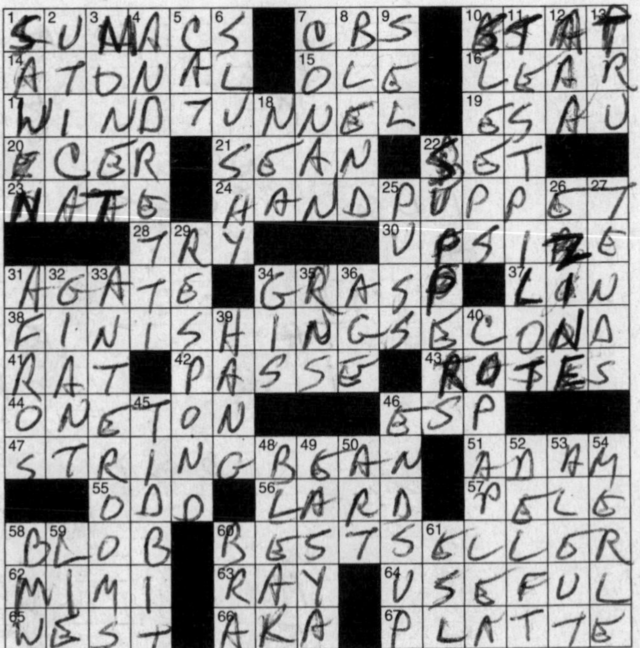

by Gail Grabowski and Nancy Salomon

45/57

ACROSS
1 All excited
5 Unexpected sports outcome
10 Small salamander
14 Earring site
15 John who was once known as the Teflon Don
16 "That's clear"
17 Houston Astro, for one
19 Stare
20 Met production
21 Chart toppers
23 Dot-com's address
25 Ump's call
26 Actors not playing major parts
34 "Quiet, please!"
35 Disdain
36 Father Christmas
37 Sounds of relief
39 Keep after
41 ___ Piper
42 Bad way to run
44 Pigpens
46 Caribbean, e.g.
47 In the driver's seat
50 What to call an officer, maybe
51 Hither's partner
52 Where to get taxis
58 Comparison shopper's quest
62 Norway's capital
63 Not bad in result
65 Mix (up)
66 Laser printer powder
67 Diva Horne
68 Spinning toys
69 Winter falls
70 Historic periods

DOWN
1 Brand for Fido
2 Trail mix
3 Double-reed instrument
4 Get ready
5 "Yuck!"
6 Experts in vote-getting
7 Flower stalk
8 Jazz singer James
9 Attaches, as a rope
10 Bedtime drink
11 Actor Morales
12 Cried
13 Golf ball props
18 Field protectors
22 Holds close
24 ___ Ness monster
26 "Naughty, naughty!"
27 "Yeah"
28 Perch
29 It's a fact
30 Navel type
31 Biscotti flavoring
32 Girder material
33 "I did it!"
34 Swedish auto
38 Tailor's tool
40 Wet, as morning grass
43 Make a sweater
45 Rudely push
48 Pre-edited versions
49 Allow
52 Purchase price
53 Regarding
54 Radar image
55 It follows 11
56 First 007 film
57 One-dish meal
59 Suggestive look
60 School for a future ens.
61 J.F.K. postings
64 Mins. and mins.

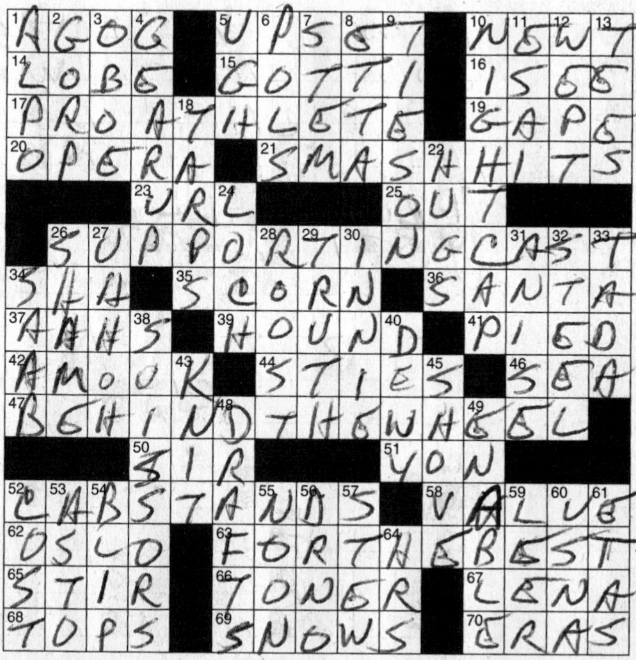

by Marjorie Berg

86

ACROSS

1 Showman Ziegfeld
4 Shakespearean character who calls himself "a very foolish fond old man"
8 Traveler's baggage handler
14 Mary's boss on "The Mary Tyler Moore Show"
15 Writer Sarah ___ Jewett
16 Bogged down
17 Beer festival mo.
18 Musical staff symbol
19 Wanderers
20 Nickname for author Ernest
23 Prunes, once
24 France's Belle-___
25 Vegetarian's protein source
28 Abominable Snowman
29 Classic New York City eatery
32 Amtrak facility: Abbr.
34 Cartoonist Drake
35 Summer along the Seine
36 Paul McCartney in the Beatles
40 Not in stock yet
42 "So that's it!"
43 Milne's "The House at ___ Corner"
45 Anka's "___ Beso"
46 Fanny Brice radio character
49 Burst of wind
53 Greek peak
54 Card below quattro
55 Postal scale marking
56 This puzzle's theme
60 Photo assignments
62 "It's ___" ("I'm buying")
63 A couple of chips, maybe
64 Dawn goddess
65 ___ Martin (cognac brand)
66 Brenda of country music
67 Geological wonder
68 Madrid Mmes.
69 Wind up

DOWN

1 Disk type
2 Place
3 Yield
4 Scottish boating spots
5 ___ Stanley Gardner
6 What Procrit may treat
7 Uses another roll on
8 Symbol of troth
9 Sufficient, in poetry
10 Ex-senator Alfonse
11 Filled in a coloring book
12 I.R.S. exam: Abbr.
13 Sour cream container amts.
21 Not quite right
22 "Super!"
26 Big bash
27 ___-friendly
29 Lawyer created by 5-Down
30 Areas between shoulders?
31 Slugger Slaughter
33 Rewards for waiting
36 Popular clown at kids' parties
37 Teachers like to hear them
38 Long, drawn-out excuse
39 One end of a bridge
41 Scoundrel
44 "Egad!"
47 Louts
48 More acute
50 Not up to it
51 Sift
52 Tried out
55 Minds
57 To be, to Henri
58 Boris Godunov, e.g.
59 Madame Bovary
60 Droop
61 Ruby or emerald

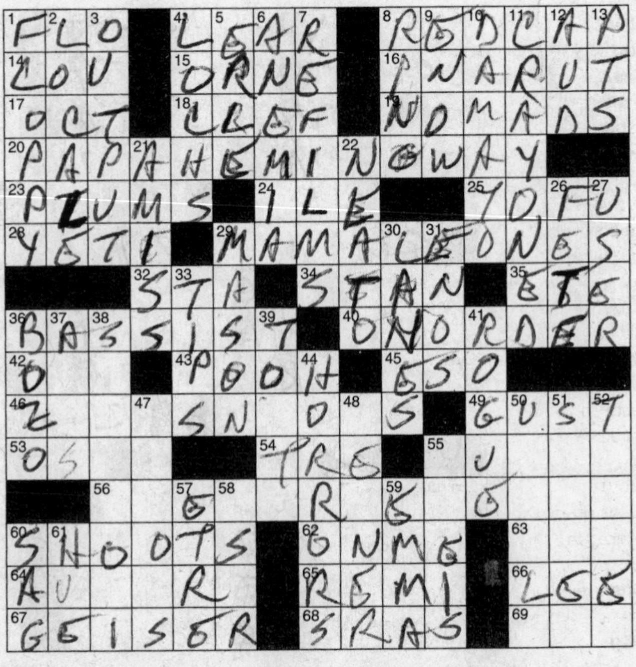

by Sarah Keller

14/26

ACROSS

1 Hunger twinge
5 Unpaid group of 7-Down
9 Sound heard hourly from Big Ben
14 Bassoon's little cousin
15 Nobelist Wiesel
16 Passenger
17 Bagpiper's wear
18 "___ Well That Ends Well"
19 Warn
20 Dutch cheese
21 Union: first stage
23 Label again, as a computer file
25 Put away for a rainy day
26 Money in South Africa
28 St. Francis' city
33 React like a threatened dog
36 Land on the Arabian Peninsula
39 Home for Adam and Eve
40 Put a cap on
41 One in a union with 37-Down
42 Lieu
43 "It's a sin to tell ___"
44 G.O.P. foes
45 Birthplace of the Renaissance
46 Interfere (with)
48 ___ of Sandwich
50 Voting no on
53 More profound
57 Union: second stage
62 100-meter race, e.g.
63 Precursor of the "Odyssey"
64 Reside (in)
65 Director Preminger
66 Washer cycle
67 Pizzeria fixture
68 City of waltzes, to natives
69 "Ciao!"
70 Overly bookish sort
71 Scent receiver

DOWN

1 Doc Holliday's game
2 Reside (in)
3 Actor Lloyd ___
4 Union: third stage
5 Overwhelm with sound
6 Jazzy Fitzgerald
7 See 5-Across
8 Physicist who pioneered alternating current electricity
9 Whooping birds
10 Site of Jack and Jill's spill
11 Prefix with -logue
12 Griffin who created "Jeopardy!"
13 Art Deco designer
22 "Terrible" czar
24 Brewer's ingredient
27 Damfool
29 Union: last stage
30 Genesis of an invention
31 Flippered mammal
32 ___ 500
33 Not shut quietly
34 Pharaoh's river
35 Surrounded by
37 One in a union with 41-Across
38 Cathedral recess
42 Beget
44 Post-Mao Chinese leader
47 NASA vehicle
49 The 3 or 5 in 3 + 5 = 8
51 Claw
52 "Uncle!"
54 Sunbather's spot
55 ___ Park, Colo.
56 Beaujolais's department
57 Lass
58 Kazan who directed "On the Waterfront"
59 Hue
60 Comfort
61 ". . . happily ___ after"

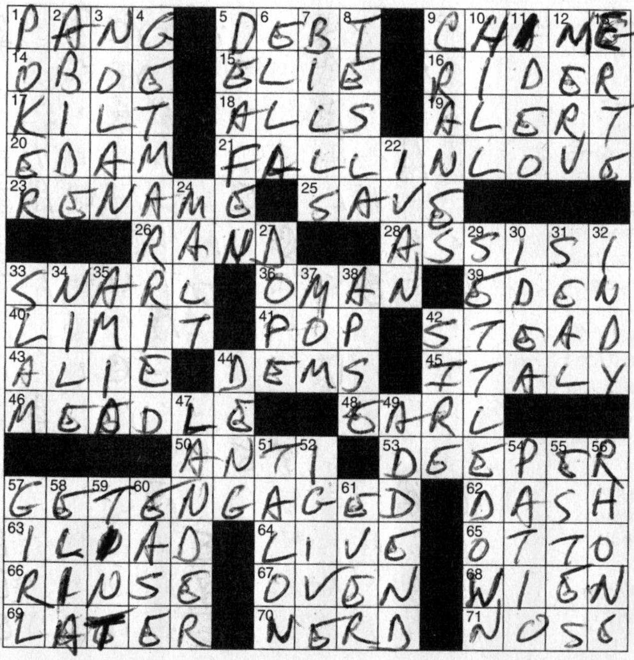

by Wesley Johnson

88

26/40

ACROSS

1 Stamp or coin collecting, e.g.
6 Artist Chagall
10 Men-only
14 "Fidelio," for one
15 Margarine
16 Frau's partner
17 Shouts of triumph
18 Rivers of comedy
19 "Green Gables" girl
20 Clueless reply
23 Hightail it
24 Statistics calculation
25 Camera type, briefly
27 Highway access
30 Squelch
34 Romances
36 Bump off
38 Skylit lobbies
39 Clueless reply
42 McQueen of "Bullitt"
43 52 cards
44 Brazilian soccer great
45 Con artists, slangily
47 Lose control on the highway
49 G-man or T-man
50 Pipe part
52 Continental currency
54 Clueless reply
60 Autobahn auto
61 Bound
62 Game for peewee batters
64 Brit's baby buggy
65 Brontë governess
66 New York Harbor's ___ Island
67 Rice wine
68 Monopoly acquisition
69 Edited out

DOWN

1 Supertrendy
2 Brightly colored fish
3 Pleasant place, metaphorically
4 Slugfest
5 Arafat of the P.L.O.
6 Voodoo spell
7 Outfielder Moises
8 Royal domain
9 Purchased apartments
10 Beatles command, baby, in "Twist and Shout"
11 Dollywood's state: Abbr.
12 Florence's river
13 Got bigger
21 Intoxicating
22 G.I.'s neckwear
25 Nothing-but-net sound
26 Numbers game
28 State of mind
29 Evergreens
31 Slugfest
32 Fine cotton fabric
33 Lightened (up)
35 Uses a shortcut
37 Head/shoulders connector
40 "Doggone!"
41 Powder lover
46 Ready for mailing, as an envelope
48 Checked for prints
51 "That's hogwash!"
53 Moscow money
54 Mushroom toppers
55 Ambience
56 Bismarck's home: Abbr.
57 Cabby's client
58 Newspaper's ___ page
59 Writer Wiesel
63 Psychedelic of the '60s

by Nancy Salomon

ACROSS

1 Take hold of
6 Anatomical pouches
10 "___ Excited" (Pointer Sisters hit)
14 Severity
15 Melville novel
16 Alcove
17 First president born outside the original 13 colonies
19 Easy tennis shots
20 Retirees, often
22 A Chaplin
23 Norma ___, Sally Field Oscar-winning role
24 Mentally sharp
26 Revolution time?
28 Ewe's mate
31 Often ___
32 Long time
35 Airhead
37 April 15 org.
38 B team
42 Driveway covering
43 Leslie Caron title role
44 Fleming who created 007
45 Shaquille of the N.B.A.
47 Kind of camera: Abbr.
49 Catch sight of
53 Kind of acid
55 Yellowstone Park animal
58 "Mazel ___!"
59 They're neither nobility nor clergy
63 Horse's hue
64 Bad way to be held by a judge
65 007 foe
66 Scheme
67 Suffered defeat, slangily
68 "I'd hate to break up ___"
69 MS. enclosure
70 Zellweger of "Bridget Jones's Diary"

DOWN

1 Lawnlike
2 Hearty steak
3 List for a meeting
4 Songs for one
5 Before, with "to"
6 World Cup sport
7 Mine, in France
8 Stallion, once
9 Actress Braga
10 Coast features
11 Frank Zappa's daughter
12 Sympathy-arousing excuse
13 Approves
18 Gun lovers' org.
21 One of the Gabors
25 S.A.T. company
27 Stimpy's pal on TV
29 Aleve competitor
30 "Mamma ___!"
33 Like some old-fashioned lamps
34 "___ won't!"
36 Prefix with angle
38 Mop wielders
39 Foam material
40 "Treasure Island" author's inits.
41 Suffix with labyrinth
42 Bridge weight unit
46 Retort to "Am too!"
48 Decorated anew
50 Place for pollen
51 Entree with a crust
52 Actress Mimieux
54 Poker pieces
56 Actor Cariou
57 Relatively cool sun
60 "To Live and Die ___"
61 Certain TV's
62 French head
63 Nutritionist's fig.

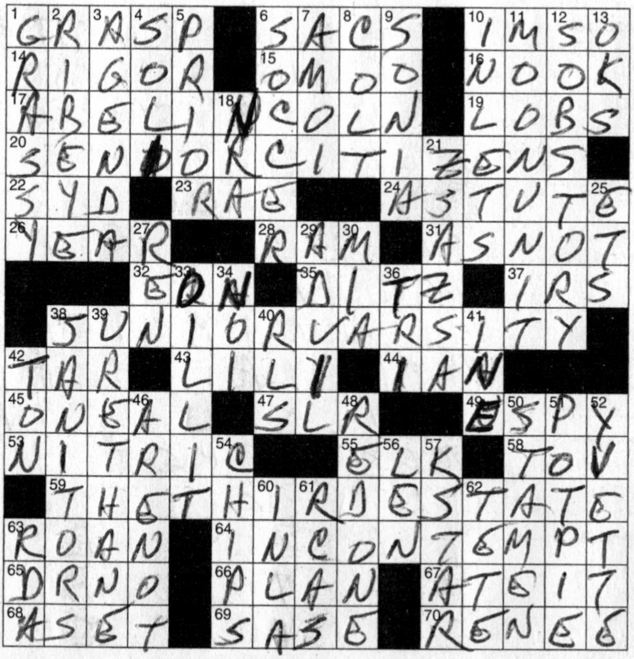

by Kevan Choset

ACROSS

1 Antisub weapon, slangily
7 Boarded up
11 Atty.'s title
14 Composer Debussy
15 Hawaiian fish, on menus
16 Thanksgiving, e.g.: Abbr.
17 1984 campaign slogan
19 ___ polloi
20 Descartes's "therefore"
21 Graceful woman
22 Folk singer Joan
23 Actresses Ireland and St. John
24 1980s White House nickname
25 The "E" in Alfred E. Smith
29 Classic drugstore name
32 Animated Disney heroine of 1998
33 Main artery
36 Sign before Virgo
37 Song from "Anything Goes"
40 Ordinal suffix
41 Dens
42 Ryan of "The Beverly Hillbillies"
43 Rotary phone user
45 Pump figures
47 Family girl
48 Bring back to court
50 Samsung or RCA product
52 In a way, slangily
53 Brewer's kiln
57 Boise's state: Abbr.
58 1975 #1 disco hit
60 It can hold its liquor
61 John Lennon's "Dear ___"
62 Mideast market
63 Hurricane center
64 Frankenstein's helper
65 Come into view

DOWN

1 Farm division
2 Talk like a drunk
3 Nail to the wall
4 Stephen King canine
5 Sidewalk stand quaff
6 Storied monster, in tabloids
7 Suspect
8 Angels' strings
9 "No way!"
10 Oscar statuette, mostly
11 Green Mountain Boys leader
12 Clog or pump
13 20 questions, say
18 Course outlines
22 Go rounds in a ring
23 Lions' "kingdoms"
24 "The Apprentice" TV genre
25 War correspondent, in modern lingo
26 Prefix with task
27 Hawaii's nickname
28 Slangy refusal
29 MapQuest offering: Abbr.
30 Sierra ___
31 Home Depot competitor
34 Bruins great Bobby
35 Italian dish cooked in broth
38 Berne's river
39 Woman's support system?
44 Roman 54
46 Buster of Flash Gordon serials
48 Columnist Mike
49 Unwanted computer message
50 Center of activity
51 June 6, 1944
52 Trudge
53 Élève's 11
54 Miles away
55 Smeltery refuse
56 Radial for a Jaguar, e.g.
58 Memo-opening letters
59 Descartes's "sum"

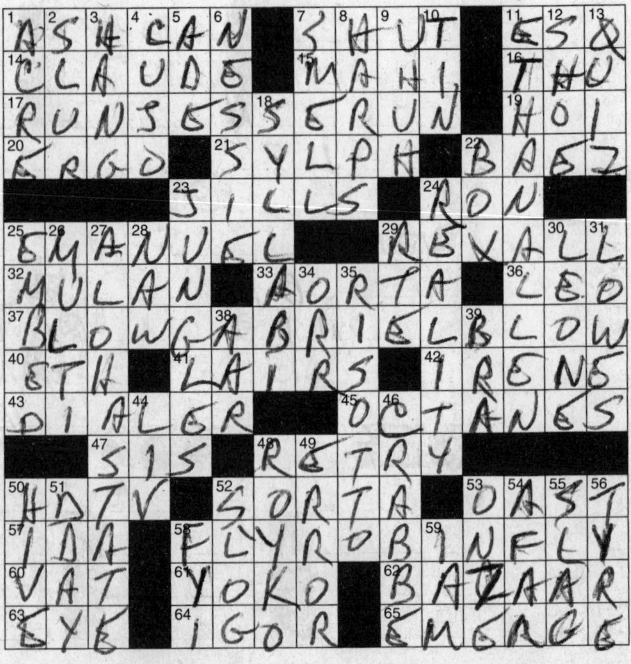

by Adam Cohen

05/17

ACROSS

1 Inclement
6 "Let me know if ___ help"
10 "Damn Yankees" siren
14 Mrs. Kramden of "The Honeymooners"
15 Grp. that outlasted the Warsaw Pact
16 Sacred bird of the pharaohs
17 Rock bottom
18 Gator's cousin
19 Captain for 40 days and nights
20 Wisconsin pro footballer
23 Craze
24 Wedge-shaped inlet
25 Reconstruction outsider
32 Length of 14 2/3 football fields
35 George Bush's home state
36 Fashion magazine
37 Airport flight info: Abbr.
38 Wine cask
39 Can.'s southern neighbor
40 Trucker's rig
42 Freeway sign with an arrow
44 Consider
45 Golden Gloves participant
48 Big inits. in long distance
49 Opposite of absorb
52 Center of Mt. St. Helens
58 Crèche figures
59 Brilliant star
60 Play much too broadly on stage
61 Stewpot
62 26- or 55-Down
63 Joe of the Dodgers
64 Hammer's end
65 "Auld Lang ___"
66 Underhanded sort

DOWN

1 Send to the gallows
2 Morning waker-upper
3 "___ cock-horse to Banbury Cross"
4 Biology or chemistry
5 Rupture
6 Old Peruvian
7 Actor Grant
8 Perched on
9 Diet food catchphrase
10 Connection
11 Penetrating wind
12 Fibber
13 Close-grained wood
21 One of TV's Simpsons
22 Undercover org.
26 Russia's ___ the Great
27 Bedroom community
28 Activity for which "it takes two"
29 Stickum
30 ". . . or ___!" (threat)
31 Paper purchase
32 Small plateau
33 Any thing
34 Holy man of Tibet
41 From Tuscany, e.g.
42 Sci-fi creatures
43 Company bigwig
44 "Yeah, sure!"
46 List ender
47 Wading birds
50 Workplace for the person named at the end of 20-, 25-, 45- or 52-Across
51 Half of octa-
52 Place between hills
53 Look at long . . . and with longing
54 Prying
55 ___ the Terrible
56 Org. helping people in need
57 Smell
58 Implement in a bucket

by Gary Steinmehl

92

17/34

ACROSS

1 Angelic music maker
5 Think ahead
9 San Diego baseballer
14 Parkay product
15 Capital of Italia
16 Instruments used in orchestra tuning
17 Pronto
20 Sack material
21 ". . . or ___ just me?"
22 Dallas-to-Duluth dir.
23 Place to hear snorts
24 Family M.D.'s
26 Adds or deletes text
28 Pronto
32 E. Lansing school
34 "Platoon" setting
35 Hoodwink
36 French roast
37 Snatches
40 Lahr who played the Cowardly Lion
41 Smooth-barked tree
43 Shoot the breeze
44 Promising words
45 Pronto
49 Skin layer
50 Head lines?: Abbr.
51 "20/20" network
54 Prince ___ Khan
56 Loony
58 Sweetums
60 Pronto
63 Area, weatherwise
64 Rebuke from Caesar
65 Latest thing
66 Calculus symbol
67 Haul in
68 Desire personified

DOWN

1 Roy ___, lead role in "The Natural"
2 Native Alaskan
3 Cook, as beans
4 Certain hotel amenity
5 Getting ready
6 Moviedom's Myrna
7 Mine, on the Marne
8 Sartre novel
9 Bonneville maker
10 Blood-typing system
11 Smaller now, in corporate-speak
12 Check, with "in"
13 Italian Renaissance art patron
18 Prego competitor
19 Rug rats
25 Lasting impression
27 Small-time
28 Lunch dish from the oven
29 S. S. Kresge, today
30 Whodunit hero Wolfe
31 Round Table title: Abbr.
32 Big name in faucets
33 Reliable source of income for a band
36 Suicide squeeze stat.
38 Innocent
39 Puts the pedal to the metal
42 Celestial Seasonings beverage
46 Part of a Latin I conjugation
47 Kind of
48 Pulitzer-winning writer James
51 Loud, as a crowd
52 "That's it!"
53 Hands over
54 Travels like a skyrocket
55 "___ Marlene," song of 1944
57 Web spot
59 Fair-sized garden
61 "Well, let me see . . ."
62 Tkt. office locale

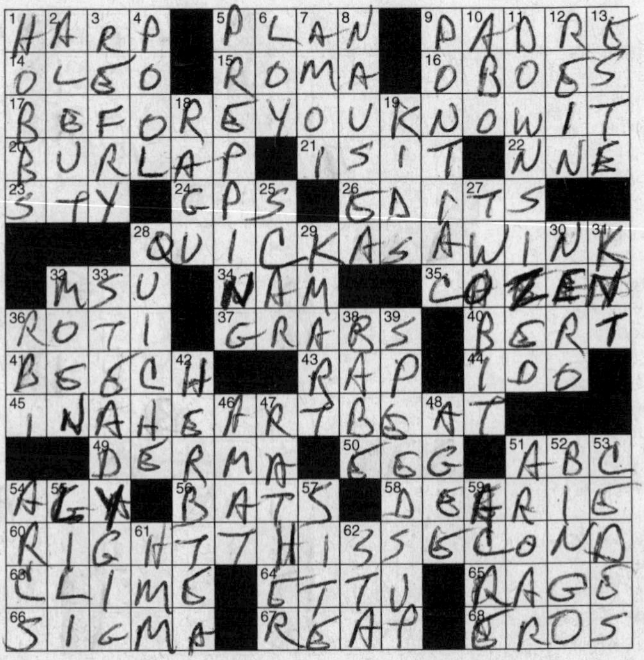

by Nancy Salomon

93

ACROSS

1 ___ Bearcat (classic car)
6 Muslim leader
10 Cover the driveway
14 Gdansk natives
15 "I Just Wanna Stop" singer ___ Vannelli
16 Manipulator
17 How often rent is usually paid
19 Perlman of "Cheers"
20 1950s prez
21 It's nothing at all
22 Herb with the Tijuana Brass
24 Oldtime crooner Julius
26 What a settlement avoids
28 Indian music
30 Difficult situations
34 "My Friend ___" (old radio/TV series)
37 Frozen waffle brand
39 Lovable ogre of film
40 Bellyache
41 What each of the longest words in 17A, 65A, 10D and 25D famously lacks
43 Online auction site
44 Mexican friend
46 MasterCard alternative, informally
47 Inquires (about)
48 Kodaks, e.g.
50 Crowd reaction
52 Jokes
54 " " " " "
58 Rocket propulsion
61 Pudding fruit
63 Blood-typing letters
64 Second-largest of the Hawaiian islands
65 Lone Ranger's cry
68 Writer Waugh
69 ___ synthesizer
70 Din
71 Small winning margin
72 Diarist Frank
73 Xenon and neon

DOWN

1 Go bad
2 Toy truck maker
3 Stomach malady
4 Golf ball raiser
5 A Gabor sister
6 Stravinsky or Sikorsky
7 North Dakota city
8 Picnic intruder
9 Angora fabric
10 Military hero's award
11 ___ Stadium (Queens landmark)
12 Suddenly change course
13 Part of Q.E.D.
18 Scanty
23 Young fellows
25 Breakfast beverage
27 Boardinghouse guest
29 Shocked
31 Wall St. figures
32 Plumbing problem
33 "The ___ the limit!"
34 Apple computer
35 Italia's capital
36 Seriously injure
38 Sock hop locale
42 Large-scale emigration
45 Underground deposits
49 Respiratory problem
51 Pointing
53 Observe furtively
55 Smiley of PBS
56 Fatter than fat
57 Tender areas
58 Fed. agent in finances
59 Saint's glow
60 Regrets
62 Seating section
66 Charged particle
67 Mauna ___ volcano

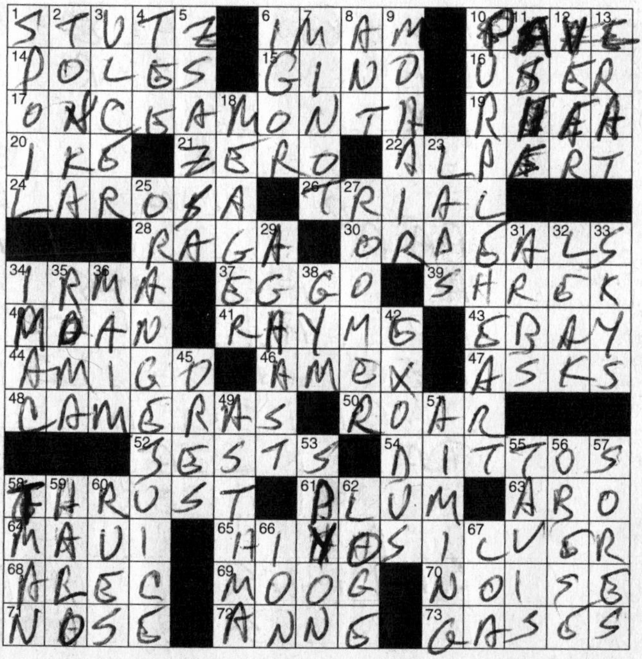

by Allan E. Parrish

94

52/04

ACROSS

1 Urban pollution
5 Booster, to a rocket
10 Winter home of the Chicago Cubs
14 Volcanic flow
15 Hang in the air
16 "We deliver for you" sloganeer: Abbr.
17 Ruthless personnel director
18 The Hunter
19 Genesis twin
20 Seasoned dancer?
23 Frequently
24 Austrian peaks, locally
28 Ancient writing material
31 Spacecraft to Jupiter
33 Missed by ___ (was way off)
34 Mantra sounds
35 Cockpit datum: Abbr.
36 Seasoned singer?
41 Missing button on an iPod: Abbr.
42 Monday night game org.
43 Extra, as a bedroom
44 The Washington Monument, e.g.
47 Emily Dickinson's home, in Massachusetts
49 Police weapon
50 Bridge authority Charles
51 Seasoned baseball player?
57 Portend
60 ___-ground missile
61 Anise-flavored liqueur
62 Sierra Club cofounder
63 ___-O-Matic (baseball game company)
64 Sitting on
65 Victories
66 Approval power
67 "Yo, ___!"

DOWN

1 Waste material
2 Passé skirt style
3 Breadmaking place
4 Quaint building decoration
5 Vowel sound in "puzzle"
6 Spanish constructions
7 Par ___ (how to send mail to France)
8 Atlas maker's subj.
9 White-tailed eagle
10 Nutritious breakfast cereal
11 Double curve
12 Resort
13 Tempe sch.
21 ___ Zimbalist Jr.
22 "Too-ra-loo-ra-loo-___"
25 Two-dimensional
26 Conger catchers
27 Possible answer to "Are we there now?"
28 Polly, who wants a cracker
29 Protozoan
30 Sign after Aquarius
31 Maker of Yukon SUV's: Abbr.
32 Communication for the deaf: Abbr.
34 Olive ___
37 Opposite of a ques.
38 Washington's ___ Stadium
39 Milo of "Barbarella"
40 Route that invites speeding
45 Pariahs
46 Rage
47 Main arteries
48 Peter Lorre role in eight movies
50 President Ford, informally
52 Free ticket
53 Round bread
54 Ballet attire
55 Popular shirt label
56 "Uh-uh!"
57 Autobahn auto
58 Yes, in Québec
59 Clamor

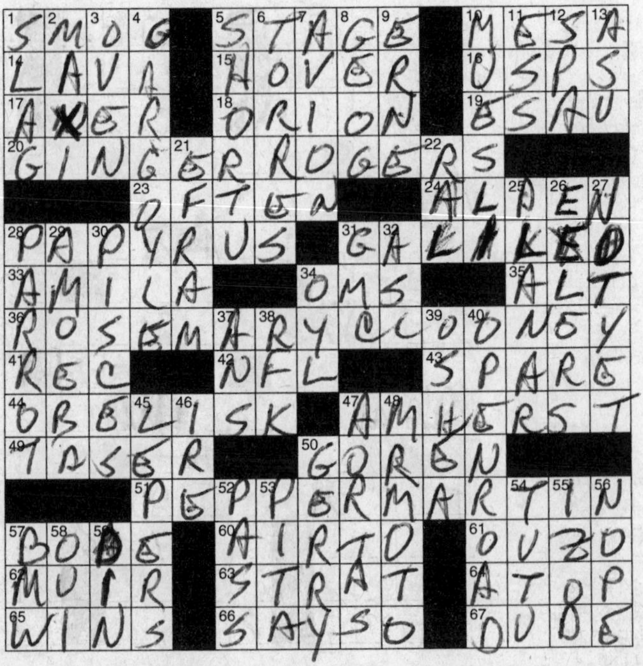

by Roy Leban

95

05/15

ACROSS

1 Borrow without intending to repay
6 College administrator
10 Eyebrow shape
14 Oak's source
15 Former attorney general Janet
16 Hawaiian feast
17 Terrific
18 Cupid's Greek counterpart
19 Ancient Peruvian
20 Part of a famous 1897 editorial
23 Author Fleming
24 Delete
25 Christmas drink
27 Christmas trimming
30 First 007 film
31 Tree's anchor
32 Ballet movement in which the knees are bent
35 Went out, as the tide
39 "Lord, is ___?"
40 Editorial, part 2
42 Swiss river to the Rhine
43 Analyze grammatically
45 Prefix with nautical
46 Thomas ___ Edison
47 Quickly, in memos
49 Spice in Christmas cookies
51 Christmas songs
54 River around the Île de la Cité
56 Attorneys' org.
57 Editorial, part 3
62 Prima donna
64 "Things aren't looking good"
65 City NNE of Paris
66 Detail
67 Greedy person's cry
68 Prudential competitor
69 Philosopher known as "the Stoic"
70 Observer
71 Vision of sugarplums dancing in one's head, e.g.

DOWN

1 Sly
2 Farming unit
3 Executes
4 Most serious
5 Complete
6 Lees
7 Like a ghost's howling
8 Ever and ___
9 More meddlesome
10 He KO'd Foreman in '74
11 Altercation
12 Tree that's the source of chocolate
13 Second-longest river of China
21 Kramden of "The Honeymooners"
22 "___ of God," 1985 film
26 Sailor, slangily
27 Misstep
28 Greek "I"
29 Film ___
30 Rudolph and team
33 Spring
34 Anger
36 Unguent
37 Roof overhang
38 Pull behind
40 Edison rival
41 Ancient Greek colony
44 ___ Paulo, Brazil
46 Artist's workplace
48 Take for granted
50 In one's birthday suit
51 Port of Spain
52 Have ___ to eat
53 Poe bird
54 Keep others awake at night, maybe
55 Upper atmosphere
58 Cry to a matey
59 Germany's Konrad Adenauer, Der ___
60 Bone near the radius
61 Stitching line
63 ___, amas, amat . . .

by Richard Hughes

96

16/32

ACROSS

1 Command to Rover
5 Feudal estate
9 Veronica of "Hill Street Blues"
14 Jai ___
15 Not taken in by
16 Stubborn as ___
17 British man-of-war
19 Bulgaria's capital
20 On a higher plane
21 Above everything else
23 Formerly, formerly
25 Nuns' garb
26 Knuckleheads
29 Neighbor of Francia
32 Landed
33 Yellow fruit
34 Nice winter coat
37 Man o' War
40 Dam-building org.
41 Comparatively close
42 "What's in a ___?": Juliet
43 It's gender
44 Kafka's "In the ___ Colony"
45 The Supreme Court, e.g.
48 Lowly worker
50 Place for things to get sorted out
53 Home in bed, ill
57 In other words
58 Portuguese man-of-war
60 Copier company
61 Natural balm
62 Three-point shot, in hoops slang
63 "Danse Macabre" composer Saint-___
64 Card catalog abbr.
65 Towel embroidery

DOWN

1 "Stop! You're killing me!"
2 Trees in an O'Neill title
3 "___ of Eden"
4 Opera script
5 They're not fair
6 Place to overnight
7 Jazz singer James
8 A. J., the racer
9 Rosh ___
10 One-celled creature
11 Civilian attire
12 "Middlemarch" author
13 Bounds' partner
18 Pair in a dinghy
22 "Casey at the Bat" writer Ernest Lawrence ___
24 Treat roughly
26 A bit cuckoo
27 Sainted Norwegian king
28 Capital near the ruins of the ancient city Pachacamac
30 Bowler's pickup
31 Indiana hoopsters
33 False start?
34 Friend of Kukla and Ollie
35 Alma mater of D.D.E.
36 Virginia dance
38 Brings to light
39 20%
43 A Rockefeller
44 Supplicate
45 Mideast princes
46 Gymnast Comaneci
47 Family girl
49 Sitcom that debuted in 1994
51 Town near Santa Barbara
52 Blanc and Brooks
54 Kind of need
55 Word with fee or ID
56 ___ Ed.
59 High ball?

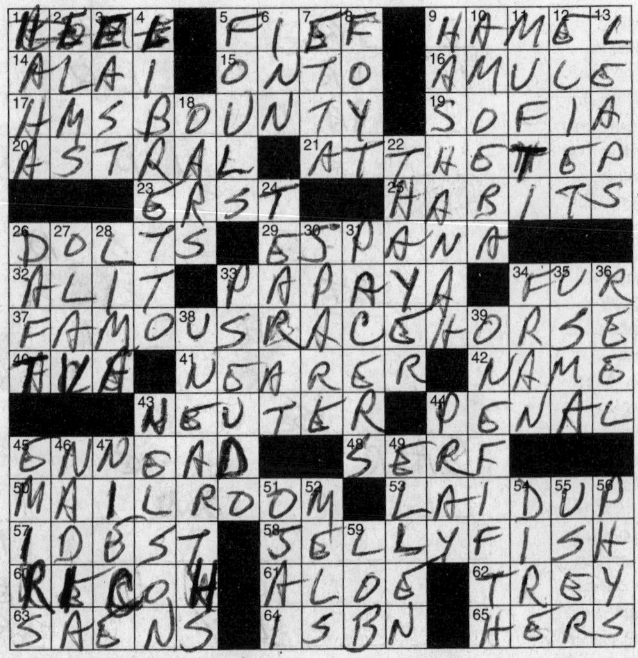

by Nancy and Holden Baker

33/43

ACROSS

1 "A guy walks into a ___ . . ."
4 State Farm competitor
9 French artist Edgar
14 From ___ Z
15 Start of a weightlifting maneuver
16 ___ Gay (W.W. II plane)
17 Wail
18 1994 John Travolta film
20 Unordinary
22 Mended, as socks
23 Litter's littlest
24 Boob tube, in Britain
26 Damon of "Good Will Hunting"
28 O_3
30 Suffix with Oktober
34 Swiss peak
35 Mouse catchers
36 Defense grp., 1954–77
37 Dentists' focus
39 Tire pressure measure: Abbr.
40 Varnish ingredient
41 The "E" of EGBDF
42 Sponsorship
44 "We Know Drama" cable channel
45 Actress Ward
46 British guns
47 McDonald's arches, e.g.
48 Place
50 Bridge guru Sharif
52 Friend of Betty and Veronica, in the comics
55 Wine server
58 "Queen of Hearts" vocalist, 1981
61 Neither's partner
62 Place to exchange rings
63 Boutiques
64 "Little" car in a 1964 top 10 hit
65 Bridle straps
66 Competitive, as a personality
67 Mind-reading ability, for short

DOWN

1 Low voice
2 Sitting on
3 British leader from whom the "bobbies" got their name
4 Former defense secretary Les
5 Line that extends for 24,902 miles
6 1960s–'80s rock group Jethro ___
7 Short snooze
8 Fed. law enforcement org.
9 Toy race car adornment
10 Price to participate
11 Enter
12 Skin cream additive
13 Hourglass fill
19 Doing nothing
21 Last word from a director
24 Tournament favorite
25 Coast Guard rank
26 Pub buddies
27 Tylenol rival
29 Mexican revolutionary Emiliano
31 City neighboring Newark, N.J.
32 Bee injury
33 Kemo Sabe's sidekick
35 "___ kingdom come . . ."
36 Some S.A.T. takers
38 Refuse holder
43 Heavy hydrogen, e.g.
46 Witnessed
47 Perry Mason's profession
49 Stadium levels
51 High-I.Q. set
52 Open slightly
53 Govern
54 Commercial prefix with bank
55 "Halt!"
56 Goes bad
57 Plunge
59 Guinness Book suffix
60 "How come?"

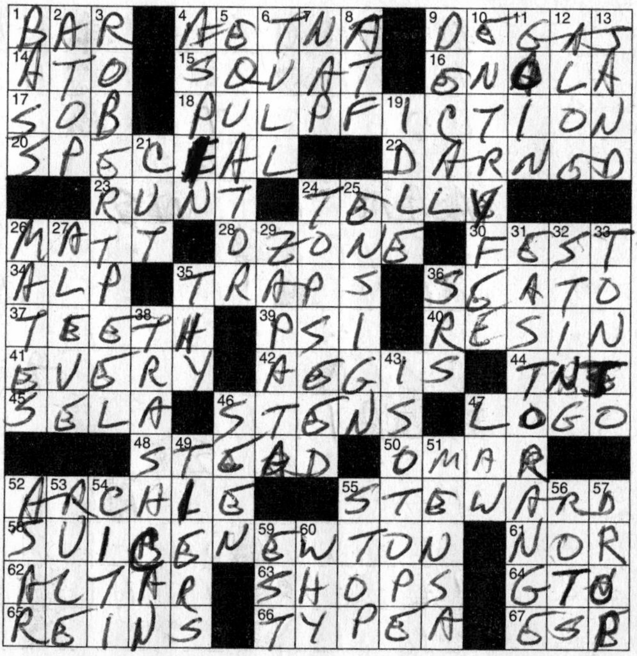

by Allan E. Parrish

98

44/59

ACROSS

1 Biblical gift-givers
5 Tattle (on)
9 Knight's "suit"
14 "Ain't that the truth!"
15 Where to get off
16 Lorna of literature
17 Flier of coffee for long distances?
19 "___ luck!"
20 Big '60s dos
21 Flustered state
22 Fleet leader
25 1981 Julie Andrews movie
26 Martians, e.g., in brief
27 Author A. Conan ___
28 Bleep out
30 Surgery ctrs.
31 Steps out of France
34 Not completely closed
37 Loco
39 Sound heard in 17- and 58-Across and 11- and 24-Down
40 Grenade part
41 Kind of engr.
42 Hoofing it
44 "This ___ test"
45 Long arms?
47 Went like a shooting star
49 Ottoman governor
51 TV spots
52 Fearful feeling
54 Private gag
56 Corners
57 Alla ___ (music notation)
58 High school grads?
62 The one with 0 in 7-0
63 Not much
64 Craving
65 Bookkeeping task
66 1936 Jean Harlow title role
67 Pizazz

DOWN

1 Capt.'s superior
2 Te ___ cigars
3 "How about that?!"
4 Behind bars
5 Cousin of quadri-
6 Praise to the rafters
7 Empty promises
8 Word unit: Abbr.
9 Wings it
10 Tooth part
11 Milk?
12 Early stages
13 Brings up
18 Violinist Zimbalist
21 "Stick around!"
22 Clay for bricks
23 Miami stop on the P.G.A. Tour
24 Witticism from Sherlock Holmes?
25 Take care of
28 Sleeve ends
29 Clumsy sort
32 Tristan's love
33 Canonical hour
35 Intelligence or good looks, e.g.
36 "Set?"
38 Chem. or bio.
43 They may be graduated
46 Smoke and mirrors
48 Off-color
49 Perennial best seller, with "the"
50 Noted bankruptcy of 2001
52 Ball's partner
53 Lacking lucre
55 "Back to you"
56 Dancer's dress
58 Essen assents
59 Electronic address
60 Turkish title
61 Cub Scout group

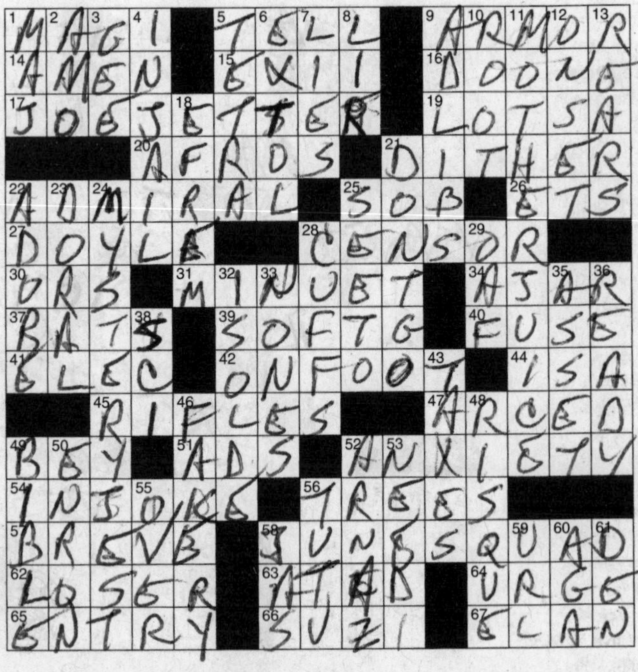

by Lee Glickstein and Nancy Salomon

ACROSS

1 Fed. food inspectors
5 Raindrop sound
9 Songwriters' grp.
14 Lecherous look
15 Cleveland cagers, briefly
16 Weigher
17 Co-star of 36-Down
19 Jabs
20 It's heard on the grapevine
21 I. M. Pei, for one
23 Red flag, e.g.
24 Lyricist Lorenz ___
25 See 41-Down
29 Online film maker
33 Star of 36-Down
38 Stallone title role
39 Out of port
40 January in Juárez
42 "___ delighted!"
43 Brouhahas
45 Co-star of 36-Down
47 Knock over
49 Fencing blade
50 The "Y" of B.Y.O.B.
52 Barge's route
57 100% incorrect
62 Whooping ___
63 '50s candidate Stevenson
64 Setting for 36-Down
66 ___ breath (flower)
67 "Guilty" or "not guilty"
68 Flex
69 Boffo show
70 Gardener's bagful
71 Counts up

DOWN

1 Part of UHF
2 Capital of South Korea
3 Film director Jonathan
4 Shady spot
5 Alternative to Macs
6 Syllables in "Deck the Halls"
7 Finished
8 Intimidate, with "out"
9 Person with goals
10 Co-star of 36-Down
11 Wedding reception centerpiece
12 Writer Waugh
13 Exterminator's target
18 Garden products name
22 "Hee ___"
26 ___-inspiring
27 Lois of "Superman"
28 "___ Jacques" (children's song)
30 Naval leader: Abbr.
31 "Dancing Queen" quartet
32 Big name in water faucets
33 Makeshift river conveyance
34 Norway's capital
35 Certain tide
36 TV series that premiered in 1974
37 Cause for a plumber
41 With 25-Across, 50%
44 Molasseslike
46 Muhammad's birthplace
48 Where Switz. is
51 Easy wins
53 Popular Caribbean island
54 Sans clothing
55 Put ___ to (halt)
56 English city NE of Manchester
57 Applies lightly
58 Dutch cheese
59 "Duchess of ___" (Goya work)
60 Cairo's river
61 Elation
65 Mouthful of gum

by Allan E. Parrish

100

ACROSS

1 Certain iron setting
6 Govt. bill
11 Mars or Milky Way
14 Really, really want
15 Toiled in the galley
16 "I love," to Livy
17 Old "Tonight Show" intro
19 Transcript fig.
20 CPR giver
21 Have a late meal
22 Unlit?
24 Scale of mineral hardness
26 Lions' lairs
29 Tee cry
30 Zeno of ___
31 Atmospheric region with a "hole"
34 Ladies of Spain
36 Word repeated after "Que," in song
37 Draft letters
38 Head honcho
42 Blood-typing letters
45 When repeated, a fish
46 Hose woes
50 Loofah, e.g.
54 Neighbor of Yemen
55 "___ girl!"
56 Hymn start
57 Fodder's place
58 Follower of Zeno
60 U-Haul rental
62 Make public
63 Haw's partner
64 Women's tennis immortal
69 Historic period
70 1940s–'50s slugger Ralph
71 More despicable
72 Thesaurus entry: Abbr.
73 Big name in printers
74 Goes up and down and . . .

DOWN

1 Connived
2 Vibrating effect
3 Made of clay
4 "___ Maria"
5 Many a teen's room
6 Saint-___ (French resort)
7 Japanese drama
8 Hold title to
9 Half a score
10 Breyers competitor
11 Supermarket helpers
12 Current units
13 Lions, at times
18 Self-defense sport
23 Son-gun link
25 Swedish auto
27 Having a snack
28 Snick-a-___
32 Poet's preposition
33 Laddie's love
35 Jazzman Zoot
39 Letterman dental feature
40 Half a train?
41 Son of Seth
42 Makes ashamed
43 9-volt, e.g.
44 Cushioned footrest
47 In a friendly manner
48 1600s stargazer
49 "Z" makers, in comics
51 "Bali ___"
52 Wield authority
53 Dutch seaport
59 Word that can follow the ends of 17-, 31-, 38-, 50- and 64-Across
61 Blue shade
65 Place to put gloss
66 Elected officials
67 Corporate V.I.P.
68 "Flying Down to ___"

by Sarah Keller

ACROSS

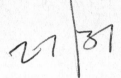

1 Opposite of highs
5 Big stingers
10 Concert blasters
14 Hawaiian island
15 Maximum poker bet
16 Bob who lost to Bill Clinton
17 Warner's statement after the fact
19 "Roots" author Haley
20 "Julius Caesar," e.g.
22 ___-fi
23 Bird's home
24 Fire leftover
27 Eve's predecessor
30 Tortilla chip dip
34 Fateful day in a 20-Across
38 Ringer
39 Not so good
40 Egg: Prefix
41 Baseball hit just beyond the infield
42 Bard of ___
43 Fateful day in a 20-Across
45 Pays a landlord
47 Require
48 "I get it!"
49 Guys-only
52 Cry to a mouse
54 "Et tu, Brute? Then fall, Caesar!," e.g.
62 Building beam
63 One who warned Caesar
64 Bronx cheer
65 Golfer Palmer, familiarly
66 Liberals, with "the"
67 ___-bitsy
68 Fabric colorers
69 Schnauzer in Dashiell Hammett books

DOWN

1 ___ Lane, admirer of Superman
2 Inauguration Day recital
3 Command to a horse
4 Broods
5 Land next to a road
6 Crooked
7 Turn on a pivot
8 Resident near the Leaning Tower
9 Make a nighttime ruckus
10 Not limited to one use
11 Gangster's gal
12 Defendant's declaration at an arraignment
13 Alluring
18 The '60s or '70s, e.g.
21 Road section requiring caution
24 Battling
25 Rudely push
26 Long-billed wader
28 ___ this minute
29 "The Jeffersons" theme "___ On Up"
31 Hotelier Helmsley
32 Laziness
33 Omega's opposite
35 Feels no remorse
36 Drum accompanier
37 John Philip Sousa offering
41 Moistens with droplets
43 "Little Women" family name
44 Grows chewers
46 VW predecessors?
50 Syrian president
51 "Mine eyes have seen the ___..."
53 Australian "bear"
54 Land SW of Samoa
55 Assist in crime
56 Fannie ___ (securities)
57 Top-notch
58 Mix (up)
59 Deli loaves
60 Adept
61 Sp. miss

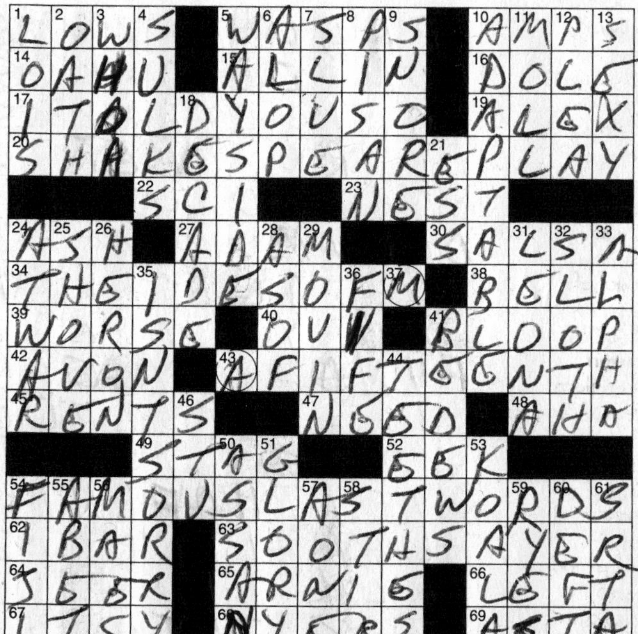

by Patrick Merrell

102

ACROSS

1 Talk like Jimmy Stewart
6 Minnelli of "Cabaret"
10 Frozen waffle brand
14 Noted Montague
15 First father
16 Potting need
17 Jellied garnish
18 Glazier's unit
19 Ditto, with "the"
20 Kingdom's dock?
23 Suffix with musket
24 Tic-tac-toe winner
25 Poet Elinor
27 Invent
30 Enzyme suffix
32 Baseball playoffs mo.
33 Mikhail of chess
34 Adage
35 Home of the Blue Devils
36 Municipality's dock?
40 Part of a financial portfolio
41 Yale, for one
42 Q-tip target
43 Put down, on the street
44 Place where you can get into hot water
45 No less than
49 Looks out for, at a heist
51 Commotion
52 Early Beatle Sutcliffe
53 Country's dock?
58 Diva Gluck
59 Breakfast food chain
60 Back, at the track
61 Depend (on)
62 Barrel of laughs
63 Hosiery hue
64 Breyers competitor
65 Adds (up)
66 Photographer Adams

DOWN

1 Hung loosely
2 More upbeat
3 Fuse unit
4 Small dam
5 Lead-in to motion
6 Traveler's work aid
7 Potato state
8 Billy of "Titanic"
9 From the U.S.
10 Composition with a viewpoint
11 Give 100%
12 Gadget-laden
13 Grand ___ Opry
21 Ball that glances off the bat and is caught by the catcher
22 Meadow mother
26 Summer in Suisse
28 Just slightly
29 Indianapolis 500 time
30 Sound of relief
31 Fond of
34 Farm pen
35 Calamitous
36 Nitpicked
37 Socially improper
38 Future aves?
39 Record-setting Ripken
40 Pharmaceutical-safety org.
44 Retired flier
45 Changes to fit
46 "The way things are . . ."
47 One of a slapstick trio
48 Prison escape route, maybe
50 Cafeteria carriers
51 Under way
54 "Java" player Al
55 Home to Columbus
56 "Chiquitita" quartet
57 Freshman, usually
58 "You ___ here"

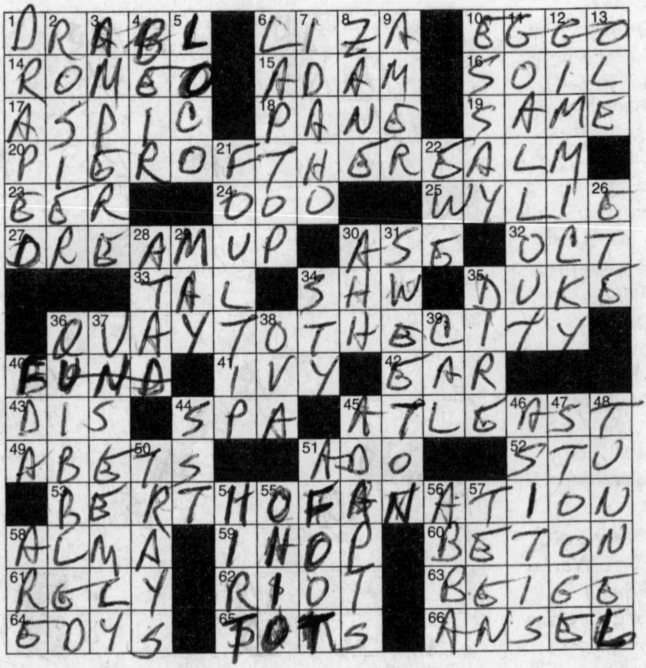

by Ron Sweet

ACROSS

1 1953 Leslie Caron title role
5 Water pitcher
9 Companion for Snow White
14 Garden of ___
15 Bad habit
16 At the proper time
17 Meteorologist's favorite movie of 1939?
20 Longtime buddy
21 Metals from the earth
22 Drunk's problem
23 One of the Jackson 5
25 Quaker ___
27 "Pow!"
30 "___ the night before Christmas..."
32 Lumberjack's "Heads up!"
36 Lotion ingredient
38 "Now it all makes sense!"
40 Dinero
41 Meteorologist's favorite movie of 1952?
44 Tennis champ Chris
45 London district
46 Jazz singer ___ James
47 Dislike with a passion
49 Writer Philip
51 "Game, ___, match!"
52 Kite part
54 Trade
56 Co. that merged with Time Warner
59 Consider
61 Meeting schedule
65 Meteorologist's favorite movie of 2000?
68 Miss America's crown
69 Scotch ___
70 Forest unit
71 Sing in the Alps
72 Speak unclearly
73 [Been there, done that]

DOWN

1 Toy block company
2 TV's "American ___"
3 Give temporarily
4 Bumbling
5 Easily-blamed alter ego
6 Mental quickness
7 Canyon effect
8 Fashionably outdated
9 Chills in the cooler
10 ESE's reverse
11 Etching liquid
12 Little squirt
13 Government agents
18 "Hold on!"
19 Miami basketball team
24 Desert resting place
26 Campfire treat popular with Scouts
27 ___ on a true story
28 Full of energy
29 "Water Lilies" painter Claude
31 Mexican mister
33 Marina sights
34 Cream of the crop
35 Charged
37 Everglades wader
39 Cultural values
42 Words with a handshake
43 Deep trouble
48 Seating level
50 Crones
53 About half of all turns
55 Trifling
56 Lawyer: Abbr.
57 Birthplace of seven U.S. presidents
58 Its symbol is Pb
60 Breakfast, lunch or dinner
62 Author Ephron
63 Sketched
64 "You can say that again!"
66 Opposite of post-
67 PC core: Abbr.

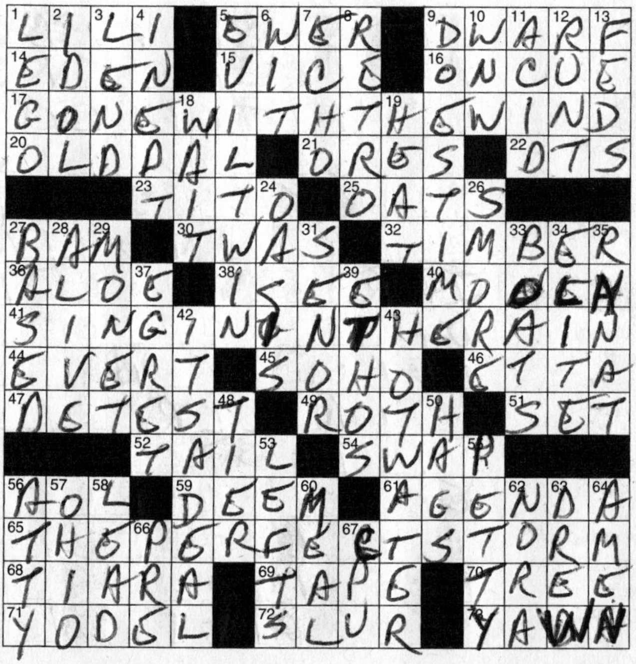

by Kyle Mahowald

104

ACROSS

1 Minty drink
6 Fallback strategy
11 Govt. property overseer
14 Loud, as the surf
15 Martini's partner
16 Mantra syllables
17 Author's sign-off?
19 College sweater letters
20 Add zest to
21 Like helium
23 Cold and wet
26 Ave. intersectors
27 Smells
28 One-named folk singer
30 A.D. part
32 "___ Bulba" (Brynner film)
33 Hardly tanned
34 Tiny fraction of a min.
37 Designer Cassini
38 One of the Osmonds
39 "Ignorance ___ excuse"
40 LP's and CD's: Abbr.
41 Microwave, e.g.
42 Yegg's job
43 Mary Hartman portrayer Louise
45 Is currently selling
46 Cellos' little cousins
48 Pricing word
49 PBS supporter
50 Keypad key
51 Compound of gold
54 Sort of: Suffix
55 Astronaut's sign-off?
60 Born, in bios
61 Mailing list items
62 Sole material
63 Norm: Abbr.
64 Search blindly
65 Mentholated cigarettes

DOWN

1 Start of a one-two
2 Suffix with strict
3 Part of PRNDL
4 Prominent donkey features
5 Unwed fathers
6 Use a button
7 Timber wolf
8 Simile center
9 Defense advisory org.
10 Two-piece wear
11 Nuclear physicist's sign-off?
12 Blue cartoon character
13 Bus. aides
18 "Later!"
22 Chuckleheads
23 Chopper part
24 Allan-___
25 Tailor's sign-off?
27 Captain Hook's henchman
29 Bargain hunter's stop
30 Risk taker
31 Lena of "Chocolat"
33 Do roadwork
35 Come after
36 Terra ___
38 Trunk growth
42 Five-time Kentucky Derby winner Bill
44 South Seas attire
45 Make well
46 Lines on leaves
47 Map enlargement
48 Plain writing
51 Spherical opening?
52 Lone Star State sch.
53 Money on the Continent
56 Former Mideast org.
57 Opposite of paleo-
58 An N.C.O.
59 Cocks and bulls

by Fred Piscop

105

ACROSS

1 Apple computers
5 1:00, e.g.
9 Eye color
14 Hideous
15 In ___ (actual)
16 New York's ___ Fisher Hall
17 Time for a Wild West shootout
18 "Excuse me . . ."
19 Pointing device
20 Fancy term for a 36-Across
23 Hornswoggled
24 Tetley product
25 Regretted
26 London's Big ___
27 Shopping place
28 Quick punch
31 Self-evident truth
34 ___ fide
35 Coke or Pepsi
36 Puzzling person?
39 Goldie of "Laugh-In" fame
40 Party giver
41 Atlas blow-up
42 Needle hole
43 Yappy dog, briefly
44 Colorado native
45 Kodak product
46 Explosive letters
47 Put down, slangily
50 Fancy term for a 36-Across
54 Secluded valleys
55 Actress Winslet
56 Stage part
57 W.W. II vessel
58 Split personalities?
59 Think tank output
60 Hairy-chested
61 Edges
62 Work station

DOWN

1 Chew (on)
2 Ancient marketplace
3 Cirrus or cumulus
4 Lip-___ (not really sing)
5 Realm for St. Peter
6 Actor Milo
7 One who takes drugs, e.g.
8 "The Night Watch" painter
9 Tiny village
10 Steer clear of
11 Mount Olympus chief
12 Formerly, once
13 Caustic substance
21 Tabloid twosomes
22 Surrounding glows
26 Cap'n's mate
27 Samuel with a code
28 Scribbles (down)
29 Cream ingredient
30 Quarterback Starr
31 Flu symptom
32 Picture of health?
33 "___ Russia $1200" (Bob Hope book)
34 Gambling professional
35 Art movie theater
37 Overcome utterly
38 "Same here!"
43 Boar's abode
44 Except if
45 Important exam
46 ___ pole
47 Electron tube
48 Cruise stopovers
49 T-bone, e.g.
50 Site of Napoleon's exile
51 Light on Broadway
52 Prepare for takeoff
53 Lines on a radar screen
54 Doublemint, e.g.

by Barry C. Silk

106

15/28

ACROSS

1 Pleasant to look at
7 "Hold on a ___!"
10 Abba of Israel
14 Promgoer's rental
15 Airport monitor abbr.
16 Nathan of stage and screen
17 Colorful ring
18 Pal in the 'hood
19 Toggery, informally
20 Christmas tree
21 Grade booster
24 Big bash
26 Helps with the dishes
27 Make even smoother
30 The late Sen. Thurmond
34 "Folsom Prison Blues" singer
38 ___-Locka, Fla.
39 Oneness
40 Chews the scenery
43 Fr. holy woman
44 Luggage receipt
48 Synagogue scroll
51 Achieve
52 Snapple competitor
54 Galley gear
58 Sub sinker
63 It may be loaded at the casino
64 Word-of-mouth
65 Fam. member
66 Assail, as a reputation
68 Not prerecorded
69 ___ y Plata (Montana's motto)
70 Puts on a happy face
71 Sly glance
72 "Spring ahead" hrs.
73 Be a snitch

DOWN

1 Office crew
2 Radium discoverer
3 Put forth, as effort
4 Prefix with classical
5 Like some chatter
6 Sweet-talk
7 Audrey Hepburn title role
8 Gofers' tasks
9 Long reptiles, in short
10 First-born
11 Modem speed unit
12 "The King ___"
13 Egg holder
22 ___ II (razor brand)
23 Apt., e.g.
25 Seaside soarers
28 Brian of the early Roxy Music
29 Harmony
31 Classroom drudgery
32 Oil grp.
33 Mardi Gras wear
34 "___ do it"
35 Not fooled by
36 Yesterday: Fr.
37 Blood: Prefix
41 ___ WorldCom (former corporate entity)
42 "This can't be!"
45 Prepares to shave
46 Gorged oneself
47 ___-Tass (Russian news agency)
49 Branch in a trophy room
50 Snickering syllable
53 New England catch
55 Not for kids
56 Star in Orion
57 Taste or touch
58 "Mama" sayer
59 Canal of song
60 Finish a drive?
61 Main idea
62 Lazarus or Goldman
67 Orchestra area

by Sarah Keller

ACROSS

1 Tough spots to get out of
5 City leader
10 Ego
14 Old radio word for the letter O
15 "___ there yet?"
16 Half a sextet
17 Charlton Heston epic, with "The"
20 Ratfink
21 Ray of the Kinks
22 Essential
25 Witherspoon of "Legally Blonde"
26 "Holy smokes!"
29 Marked, as a survey square
31 Whodunit board game
32 New Guinea native
34 C.E.O.'s degree
37 Home for Pooh and Tigger
40 Baseballer Mel
41 Large system of newsgroups
42 Smog
43 Unappetizing dishes
44 Try to pick up, as at a bar
45 Laissez-___
48 Join forces (with)
51 Popular Honda
53 Runs full speed
57 Chain in the upper St. Lawrence River
60 Ages and ages
61 False move
62 Jazzy improv style
63 One bit of medicine
64 Hot dog picker-upper
65 Amerada ___ (oil giant until 2006)

DOWN

1 Writes (down)
2 Assist in wrongdoing
3 Pre-stereo sound
4 Supported, as a motion
5 Mrs. Eisenhower
6 Like gunmen and octopuses
7 Nay's opposite
8 Possess
9 Foxx of "Sanford and Son"
10 Filmmaker Spielberg
11 Bert's roommate on "Sesame Street"
12 Reduced-calorie beers
13 "All That Jazz" choreographer Bob
18 Bullfight cheers
19 Corps member
23 Wide area
24 Two of cards
26 Sound in a big, empty room
27 Excess supply
28 Uncle's partner
30 It's thrown at a bull's-eye
32 Mexican money
33 Good (at)
34 Castle encircler
35 Old TV clown
36 Chief Yemeni port
38 Kings and queens
39 Auto accident injury
43 Complain
44 Hockey great Bobby
45 Destined
46 Sound preceding "God bless"
47 Desktop pictures
49 Growing older
50 Sail supports
52 Loony
54 Formerly
55 Some handhelds: Abbr.
56 Speedy fliers, for short
58 Modern: Prefix
59 Kipling's "Gunga ___"

by Jim Hyres

108

38/53

ACROSS

1 Big stinger
5 Org. whose approval is much sought
8 "Le ___ Prince"
13 Opera solo
14 Costa ___
16 The O in FeO
17 Call in a bakery
18 Tennis's Arthur
19 Slangy send-off
20 1986 Prince movie, after 29-Down
23 Calendar box
25 Opponent's vote
26 Cry from a butterfingers
27 Map miniatures
29 Letter carriers' org.
30 "No seats left" sign
33 Martin or McQueen
34 Initial stake
35 Not at home
36 By night, with 29-Down
39 Rightmost column
40 Suffix with young or old
41 Smallest
42 Thesaurus feature: Abbr.
43 Minnesota Twin, e.g., briefly
44 Dance at 23-Down
45 Set-to
46 Not dis, in Brooklyn
47 Sun. talk
48 Business sign, after 29-Down
53 Orangeish shade
54 Respite
55 Grub
58 Popular vodka, informally
59 Wash
60 Oscar winner Sorvino
61 Has, as a party
62 Place to hear a 13-Across, with "the"
63 Taking care of business

DOWN

1 Pallid
2 Exist
3 Year "The Graduate" came out, in short
4 Walkway
5 Set-to
6 Like good gossip columns
7 Overexerciser's woe
8 Growths that may be removed by surgery
9 Tests
10 ___ Puente, the Mambo King
11 Prefix with logical
12 Beach bird
15 Former Ford minivan
21 Type in
22 Rodeo performer
23 Studio 54 and Xenon, famously
24 Cleopatra's paramour
28 Preceding nights
29 See 20-, 36- and 48-Across
30 Laundry challenge for a gymgoer
31 Fight down and dirty
32 Food in a shell
34 In the end
35 Hydrocarbon suffixes
37 Singer K. T. ___
38 Movie for which Jane Fonda won an Oscar
43 Some old computers
44 Classic Olivier role
45 Silvery food fish
46 Dig (into)
48 Snack
49 Prefix with plasm
50 "Look ___ Talking"
51 U.S. Pacific island
52 Captain of fiction
56 Prefix with color or cycle
57 Posed

by Tony Orbach

54/05

ACROSS
1 Subdued color
7 Lift in Aspen
11 Height: Abbr.
14 Title girl in Kay Thompson books
15 "Othello" villain
16 Pastoral place
17 Golf locale
19 Prohibit
20 Letters on a Cardinal's cap
21 Rock musician Brian
22 Diving board's part of a swimming pool
24 Ambles (along)
27 Johnson of "Laugh-In"
28 Thom ___ shoes
30 Extremely low, as prices
34 Strokes on a green
36 Game authority
37 Brays
40 Views, as through binoculars
44 Online correspondence
46 Quick bite
47 Informal group discussion
52 Choir voice
53 Roundish
54 Walks about looking for prey
56 Frog's seat
60 Figure skater Midori ___
61 ___ Lingus
64 On the ___ (fleeing)
65 Pivoting span on a river
68 Summer in Montréal
69 Encl. with a manuscript
70 Give, as duties
71 One side in checkers
72 Little 'un
73 Tyrannical leader

DOWN
1 Chest muscles, briefly
2 Tremendously
3 One's special person in life
4 ___ Lizzie (Model T)
5 ___ Park, Colo.
6 Loewe's partner on Broadway
7 The first O of O-O-O
8 Like Yul Brynner or Telly Savalas
9 Tropical fever
10 Justice's attire
11 Queen Victoria's prince
12 Shack
13 Two-trailer rig
18 Toy that does tricks
23 Fatherly
25 Furtively
26 Jr. high, e.g.
28 Speedometer letters
29 Billiards rod
31 Keystone officer
32 Automatic tournament advance
33 Bullring hurrahs
35 Identical
38 "What ___ I saying?"
39 ___-boom-bah
41 Spicy chip topping
42 Malfunction, with "up"
43 Bout ender, for short
45 Place for gloss
47 Hair salon item
48 Fly
49 Picked up stealthily
50 It goes on a photocopier: Abbr.
51 "Pretty good!"
55 Poorer
57 "Hey, you!"
58 Not at home
59 Part of the spine
62 Frozen waffle brand
63 Apartment payment
66 Previously named
67 Magazine no.

by Gail Grabowski

110

ACROSS

1 Play lookout for, for example
5 Praises
10 Vegetarian's no-no
14 Lollapalooza
15 Beginning
16 "Cogito, ___ sum"
17 V.I.P. #1
20 Blazing, as the eyes
21 Stirs up
22 Forest rangers' worries
25 U.F.O. fliers
26 Ammo holder
28 Fizzler
30 Like zoo animals
34 Very, in Versailles
35 Maze goal
37 "Where ___?"
38 V.I.P. #2
41 Dr. J's org., once
42 Unit
43 James who wrote "A Death in the Family"
44 Marooned, maybe
46 Chicago-to-Tampa dir.
47 Pants part
48 Barely lit
50 Blue eyes or curly hair
52 The "E" of PETA
56 Turn
60 V.I.P. #3
63 Group in a spies' network
64 Harden
65 Property right
66 London's ___ Park
67 Jargons
68 Actress Heche

DOWN

1 Aquatic plant
2 Small town
3 Carrier to Israel
4 Sushi staple
5 Running horse
6 Bibliographical suffix
7 Part of the Defense Dept.
8 ___ vu
9 Gaze intently
10 One of the Gorgons
11 Botches one
12 Chills and fever
13 Male turkeys
18 Mr. Unexciting
19 Cut irregularly
23 Decrees
24 Orange label
26 Corn holders
27 Over 18, say
29 One on the Atkins plan
31 Railroad measure
32 Roastmaster
33 It holds back the sea
34 Spicy cuisine
35 When said three times, a 1964 Beach Boys hit
36 Pigpen
39 Noble Italian family name
40 Spanish scarf
45 Fit to serve
47 Fuzzy fruit
49 Wizardry
51 "Angela's ___" (1996 best seller)
52 Inscribe permanently
53 "If ___ only knew!"
54 Grasped
55 Musical Horne
57 Conceited
58 1950s British P.M.
59 The Beatles' "Penny ___"
61 Sister
62 TV screen: Abbr.

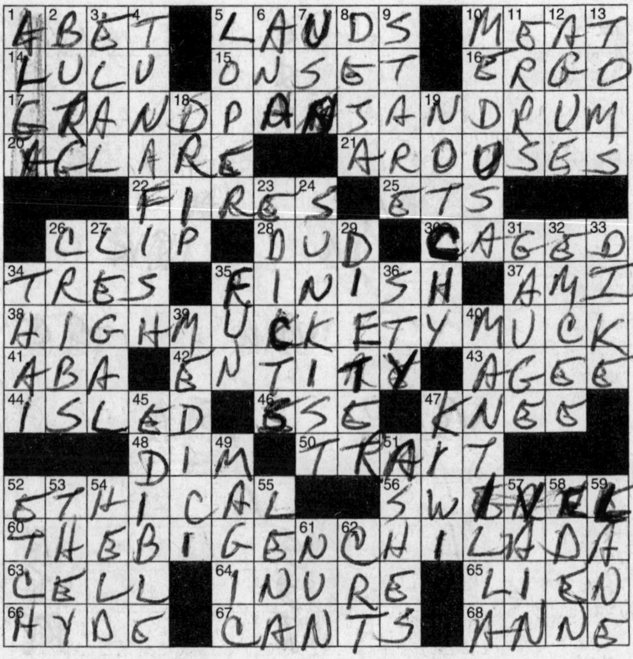

by Bill Ballard

111

34/43

ACROSS
1 Timber wolf
5 Gymnast Comaneci
10 Little tricksters
14 Grad
15 Addicts
16 One who nabs 15-Across
17 Nothing more than
18 Eats elegantly
19 French cheese
20 Like some Christians
22 Four-door
23 Do cross-country
24 When the stomach starts grumbling
26 Air conditioner capacity, for short
29 Co. name completer
31 Boar's mate
32 Not behaving conservatively
39 Genesis garden
40 French sea
41 Dublin's land
42 Not just gone
47 ___ Jima
48 Science guy Bill
49 CD predecessors
50 Does a U-turn
55 Place to relax
57 Enlighten
58 Utterance that sums up 20-, 32- and 42-Across
63 Misshapen citrus
64 Chicago airport
65 "A Clockwork Orange" protagonist
66 Unload, as stock
67 Voting machine part
68 5,280 feet
69 Dutch cheese
70 Clothe
71 Quaker ___

DOWN
1 Gentle animal
2 Toast spread
3 Famous duelist
4 Black cats, traditionally speaking
5 Prodding
6 One side of the Urals
7 Overalls material
8 "Me, Myself & ___" (2000 flick)
9 Ninny
10 Not on one side or the other
11 ___ Gras
12 Trojan War king
13 Verona, in "Romeo and Juliet"
21 Related
22 ___ gin fizz
25 Arson aftermath
26 Ran, as colors
27 Seashore washer
28 Eye layer
30 Deep sleep
33 Sundance entry, informally
34 Actor Beatty
35 1982 Disney film
36 Use a rotary phone
37 Basic of golf instruction
38 Lampreys, e.g.
43 Twisted
44 Letters of distress
45 Dish sometimes served "on the half-shell"
46 Officials elected for two yrs.
50 Employ again
51 Nosed (out)
52 Mediterranean estate
53 Old-fashioned anesthetic
54 Trim
56 Site of an 1836 massacre
59 Son of Zeus
60 Russian gold medalist ___ Kulik
61 Had emotions
62 Alimony receivers
64 On in years

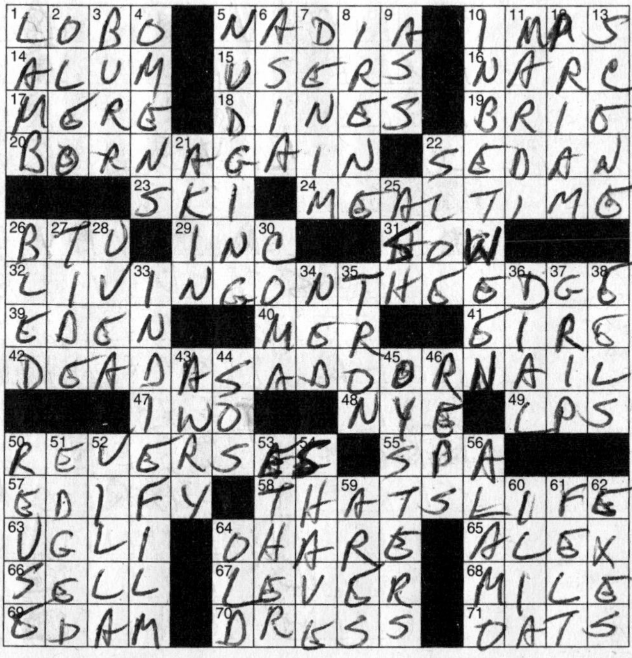

by Michael Doran

112

43/100

ACROSS

1 Tupperware sound
5 Viva ___ (by word of mouth)
9 Jazz genre
14 State firmly
15 Skeptic's scoff
16 Unescorted
17 Where to get hitched in a hurry
18 Brummell or Bridges
19 Laundry soap introduced in 1918
20 See 40-Across
23 Cozy room
24 Demagnetize, as a tape
25 "Heads up!" and others
27 Run-of-the-mill
30 Kingdom divisions, in biology
31 "What have we here?!"
32 Jill of "Diamonds Are Forever"
35 Stash
38 "Please," in Potsdam
40 Clue to 20- and 55-Across and 11- and 29-Down
41 Paris's river
42 Crude sort
43 Acela Express runner
45 17-Across's state: Abbr.
46 Breaks in relations
48 Hair snarl
50 Cloak's partner
52 Sudden outpouring
54 Make a miscue
55 See 40-Across
60 Regional flora and fauna
62 ___ Domini
63 General or major
64 Run-of-the-mill
65 Frees (of)
66 X-rated
67 Great Plains home
68 Ripken Sr. and Jr.
69 Thanksgiving dish

DOWN

1 Cutting remark
2 Iris's place
3 Patronize Hertz or Avis
4 Like some presidents
5 Pulsing with energy
6 Takes orders from
7 Stop
8 Needle case
9 Just
10 ___ Lilly and Co.
11 See 40-Across
12 Beginning
13 Lowly workers
21 Irregularly notched, as a leaf
22 Journalist Paula
26 Ultimatum ender
27 Ty of Cooperstown
28 Kent State state
29 See 40-Across
30 Rx dispenser: Abbr.
33 Photocopier problems
34 Cereal grain
36 Scott Turow title
37 "___ Only Just Begun"
39 H.S. math class
41 Do figure eights, say
43 Longfellow's bell town
44 Totally baffled
47 Like fillies but not billies
49 Close at hand
50 Coming-out
51 Get up
52 Braga of film
53 Gearshift sequence
56 Pusher's pursuer
57 Hearty party
58 E pluribus ___
59 Squeaks (out)
61 ___-Bo (exercise system)

by Allan E. Parrish

01/14

ACROSS

1 Casino game
5 Symbol on a "one way" sign
10 Numbered musical work
14 Patron saint of Norway
15 "Yeah"
16 Prefix with physical
17 Homeless child
18 Mother ___ stories
19 Checkbook record
20 Mother in a 1960s sitcom
23 Web address: Abbr.
24 Naturalness
25 Sen. Feinstein
27 Go away
30 Mississippi city
32 Arkansas's ___ Mountains
33 Be in harmony (with)
34 Diner sign
37 Vessel for ashes
38 Thirst quenchers
41 Poker prize
42 Historical
44 Pinnacle
45 Port-au-Prince's land
47 It's a bore
49 Los Angeles baseballer
50 Golden period
52 Drop of sweat
53 "Hold On Tight" band
54 1965 Natalie Wood title role
60 Emcee's need
62 Big African critter
63 Opposite of 15-Across
64 France's Cote d'___
65 Fund contributor
66 Laced up
67 Partner of rank and serial number
68 Gushes
69 Lyric poems

DOWN

1 Chickens and turkeys
2 Jai ___
3 Train transport
4 Extended slump
5 Month without a national holiday
6 River of Lyon
7 Greek R's
8 Un-elect
9 Apple-polisher
10 Meditative sounds
11 Merrie Melodies "co-star"
12 Reversal
13 Valuable fur
21 Pre-euro German money
22 ___ Bravo
26 Paul Bunyan's tool
27 Arrange, as the hair
28 Book before Nehemiah
29 "Li'l Abner" mother
30 Gang member, maybe
31 Wild goat
33 Make sport of
35 Lug
36 Recipe direction
39 Holders of referee whistles
40 River hazard
43 Small amount
46 Extend, as a house
48 Roll of bills
49 Styles
50 Charles Atlas, for one
51 "My Fair Lady" lady
52 Already
55 Breakfast restaurant chain
56 Trig function
57 Empty space
58 Fencing blade
59 Wines that aren't whites
61 Afore

by Merle Baker

114

14/29

ACROSS

1 Job detail, briefly
5 24/7 auction site
9 Jazz group
14 Sledder's spot
15 Sub builder?
16 Burger layer
17 Pastel shade
18 Loafing
19 Pottery finish
20 Bad place for the modest
23 Tractor name
24 Many-headed serpent
25 ___ Lanka
28 Since 1/1, to a C.P.A.
29 It has 21 spots
31 Orchestra's percussion or strings, e.g.
33 Coniferous tree
35 Library ID
36 Band with the 1998 #1 hit "One Week"
42 Bard's river
43 Chief exec
44 Played a knight game?
48 ___ Amin
49 Chum
52 Leave speechless
53 "Peachy!"
55 Met offering
57 1997 steelworkers-turned-dancers film
59 Red River capital
62 Calvary letters
63 Pond gunk
64 Shady spot
65 Like eggs
66 Beget
67 Meager
68 Therefore
69 North Carolina university

DOWN

1 Sterne's "Tristram ___"
2 Card game for two
3 Gave the slip to
4 "___ de Lune"
5 Trim to fit, maybe
6 Nighttime inspection
7 Brass or pewter
8 Rates of return
9 French brandy
10 Just
11 Hamm of soccer
12 Dickens's pen name
13 "That's ___ for the books!"
21 Family auto
22 Smelter input
25 "Certainly!," south of the border
26 Boxer's wear
27 Vacationers' stops
30 Nest-egg letters
32 In good order
33 Fisheye ___
34 With it
36 Mexican peninsula
37 Declare openly
38 Philandering sort
39 Oil company structure
40 Played first
41 Self-evident truth
45 Casual top
46 Ram's mate
47 Desecrate
49 Tentatively schedule, with "in"
50 Conductor Toscanini
51 Nonprofessionals
54 Like some eclipses
56 Oater group
57 Animator's creation
58 Italian resort
59 Suffers from
60 Circle segment
61 Magic and Wizards org.

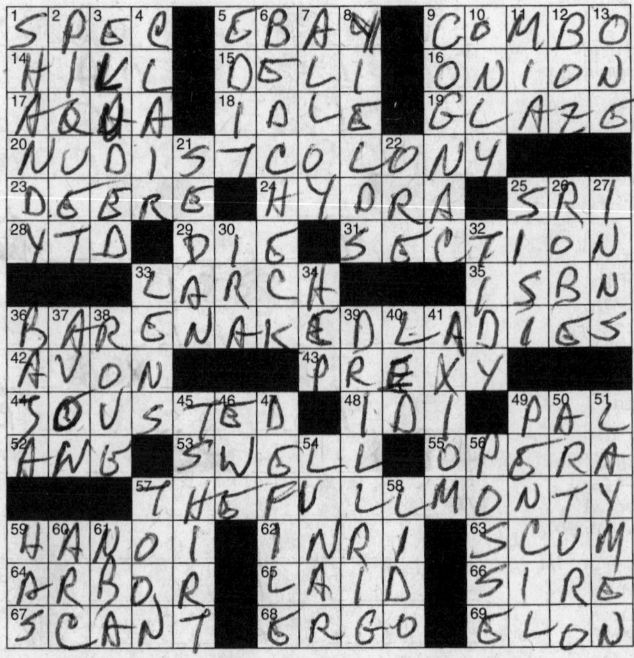

by Janet R. Bender

29/38

ACROSS

1 Did laps in a pool
5 Foolhardy
9 "She loves me . . . she loves me not" flower
14 "Horrors!"
15 "Cómo ___ usted?"
16 Blast from the past
17 Spick-and-span
18 Genesis twin
19 F.B.I. worker
20 Achieve initial success
23 Singletons
24 Bullfight cheer
25 Suffix with lion
28 Oar-powered ship
31 Like a fiddle
34 "Scratch and win" game
36 Pub brew
37 Sweep under the rug
38 Estimates
42 Intl. oil group
43 Take to court
44 Use crib notes
45 Cheyenne's locale: Abbr.
46 Kind of underwear
49 Foxy
50 "___ Drives Me Crazy" (Fine Young Cannibals hit)
51 Western tribe
53 Completely mistaken
60 Improperly long sentence
61 Risk-free
62 Number not on a grandfather clock
63 Space shuttle gasket
64 With warts and all
65 Elm or elder
66 ___ Park, Colo.
67 Camper's cover
68 Hankerings

DOWN

1 Spiritual, e.g.
2 Cry on a roller coaster
3 Med. school class
4 E pluribus unum, for instance
5 "___ Madness" (1936 antidrug film)
6 Whence St. Francis
7 Night twinkler
8 Düsseldorf dwelling
9 Within one's power
10 Pond buildup
11 March 15, e.g.
12 Trig term
13 "Are we there ___?"
21 In first place
22 Marisa of "My Cousin Vinny"
25 Arm joint
26 Unrinsed, maybe
27 Fifth-century pope
29 Autumn yard worker
30 Santa's little helper
31 Pink-slips
32 Perfect
33 Short-tempered
35 Nurse's skill, for short
37 "What'd you say?"
39 Gray
40 Feel sorry about
41 Symbol at the head of a musical staff
46 First ___ first
47 Breakfast bread
48 Swear (to)
50 Masonry
52 Nearing retirement age, maybe
53 Yours and mine
54 The "U" in I.C.U.
55 Future atty.'s exam
56 Facilitate
57 Dublin's land
58 Legal claim
59 Goes kaput
60 Salmon eggs

by Gregory E. Paul

116

ACROSS

1 Spain and Portugal
7 ___ alai
10 Amtrak stop: Abbr.
13 Vietnamese port
14 End abruptly
16 Tense
17 Source of a cry at night
18 Wound
19 ___ Maria
20 Tree-lined road: Abbr.
21 Contribute
22 Uses the HOV lanes, perhaps
24 Butt of jokes
27 Blond shade
29 Krypton or radon
30 Security numbers
33 Groovy
36 ___ apso (dog)
37 It's south of Eur.
38 Sylvester's co-star in "Rocky"
40 Lay turf
41 "As luck would have it . . ."
44 Chemin de ___ (French railway)
45 Med. care provider
46 With a discount of
47 Victoria's Secret item
51 Hush-hush D.C. org.
53 Lena of "The Unbearable Lightness of Being"
54 Guitarist Nugent
55 Seasonal mall employees
59 "Praise be to God!"
61 After-class aides
62 Inclination
63 Even (with)
64 Seattle-to-Las Vegas dir.
65 Rhoda's TV mom
66 Talk show groups

DOWN

1 Person on a poster
2 Undoing
3 Chemical endings
4 Gives off, as heat
5 ___ We Trust
6 Slates
7 Louis-Dreyfus of "Seinfeld"
8 Not yet apprehended
9 Suffix with expert
10 Simply smashing
11 Shrimper's net
12 Courtroom figs.
14 Shore dinner special
15 Some needles
23 Trattoria course
24 Women, casually
25 Dos cubed
26 Military sch.
28 Leave a permanent mark on
31 Bank features
32 Large barrel
33 Run away
34 Is unwell
35 Howls like a dog
39 Brave, for instance
42 Rich, as a voice
43 24-hour
44 Penalized, as a speeder
47 Paint layers
48 "Deutschland über ___"
49 Creator of Pooh and Piglet
50 Nikon rival
52 Place for sweaters?
56 Hit the bottle
57 ___ Sea, east of the Caspian
58 Lith. and Lat., once
60 Wreath

by Eric Berlin

ACROSS
1 Likely
4 Hot dish with beans
9 Bridge maven Charles
14 Justice Sandra ___ O'Connor
15 Appealingly shocking
16 Licorice flavoring
17 Antique auto
19 Frank of rock's Mothers of Invention
20 Vegetable oil component
21 The "S" of CBS
23 Black currant
25 Humiliated
29 Tea server's question
33 Out of one's mind
36 Van Susteren of Fox News
37 Alternative to a nail
38 "That's ___!" (angry denial)
40 Conductor's stick
42 Long-eared hopper
43 Neuters
45 Danger
47 Fashion inits.
48 Cause of an out
51 Refuses
52 Smoothed
56 Drops
60 Baghdad resident
61 ___ Mongolia
64 Small frosted cake
66 Item confiscated at an airport
67 Goofy
68 Wrestler's locale
69 Seasoned sailors
70 Parachute pulls
71 They: Fr.

DOWN
1 ___ committee
2 Newswoman Zahn
3 Varieties
4 Asexual reproduction
5 Where spokes meet
6 Showy flower
7 Showy flower
8 "Beware the ___ . . ."
9 Park shelters
10 Parading . . . or a hint to this puzzle's theme
11 ___ Van Winkle
12 Psychic's claim
13 Educator's org.
18 Japanese soup
22 Punch out, as Morse code
24 Kosovo war participant
26 Not stay on the path
27 Pitchers
28 Wooden pin
30 Bounded
31 Absolute
32 New Zealand native
33 A brig has two
34 ___ male (top dog)
35 Locked book
39 Command to people who are 10-Down
41 "Just do it" sloganeer
44 Gentlemen of España
46 An original tribe of Israel
49 Scatter, as seeds
50 Feudal figure
53 Ashley's country-singing mother
54 Sweet'N Low rival
55 Mud, dust and grime
57 Like "The Lord of the Rings"
58 It's north of Carson City
59 Movie rating unit
61 Approves
62 Spanish article
63 Up to, informally
65 Polit. maverick

by Joy M. Andrews

118

34

ACROSS

1 Trunk item
6 Job seeker's success
11 Gridlock
14 Poe's middle name
15 Bisect
16 Mentalist Geller
17 All-freshman team?
19 Zero
20 Ugly Duckling, in reality
21 Reflect (on)
22 Arcade coin
24 So-so
26 Bridle's partner
27 Peter Cottontail?
32 Tonsil neighbor
33 Smallish field
34 Put on TV
37 Boone, to rustics
38 Have a ball?
40 Blue Triangle org.
41 Inventor Whitney
42 Fill-in
43 Heart of France
44 Answer to "Who wrote 'The Highwayman'?"
48 Historical Scottish county
50 Summoned Jeeves
51 M-1, for one
52 Tokyo ties
54 Charlie Chaplin's widow
58 '60s muscle car
59 Milliner on the move?
62 Poet's preposition
63 Zoo critter
64 Campfire treat
65 "Shame on you"
66 Supersized
67 Tournament favorites

DOWN

1 ___-serif
2 Furrow former
3 Thomas ___ Edison
4 Drops from on high
5 Letter accompanier: Abbr.
6 "Yeah, right"
7 Web site sect. for newbies
8 Chimney channel
9 Zsa Zsa's sister
10 Bureaucratic tangle
11 Place for miscellaneous stuff
12 Sharon of Israel
13 Eeyore's creator
18 Oscar winner Jannings
23 Lyrical lines
25 Dr. J's old league: Abbr.
26 Nimble
27 Au naturel
28 Horse course
29 Item in a musician's pocket
30 Arthur Marx, familiarly
31 Columbus Day mo.
35 Hosp. areas
36 Like a compliant cat
38 Banana waste
39 Early hrs.
40 "Dunno"
42 Aspirin alternative
43 Bamboozle
45 Olive in the comics
46 Milk container?
47 Redeem, with "in"
48 Insider's vocabulary
49 Priests' administrations
52 "Rubáiyát" poet
53 Screen door sound
55 Oklahoma Indian
56 One who's unhip
57 Aphrodite's lover
60 ___ pro nobis
61 Big jerk

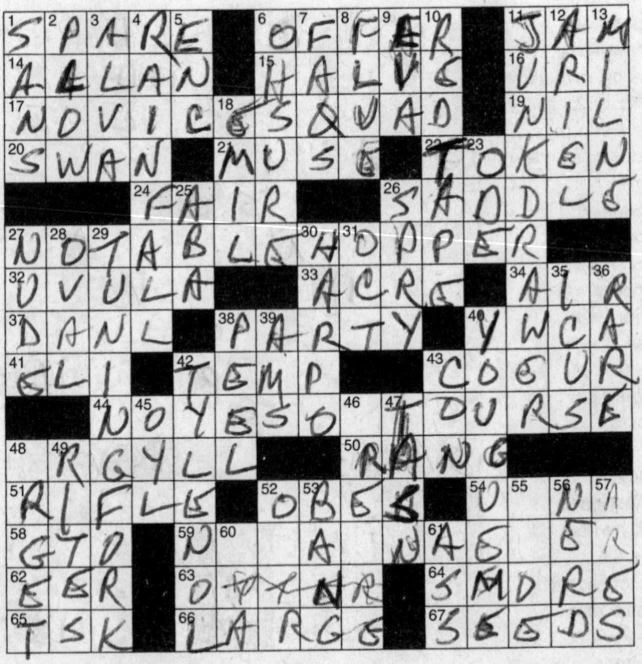

by Lee Glickstein and Nancy Salomon

119

5/7/16

ACROSS
1 Boeing 747's and 767's
5 The Monkees' "___ Believer"
8 "Am not!" rejoinder
14 Forced out
16 Wash receptacles
17 With 56-Across, lawyer who argued in 19- and 49-Across
18 Pre-Mexican Indians
19 With 49-Across, noted decision made 5/17/54
21 Buying binge
24 Musical talent
25 Eight: Fr.
26 Stuart queen
29 Went after congers
34 Aged
35 On the briny
36 Curious thing
37 Decision reversed by 19- and 49-Across
40 One sailing under a skull and crossbones
41 Locust or larch
42 Spanish aunt
43 Belgian painter James
44 Chief Justice ___ Warren, majority opinion writer for 19- and 49-Across
45 Rolodex nos.
46 Select, with "for"
48 Stanford-___ test
49 See 19-Across
55 Sitting room
56 See 17-Across
60 Groups of starting players
61 Forebodes
62 Vice President Dick
63 Ave. crossers
64 Mary ___ Lincoln

DOWN
1 Stick (out)
2 Book after Galatians: Abbr.
3 Capote, for short
4 Iced dessert
5 Langston Hughes poem
6 Cat's cry
7 Annex: Abbr.
8 Addis ___, Ethiopia
9 Symbol of sharpness
10 "Cómo ___ usted?"
11 Echelon
12 How a lot of modern music is sold
13 Secret W.W. II agcy.
15 Brute
20 Flying geese formation
21 Quaint establishment
22 Arrive, as by car
23 Passengers
26 "___ sow, so shall . . ."
27 Reno's state: Abbr.
28 U.S./Can./Mex. pact
30 University URL ending
31 Pay attention
32 French star
33 Ruler by birth
35 Houston landmark
36 Pitcher Hershiser
38 ___ Paulo, Brazil
39 Go off track
44 And so forth
45 Soldier's helmet, slangily
47 Short-winded
48 Bruce Springsteen, with "the"
49 ___ of office
50 Gratis
51 Flair
52 Concert equipment
53 Pucker-inducing
54 Angers
55 ___-Man (arcade game)
57 Past
58 Was ahead
59 "Acid"

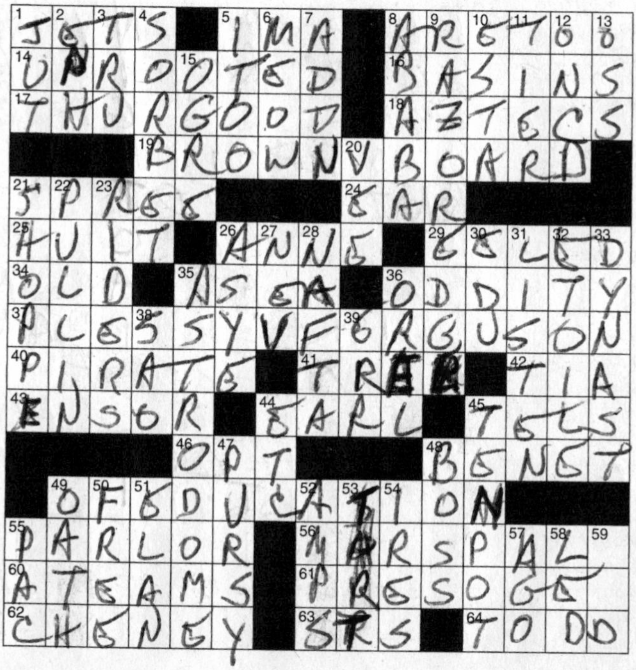

by Ethan Cooper

120

17

ACROSS

1 Wise competitor
5 Quack
10 On vacation
14 Snack sold in a stack
15 Crystal set
16 Lens holders
17 Soccer commentator's cry
18 Shelley's "Adonais" is one
19 List-ending abbr.
20 "Aha!"
23 Caper
24 Little one
25 Four-bagger
27 Hosp. workers
28 Top worn with shorts
30 "All in the Family" network
32 Arctic bird
33 Soccer star Hamm
34 ___ correspondent
35 Singer/songwriter Laura
36 Honky-tonk instruments
40 Mountaintop
41 Aurora's counterpart
42 Wonderment
43 Deli sandwich, for short
44 Corots, Monets and such
45 Sp. Mrs.
46 Qualifiers
49 Red Sea peninsula
51 Cartoon collectible
53 Spokes, e.g.
55 Passable
58 Some drive-thru features, briefly
59 Not as friendly
60 Tennis score after deuce
61 Old-fashioned dance
62 "___ luck!"
63 Evening, in ads
64 Retailer's gds.
65 "Mmm, mmm!"
66 Leave in, to an editor

DOWN

1 River blockage
2 In the vicinity
3 Bakery supplies
4 Longtime Chicago Symphony maestro
5 Air Force One passenger: Abbr.
6 Soft, white mineral
7 Keats's "___ a Nightingale"
8 Bedtime drink
9 Ma with a bow
10 "All systems ___!"
11 How a 43-Across is usually prepared
12 All Olympians, once
13 Designer monogram
21 Play segment
22 Sounds of doubt
26 "King Kong" studio
29 Raring to go
31 Hare's habitat
33 Mystery man
34 Scale amts.
35 Del.-to-Vt. direction
36 Elated
37 Spot and Felix, e.g.
38 Après-ski treat
39 Tony, Oscar or Hugo
40 Middle manager's focus?
44 Balloon filler
45 Most guileful
46 "Hurray for me!"
47 Limited
48 Major paperback publisher
50 Bridal path
52 Gives off
54 Bates and King
56 Pinball stopper
57 Horse-drawn vehicle
58 Pitching ___

by Elizabeth C. Gorski

11/27

ACROSS

1 Dreadful, as circumstances
5 One not of high morals
10 Spanish house
14 TV's "American ___"
15 Come back
16 Shakespeare, the Bard of ___
17 1970 Richard Thomas film adapted from a Richard Bradford novel
20 Mao ___-tung
21 Hula shakers
22 To no ___ (uselessly)
23 Outlaws
24 Wall Street business
26 Jumped
29 Long baths
30 Ayatollah's land
31 Kunta ___ of "Roots"
32 Duo
35 1975 Al Pacino film
39 Lamb's mother
40 Landlord payments
41 Shrek, for one
42 Slight hangups
43 Reveries
45 Oilless paint
48 Cure
49 Lily family plants
50 Arias, usually
51 King topper
54 1941 Priscilla Lane film whose title was a #1 song
58 Advance, as money
59 Lollapalooza
60 Bridle strap
61 Football positions
62 "I'm innocent!"
63 Poet ___ St. Vincent Millay

DOWN

1 Earth
2 Midmonth date
3 Was transported
4 Raised railroads
5 Difficult
6 Harvests
7 Intermissions separate them
8 Silent
9 ___-am (sports competition)
10 Sail material
11 Birdlike
12 ___ boom
13 Corner
18 Mongol title
19 Fouler
23 Wedding reception staple
24 Type assortments
25 "I can't believe ___..." (old ad catchphrase)
26 Lateral part
27 Ship's front
28 Fury
29 Sorts (through)
31 Australian hopper, for short
32 "Gladiator" garment
33 Fish bait
34 Halves of a 32-Across
36 James of "Gunsmoke"
37 Wine vintage
38 Christmas song
42 Zips (along)
43 X out
44 Cause for umbrellas
45 Billiards furniture
46 Actress Burstyn
47 Knoll
48 Yawn-inducing
50 Yards rushing, e.g.
51 Elderly
52 Goatee site
53 Sicilian volcano
55 Son of, in Arabic names
56 Recent: Prefix
57 Fury

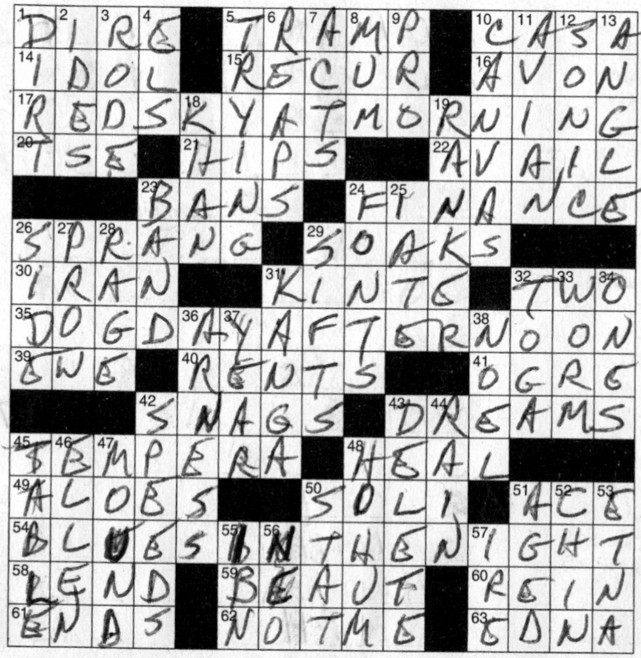

by Frederick J. Healy

122

ACROSS

1 Doze (off)
4 Following
9 Infield fly
14 Pub offering
15 "Death, Be Not Proud" poet
16 "Maria ___," 1940s hit
17 At leisure: Abbr.
18 Pact made at The Hague?
20 Legacy sharer
22 Directors Spike and Ang
23 Co., in France
24 Talks wildly
26 One more
28 Emulated O. Henry?
31 Many eras
32 Distress signal
33 ___ to go
37 Six-time U.S. Open tennis champ
40 Fool
42 Dweeb
43 Longing
45 Onetime neighbor of Israel: Abbr.
47 Neckline style
48 Where chocolate candy is made?
52 Procession
55 Sensation
56 Mancinelli opera "___ e Leandro"
57 They're welcome on the back
59 Epoch of 50 million years ago
62 Part of a shirtmaker's education?
65 Female rabbit
66 Place to moor
67 Stan's foil, in old films
68 Not well
69 Reluctant
70 Interminably
71 Taboos

DOWN

1 D.E.A. agent
2 Butter alternative
3 Removes from power
4 Summing
5 Quarters
6 Explosive
7 Abbr. at the bottom of a business letter
8 Consider again
9 Kind of ad
10 Corrida cry
11 Miss ___ of the comics
12 Loosen
13 Reimburser
19 Pavarotti, notably
21 ___ de Cologne
25 Portico in Athens
27 Beginner
28 Work in the garden
29 Wander
30 Promulgate
34 Gets elected
35 ___-do-well
36 Joel of "Cabaret"
38 Estrangement
39 God's way, in religion
41 Umpire's call
44 Mystery writer's award
46 Arrived quickly
49 Mounts
50 Was too sweet
51 Middle X or O
52 Rhodes of Rhodesia
53 College town on the Penobscot River
54 University of Missouri locale
58 W.W. II battle town
60 ___ contendere
61 Fish caught in pots
63 Tennis call
64 Suffix with mod-

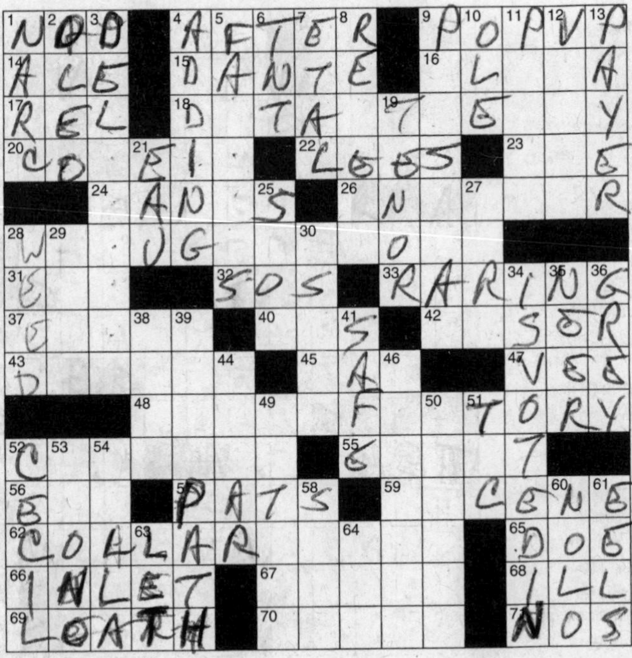

by Richard Chisholm

123

42/54

ACROSS

1 Gun-toting gal
5 ___ vu
9 Put forth, as a theory
14 Singer Brickell
15 Greek counterpart of 27-Down
16 Wonderland girl
17 Mediocre
18 "___, vidi, vici" (Caesar's boast)
19 Ohio birthplace of William McKinley
20 Bridge
23 Widespread
24 April 15 deadline agcy.
25 Fond du ___, Wis.
28 Take the witness stand
31 Classic muscle car
34 Caribbean resort island
36 "___ we having fun yet?"
37 Conclude, with "up"
38 Bridge
42 Spew
43 Washington's ___ Stadium
44 Below
45 Young fellow
46 Feature of Texaco's logo, once
49 Period in history
50 Sawbuck
51 Periods in history
53 Bridge
61 Ancient Greek marketplace
62 Prayer's end
63 Govern
64 Laser printer powder
65 Left, at sea
66 Vicinity
67 War horse
68 Some Father's Day callers
69 Sign of boredom

DOWN

1 Flat-topped hill
2 Reason to say "pee-yew!"
3 "Schindler's ___"
4 Sainted ninth-century pope
5 Concoct
6 Puts up, as a tower
7 Mitchell who sang "Big Yellow Taxi"
8 India's locale
9 Kitchen closet
10 Miscellanies
11 Building next to a barn
12 Noted rapper/actor
13 Radio host John
21 Deadly
22 Prisoner who'll never get out
25 Sports jacket feature
26 Inviting smell
27 Roman counterpart of 15-Across
29 Bulletin board stickers
30 Savings for old age: Abbr.
31 Exam mark
32 Worker with circus lions
33 "La Bohème," e.g.
35 Except that
37 Chicago-based Superstation
39 Where the action is
40 TV's "Mayberry ___"
41 German engraver Albrecht
46 Offer on a "Wanted" poster
47 Alehouse
48 C.I.A. operatives
50 Number of points for a field goal
52 Deodorant type
53 Stetsons, e.g.
54 Gershwin's "___ Rhythm"
55 Sold, to an auctioneer
56 Puppy sounds
57 1847 Melville novel
58 Mysterious quality
59 Whole bunch
60 Actor Connery

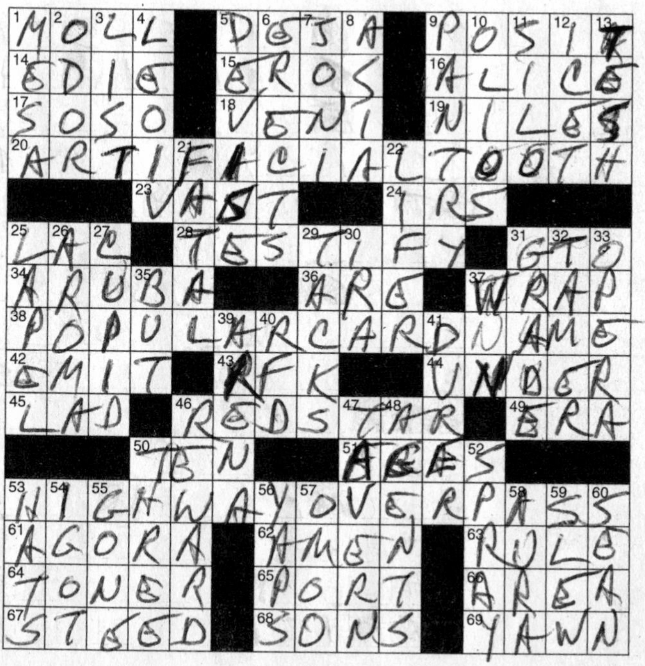

by Gregory E. Paul

124

ACROSS

1 Verboten: Var.
5 Boats' backbones
10 "The Nazarene" writer Sholem
14 Park and Lexington, e.g., in N.Y.C.
15 Decorated Murphy
16 Starlet's goal
17 Ceremony for inventors
19 In alignment
20 Off the track
21 Rankled
23 Lager holder
24 Burlesque star Lili St. ___
25 One of Alcott's "Little Women"
26 Jean Arp's art
28 Stair part
31 Greeting for a villain
34 Holy Iraqi
37 In reserve
38 Bat material
39 Is headed for a fall
41 Baseball rarity
42 Ill will
44 Lantern-jawed celeb
45 Hide's partner
46 High-strung
47 Shiites or Amish
49 Easy card game
50 Place to relax
52 Sophisticates they're not
56 Soak through
59 Coin flipper's phrase
60 "How sweet ___!"
61 Low-cal beer in reserve?
63 Ides of March rebuke
64 Actor Delon
65 In perpetuity
66 Leak slowly
67 Jack who was famously frugal
68 Laura of "I Am Sam"

DOWN

1 Spanish appetizers
2 Sailor's "Stop!"
3 Midler of stage and screen
4 Cyber-handles
5 Name in a stuttered 1918 song title
6 Where Lux. is
7 Uplift spiritually
8 Pepsi bottle amount
9 Meets, as a bet
10 Sister of Apollo
11 Bad place to build?
12 Whodunit board game
13 Pay mind to
18 "Peter Pan" dog
22 Gogol's "___ Bulba"
24 Caravan beast
27 Conk out
29 Falco of "The Sopranos"
30 Need a bath badly
31 Dish that's "slung"
32 Culp/Cosby TV series
33 Word processor for sailors?
35 Munched on
36 Brainy group
39 ___ Haute, Ind.
40 Sturgeon delicacy
43 Joins forces (with)
45 Silenced
48 Crack from the cold
50 Played out
51 Praline nut
53 Critic Barnes
54 Check falsifier
55 Howard of morning radio
56 They're cut into wedges
57 Sermon ending?
58 Simple rhyme scheme
59 Big Apple college inits.
62 They're related

by Fred Piscop

ACROSS

1 True-blue
6 Toy gun poppers
10 Smooch
14 "Good Night" girl of song
15 Arthur ___ Stadium in Queens
16 Peak
17 River triangle
18 Signify
19 Horn's sound
20 Logic
23 ___ capita
24 Buffalo's lake
25 Money in the bank, e.g.
30 Declare
33 Seizes without authority
34 Old what's-___-name
35 George W. Bush's alma mater
36 Michael who starred in "Dirty Rotten Scoundrels"
37 Snorkeling accessory
38 Wolf calls
39 Broadway hit with 7,000+ performances
40 With it
41 Immobilize
42 Swelling reducer
43 Highway stops
45 Ritzy
46 Little rascal
47 Question of concern, with a hint to 20-, 25- and 43-Across
54 Corner square in Monopoly
55 Den
56 Unsophisticated
57 Loafing
58 Dublin's home
59 Lyrics accompany them
60 2000 "subway series" losers
61 Toy used on hills
62 Commence

DOWN

1 Eyeball covers
2 Nabisco cookie
3 Shout
4 Against
5 Weapon in the game of Clue
6 Tripod topper
7 On the open water
8 Adds gradually
9 Mexican misters
10 Couric of CBS News
11 Computer symbol
12 Haze
13 Movie backdrop
21 Commies
22 Tiny criticism
25 Emmy-winner (finally!) Susan
26 Author ___ Bashevis Singer
27 Truly
28 Vases
29 Harbor sights
30 Took care of
31 Totally tired
32 Sí and oui
35 Quotable Yank
37 Swerve back and forth, as a car's rear end
38 Very short shorts
40 Big bothers
41 Soccer star Mia
43 Caught
44 In layers
45 Sees a ghost, maybe
47 Walk through water
48 Sword handle
49 Put on the payroll
50 Tightly stretched
51 Turner who sang "I Don't Wanna Fight"
52 At any time
53 Sabbath activity
54 ___-dandy

by Lynn Lempel

126

37/54

ACROSS

1 10K, e.g.
5 Wheedler's tactic
10 Jungle crushers
14 ___ Bator
15 Land of a billion
16 Basilica area
17 Start of an Oscar Wilde quote
20 Revolutionary Allen
21 Comics shriek
22 Out of bed
23 Bakers' wares
25 Strange sightings
27 Quote, part 2
31 Cost-controlling W.W. II agcy.
34 Jacob's twin
35 Et ___ (and the following)
36 Cozy spots
38 "I cannot ___ lie"
40 Make a knight, e.g.
42 Utter disorder
43 See 61-Down
45 Dr. Seuss's Sam ___
47 "Rule Britannia" composer
48 Spain's Juan Carlos, for one
49 Quote, part 3
52 ___ En-lai
53 Slinky's shape
54 Bawdyhouse manager
57 Bleachers cry
59 ___ Jean Baker (Marilyn Monroe)
63 End of the quote
66 Excursion
67 Met offering
68 Civil wrong
69 Coin flip
70 Theroux's "endless night"
71 Summers in Québec

DOWN

1 Deserving a slap, maybe
2 Touched down
3 Country singer Johnny
4 Summarize
5 Tonic's partner
6 Brand-new
7 ___ fixe (obsession)
8 Meeting of spacecraft
9 "Mangia!"
10 Groundwork
11 Chooses, with "for"
12 1975 Wimbledon winner
13 Perceived
18 "Sleep ___"
19 Like many an O. Henry story
24 Pothook shape
26 Half a sawbuck
27 Awful smell
28 Grenoble's river
29 Come from behind
30 Furnish with gear
31 Midwest air hub
32 Hacienda drudges
33 Pack animals
37 A Brontë sister
39 Cause of wheezing
41 Graph with rectangular areas
44 "___ 'nuff!"
46 Meadow call
50 The Continent
51 Actress Lollobrigida
52 Roughs it
54 Feminist Lucretia
55 Michael Jackson's old do
56 Honored guest's spot
58 Neighborhood
60 Knee-slapper
61 With 43-Across, approximately
62 Little scurriers
64 Auction assent
65 "Uh-uh!"

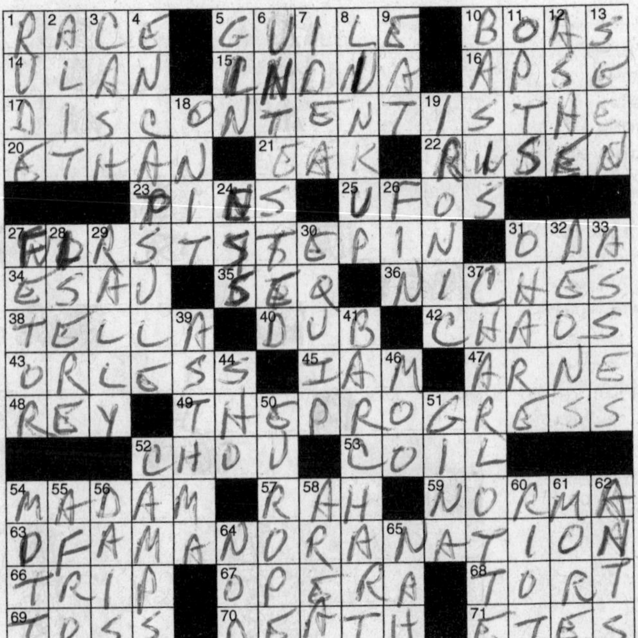

by Ed Early

ACROSS

1 Literature Nobelist Bellow
5 Slender
9 Gregorian music style
14 Port or claret
15 Left a chair
16 Edmonton hockey player
17 Vicinity
18 Out of the wind
19 Handsome wood design
20 Place to pull in for a meal
23 Seafood in shells
24 Site of one-armed bandits
27 Place for a pig
28 New York ballplayer
29 Ryan of "When Harry Met Sally"
30 Four-star officer: Abbr.
31 F.D.R. radio broadcast
34 As well
37 Responses to a masseur
38 German chancellor ___ von Bismarck
39 Highest-priced boxing ticket
44 It may be served with crumpets
45 Snoop around
46 Old cable inits.
47 "Sesame Street" broadcaster
50 Modern affluent type
52 Teen meeting place
54 Kindly doctor's asset
57 Setting for Theseus and the Minotaur
59 Plumb crazy
60 Skin outbreak
61 Broadcasting
62 Whiskey drink
63 Display
64 Desires
65 Statement figures: Abbr.
66 "Bonanza" brother

DOWN

1 Groups of bees
2 Clear of stale smells
3 Apprehensive
4 Clues, to a detective
5 Movie preview
6 Not change course
7 "Gotcha"
8 Must-have item
9 Just-made-up word
10 Actor/dancer Gregory
11 O.K.
12 Org. that funds exhibits
13 Have a go at
21 Big rig
22 Decorated, as a cake
25 Well-groomed
26 Not fooled by
29 Fail to qualify, as for a team
31 London weather, often
32 That girl
33 Barracks bunk
34 Bohemian
35 In ___ of (replacing)
36 Vegetable in a crisp pod
40 Tarantulas, e.g.
41 Angers
42 Captivates
43 Tennis star Kournikova
47 Pullover raincoat
48 ___ Aires
49 Scatters, as petals
51 Mini, in Marseille
53 Grind, as teeth
55 Rick's love in "Casablanca"
56 Fate
57 It may be put out to pasture
58 Genetic stuff

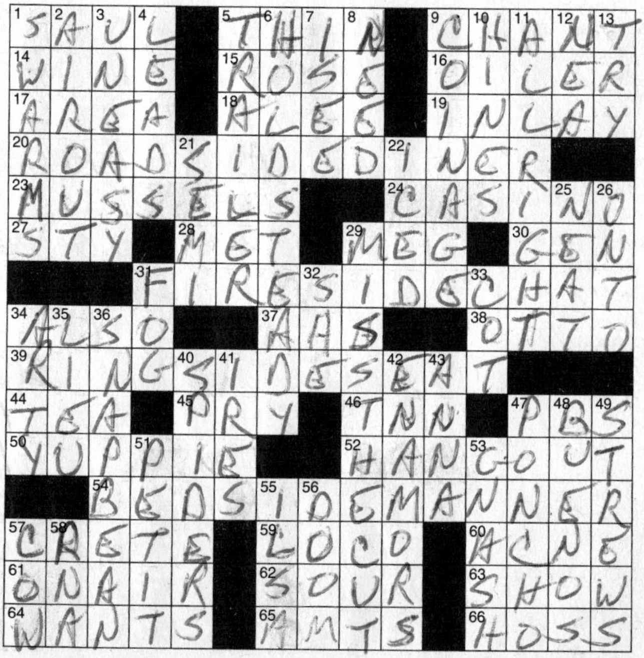

by Craig Kasper

128

05/20

ACROSS

1 Rugged rock
5 Incite
9 Unlike a dirt road
14 Whopper
15 White-tailed eagle
16 Spry
17 Fusses
18 Makes lace
19 Like maples but not firs
20 Area between two scrimmage lines
23 Jul. follower
24 Largest of the British Virgin Islands
29 Chemical process also called hyperfiltration
33 Attention-getter
34 Radio feature
35 Successful
36 Flared-spout pitcher
38 Military newbie
41 Heredity unit
42 Grief
44 Rotators under the hood
46 ___ Lingus
47 Make crazy
51 Increased
52 Took off
53 Yellowstone employees
59 Video game pioneer
63 Bluish green
64 "The Grapes of Wrath" figure
65 Get ready for Web-surfing
66 Northern Oklahoma city
67 Take a break
68 Hard stuff
69 Lightning catchers
70 Inquires

DOWN

1 Family group
2 Obnoxious
3 Baseball brothers' name
4 Holst who composed "The Planets"
5 "Stop living in your fantasy world!"
6 Kind of hygiene
7 1998 animated film with the voice of Woody Allen
8 Spanish explorer who discovered the Mississippi
9 Capital of Sicily
10 Get on in years
11 By way of
12 Keebler worker?
13 Susan of "L.A. Law"
21 Regretted
22 Rejections
25 Chinese mafia
26 Bony
27 Toy train maker
28 "___ your instructions . . ."
29 Express differently
30 Lash site
31 Mineo of "Exodus"
32 Vote in
33 Gossipy Hopper
37 Gad about
39 Relative of "Phooey!"
40 Green gems
43 Timber from Maine
45 Long-necked bird
48 Hagen of Broadway
49 Luggage carrier
50 Some wool
54 Gambler's game
55 Police cry
56 Stretches (out)
57 Hazard
58 Nears the western horizon
59 Vestment for a priest
60 As well
61 Back then
62 Role on "Frasier"

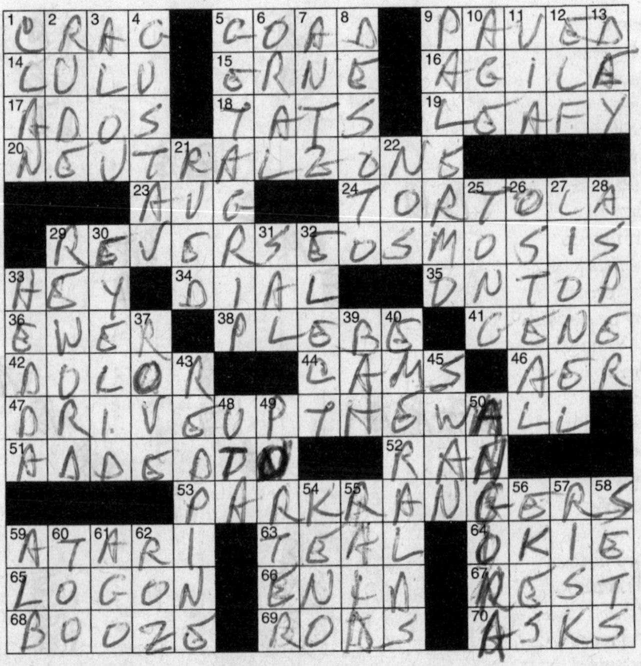

by Nancy Kavanaugh

20/33

ACROSS

1 End-of-week cry
5 Makes, as tea
10 Wise ___ owl
14 Folk singer Guthrie
15 Soprano Callas
16 Popular building block
17 1959 Doris Day/Rock Hudson comedy
19 Actress Singer of "Footloose"
20 Victor's entitlement
21 Errors
23 See 24-Across
24 With 23-Across, Neptune, e.g.
26 Back street
27 Clearance item's caveat
29 Wrestler's win
30 Had a bite
31 Disposable pen maker
32 Davenport
33 Church official
37 What a full insurance policy offers
40 Bronze and stainless steel
41 Bed size smaller than full
42 ___ Paul's seafood
43 Spider's prey
44 Conger or moray
45 Mosquito repellent ingredient
46 First lady after Hillary
49 Put two and two together?
50 California's Big ___
51 Evidence in court
53 Tetley competitor
56 Radio tuner
57 Piano player's aid
60 France, under Caesar
61 "___ Doone" (1869 novel)
62 Not us
63 Building additions
64 Vote into office
65 Jekyll's alter ego

DOWN

1 Bugler's evening call
2 Hang on tight?
3 Not according to Mr. Spock
4 Shakespearean volumes
5 Some luxury cars
6 Squealer
7 Time in history
8 "The Flintstones" mother
9 Pseudonym of H. H. Munro
10 Post-danger signal
11 1988 Olympics host
12 Be of one mind
13 Clamorous
18 Outdated
22 Lustrous fabric
24 Go (through), as evidence
25 Made into law
27 "Mamma Mia" pop group
28 Window box location
29 Verse-writing
30 Tablet with ibuprofen
32 Bygone space station
34 Averse to picture-taking
35 Meanie
36 Home in a tree
38 Without any extras
39 Was beholden to
45 University of Minnesota campus site
46 Overhang
47 Like some symmetry
48 Mover's rental
49 Playwright ___ Fugard
50 Uncle ___
52 Ireland, the Emerald ___
53 Ballpark figure?
54 Went out, as a fire
55 Pinnacle
58 Before, in 29-Down
59 Business letter abbr.

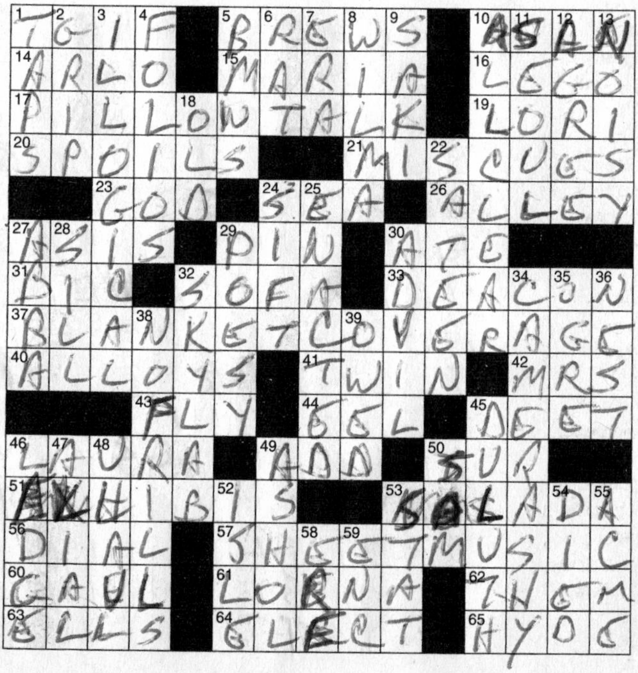

by Craig Kasper

130

ACROSS

1 Luau instruments, for short
5 Noted plus-size model
9 Nice to wear
14 Like Playboy models
15 "Hud" Oscar winner Patricia
16 Be nuts about
17 Qatari V.I.P.
18 Turns abruptly
19 Novelist Ephron
20 Old telephone feature
23 Proofreader's mark
24 G.P.A., slangily
25 Put a value on
27 When summer starts
30 Cry over
32 Geographical septet
33 Kabob holder
35 Pitcher part
38 See 41-Across
40 Historic time
41 With 38-Across, what the four key parts of this puzzle are
43 Uno + due
44 Conductor Toscanini
47 State openly
48 Brawl site in a western
50 Horrifies
52 Yalta's peninsula
54 Stowe equipment
55 Hearty party
56 Gymgoer's goal
62 Earth's ___ layer
64 19-Across's sister
65 Medieval chest
66 Wades across, say
67 "The heat ___!"
68 Bring up
69 Rendezvous
70 Rock's Rundgren
71 The end of each of 20- and 56-Across and 11- and 29-Down is a popular one

DOWN

1 Addict
2 ___ sabe
3 Turnpike toll-paying locale
4 Big Orange of college sports
5 Pepsin and rennin, for two
6 Gettysburg victor
7 Yule trio
8 Adamson's lioness
9 Crude dude
10 Ukrainian port
11 Fuji flow
12 Part of a Happy Meal
13 "The Second Coming" poet
21 Seek a seat
22 Poor, as excuses go
26 Put into slots
27 "___ that special?!"
28 Within earshot
29 "Howards End" director
30 Kicked off
31 Fancy pitcher
34 Green Hornet's sidekick
36 Hit Fox show, in headlines
37 Mass seating
39 Mall attraction
42 Eminem and Dr. Dre, for two
45 Gad about
46 Bay Area city
49 Makes right
51 Pizza order
52 Video game heroine Lara ___
53 Stubble remover
54 New England catch
57 Complex dwelling
58 "Eh"
59 Black-and-white treat
60 Final Four org.
61 Tombstone lawman
63 Ballpark fig.

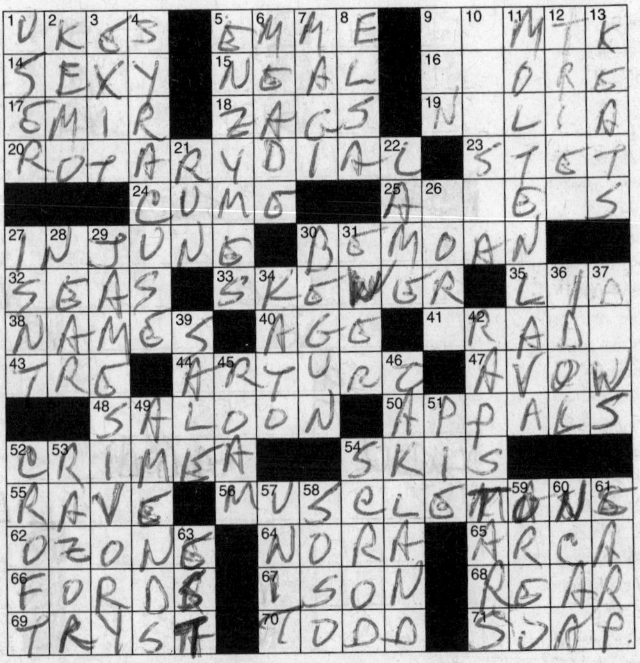

by Allan E. Parrish

ACROSS

1 Crossword pattern
5 Dinner and a movie, perhaps
9 No longer fresh
14 Prefix with space
15 Sharif of "Funny Girl"
16 Swatch competitor
17 Convention group
18 Sitarist Shankar
19 Christopher of "Superman"
20 Polyester, e.g.
23 Battering device
24 Words before tear or roll
25 Astroturf, e.g.
34 Everest or Ararat
35 Comic strip orphan
36 Country singer Brenda
37 Johnson of "Laugh-In"
38 Vision-related
39 Darn, as socks
40 Lunar New Year
41 Grand Canyon transport
42 Contemptible person
43 Oleomargarine, e.g.
46 Airport monitor abbr.
47 Blonde shade
48 Fake 50, e.g.
57 Throng
58 Banjo-plucking Scruggs
59 Hand lotion ingredient
60 Indy-winning Al, Jr. or Sr.
61 Canal of song
62 It's trapped on laundry day
63 Sirs' counterparts
64 Give temporarily
65 Falls behind

DOWN

1 Chews the fat
2 Depend (on)
3 "Pumping ___"
4 Marxism, for one
5 Starting notes in music
6 Amo, amas, ___ . . .
7 Rikki-Tikki-___
8 Guitarist Clapton
9 Eerie
10 Item of men's jewelry
11 From the United States: Abbr.
12 Jeans purveyor Strauss
13 Business V.I.P.
21 Sword handle
22 ___ acid (B vitamin)
25 Maker of precious violins
26 Composer/author Ned
27 ___-frutti
28 Isle in the Bay of Naples
29 Emcee's spiel
30 Negatively charged particle
31 Alaskan native
32 "Common" thing that's not always common
33 Passover feast
38 Bizarre
39 Closet larvae repellent
41 Does deals without money
42 Earthy desire
44 Bicycle for two
45 Tried to save a sinking boat
48 Buddy
49 One of the O'Neills
50 ___ Major
51 Rod's partner
52 Price of a ride
53 "___ go bragh"
54 Pelvic bones
55 Beyond the end line
56 Answer to "Shall we?"

by Sarah Keller

132

ACROSS

1 Opportunity to hit
6 Shoots 18, say
11 Rocks in a bar
14 Long green
15 The Beatles' "Eight Days ___"
16 Turf
17 Result of eating ice cream too fast, possibly
19 Moth-eaten
20 Best guess: Abbr.
21 Fastens with a band
22 "That is ___ . . ." (in other words)
24 Town next to Elizabeth, N.J.
26 Flexible, electrically
27 Fondue dip
32 Bops hard
35 Light as a feather
36 Pot's top
37 Spa wear
38 En ___ (all together)
40 Place for a ham
41 Where Schwarzenegger was born: Abbr.
42 "Lost our lease" event
43 Airplane seating option
44 Entreater's words
48 Asta's mistress
49 The whole ___ (everything)
53 Must, slangily
55 Debaters debate it
57 Shaq's alma mater: Abbr.
58 Copy
59 Sunshine State vacation area
62 Snore letter
63 3 on a par-5 hole, e.g.
64 Largish combo
65 Golfer Ernie
66 Collar inserts
67 Quaint footwear

DOWN

1 Color of waves of grain, in song
2 Sculpted figure
3 Bath toys
4 2001 role for Will Smith
5 Comb stoppers
6 Attic
7 Was in the red
8 Dregs
9 Shriner's topper
10 Missing many details
11 Kind of triangle
12 RC, for one
13 Whirling water
18 "___ 'er up!"
23 Pindar work
25 One-named supermodel
26 Plot unit
28 Studio prop
29 Insult, slangily
30 Spot for a warm pie
31 Falco of "The Sopranos"
32 Shawl or stole
33 Billing unit
34 Some voters
38 Yucatán native
39 Gran Paradiso, for one
40 Per ___
42 Attacks from the air
43 Sub sinkers, in slang
45 Young 'un
46 Catches sight of
47 Like gastric juice
50 Dementieva of tennis
51 So far
52 Corrodes
53 Stare intently
54 Kadett automaker
55 Fraternity party attire
56 Paris airport
60 Long. crosser
61 Keystone lawman

by Jim Hyres

ACROSS

1 What a surfer rides
5 Do agricultural work
9 Pre-euro German money
14 Violinist Leopold
15 Side squared, for a square
16 When added up
17 Porn classification
19 AM/FM device
20 Rainbow's shape
21 Attractive
23 Nova ___
26 Battle exhortations
27 Followers of the Vatican
29 Dockworker's org.
30 Postponed
31 Driver entitled to free maps, perhaps
37 Sprinted
38 Grp. battling consumer fraud
39 Genetic letters
40 Big shoe request
44 Accumulate
46 Lumberjack's tool
47 Binds, as wounds
49 Sign-making aids
54 Gets the soap off
55 Part of a grandfather clock
56 "Then what . . . ?"
57 Handy ___ (good repairmen)
58 English king during the American Revolution
63 Feed, as a fire
64 Jazz's Fitzgerald
65 Horse color
66 Customs
67 Leave in, to a proofreader
68 At the ocean's bottom, as a ship

DOWN

1 Floor application
2 Secondary, as an outlet: Abbr.
3 Annoy
4 Inconsistent
5 Wealthy sort, slangily
6 ___ Ben Canaan of "Exodus"
7 Extend a subscription
8 ___ cum laude
9 Act of God
10 Horrid glances from Charles Grodin?
11 Hub projections
12 Kevin of "A Fish Called Wanda"
13 Wades (through)
18 Stand up
22 Bad, as a prognosis
23 Mold's origin
24 Something not really on Mars
25 Hypothesize
28 Kemo ___ (the Lone Ranger)
32 Pres. Lincoln
33 Help in crime
34 Button material
35 Follow
36 Metal filers
41 Beard named for a Flemish artist
42 Forgives
43 Astronaut Armstrong
44 Imitating
45 Darners
48 Mount where an ark parked
49 Charley horse, e.g.
50 ___-one (long odds)
51 Witch of ___
52 Olympic sleds
53 Refine, as metal
59 Bullring call
60 Debtor's note
61 Writer Fleming
62 It's kept in a pen

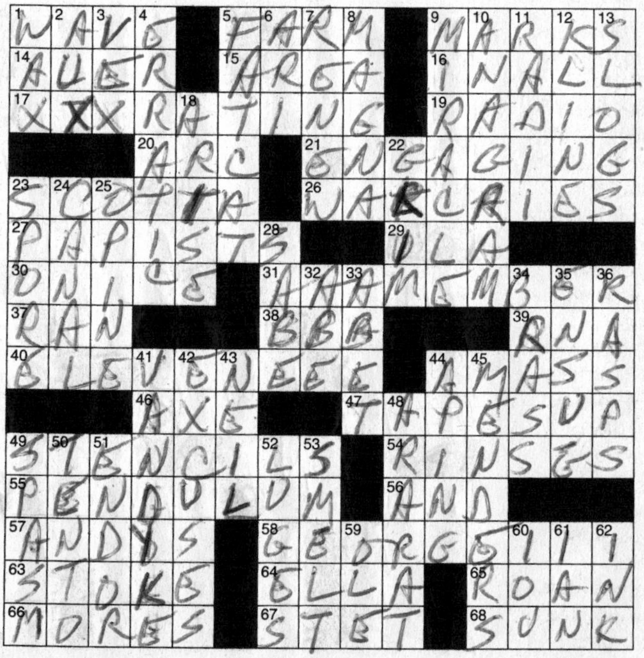

by Patrick Merrell

134

19

ACROSS

1 "___ as I can tell . . ."
6 Hurdles for future attorneys: Abbr.
11 Pudding fruit
14 Florida's Key ___
15 Florida's ___ Center
16 Form 1040 datum: Abbr.
17 Danish theologian (speller's nightmare #1)
19 Swe. neighbor
20 "As I Lay Dying" character
21 Afternoon: Sp.
22 What "nobody can" do, in song
23 Musical for which Liza Minnelli won a 1978 Tony
25 "___ it a shame"
27 German philosopher (speller's nightmare #2)
32 Walloped, old-style
35 Learning style
36 Cpl., for one
37 Astronomical ring
38 Pipe cleaner
40 '20s touring cars
41 First daughter in the Carter White House
42 Certain Scandinavian
43 With regrets
44 Swedish statesman (speller's nightmare #3)
48 Locked (up)
49 Printing goofs
52 Romulus or Remus
54 City maps
57 Seldom seen
59 Colonial ___
60 Russian composer (speller's nightmare #4)
62 "Out of sight!"
63 Freak out
64 Navel variety
65 Brit. lawmakers
66 Reliance
67 Ceaselessly

DOWN

1 ___-Seltzer
2 Francis or Patrick, e.g.
3 Sassy
4 Accepts, as terms
5 Seoul soldier
6 Smooth, in music
7 Trade jabs
8 Military sch.
9 Railed against
10 The "S" in E.S.T.: Abbr.
11 Tweaked
12 Fe, to a chemist
13 Politico Hart
18 Design on metal
22 Cloning need
24 One-spot
26 "___-Devil"
28 Fraternity fun
29 Almost forever
30 Earth Day subj.
31 Pinkish
32 Head of old Iran
33 Papa's partner
34 Quadrennial events
38 Impoverished
39 T.L.C. givers
40 Speed reader?
42 Cheer leader?
43 Camera type, briefly
45 Game pieces
46 On-the-go group
47 Roughly
50 Spoonful, say
51 Alan of "The In-Laws"
52 Time in office
53 Trendy sandwich
55 Island party
56 Dangerous slitherers
58 Ogled
60 Nonunion workers: Abbr.
61 Pooh's pal

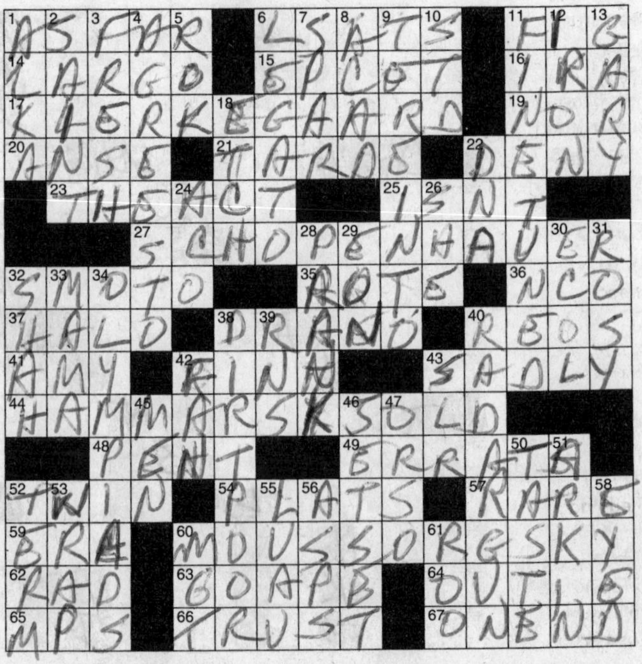

by Matt Skoczen

ACROSS

1 Food lover's sense
6 Home for alligators
11 "Open ___ 9" (shop sign)
14 Pays to play poker
15 Talk show group
16 Early afternoon hour
17 "Pronto!"
19 Tribe related to the Hopi
20 Historic times
21 Use a hose on, as a garden
23 Rev. William who originated the phrase "a blushing crow"
27 "What so ___ we hailed . . ."
29 Singer Don of the Eagles
30 Opt for
31 Parking lot posting
32 Dahl who wrote "Charlie and the Chocolate Factory"
33 Subject of "worship"
36 Sound in a cave
37 Pocketbook
38 Ditty
39 Itsy-bitsy
40 Free-for-all
41 "I do" sayer
42 "Tom ___" (#1 Kingston Trio hit)
44 Smashed and grabbed
45 Adds up (to)
47 "___ keepers . . ."
48 Boxing matches
49 Skin soother
50 Sphere
51 "Pronto!"
58 Gibson who was People magazine's first Sexiest Man Alive
59 Hair-raising
60 Dickens's ___ Heep
61 "Later!"
62 Coral ridges
63 Shindig

DOWN

1 Bar bill
2 At ___ rate
3 Mudhole
4 Golf ball support
5 Ancient Jewish sect
6 Javelin
7 The "W" in V.F.W.
8 Plus
9 "Oh, give ___ home . . ."
10 Layered building material
11 "Pronto!"
12 Computer chip company
13 Suspicious
18 Card below a four
22 "The Sound of Music" setting: Abbr.
23 Nagging sort
24 Result of a treaty
25 "Pronto!"
26 Skillet lubricant
27 Moon stage
28 Part in a play
30 Actor Feldman
32 Contest specifications
34 Below
35 Requires
37 Hit with snowballs, say
38 Walked on
40 Loch Ness dweller, they say
41 Studies hard
43 Ump's call
44 Animal with a cub
45 Mushroom cloud maker
46 Amsterdam of "The Dick Van Dyke Show"
47 Goes by jet
49 "___ I care!"
52 Part of a giggle
53 Bad temper
54 ___-la-la
55 Atmosphere
56 Turner who led a revolt
57 "___ will be done"

by Gregory E. Paul

136

ACROSS

1 Military bigwigs
6 Pad user
11 Gullible one
14 Consume
15 Luau serving
17 Wine bouquet
18 Consider, as a thought
19 Periodic arrival that causes much angst
21 Big times
22 Hardly a he-man
23 Member of a board of dirs.
24 Flower part
28 ___ Paulo
29 ___-all (score)
30 Really good joke
34 Seat at a wedding
37 What a 52-Across on a group of 19-Acrosses is
40 Whitney and others: Abbr.
41 Aim
42 Roman writer
43 Some Harvard grads: Abbr.
44 Certain Wall Street activities
46 Some are pale
48 La ___
51 Money guarantor, for short
52 Student's dream
57 "Hail, Stanford, Hail!," for one
59 Swashbuckling Flynn
60 Song from "No, No, Nanette"
61 Aptly named English novelist
62 Yearbook sect.
63 Kind of code at some schools
64 "The Sixth ___"

DOWN

1 Symbol on California's flag
2 Like a 52-Across
3 On
4 Clash of heavyweights
5 Spread out
6 Writer's guidelines
7 Turner and Louise
8 Diary bit
9 Penury
10 Sculler
11 Flat replacement
12 TV spy series starring Jennifer Garner
13 What stylophiles collect
16 Wing: Prefix
20 Equipment in kids' toy "telephones"
23 Prefix with legal
24 Dis
25 Perfectly
26 Gardner and others
27 ___ culpa
28 "Frasier" setting
31 Cereal grain
32 Actress Charlotte
33 Dodge City's home: Abbr.
34 Invoice stamp
35 House shader
36 Methods
38 Broadcasts
39 Like
43 Coffee for late at night
45 Go-carts
46 Grace ___ of "Will & Grace"
47 Certain beans
48 Tre + quattro
49 Ships' workers
50 Big dos
51 Saturated substances
52 Henry VIII's sixth
53 Place for a knot
54 Mother's mother, informally
55 Miniature sci-fi vehicles
56 Sheltered, at sea
58 Stylish, in the '60s

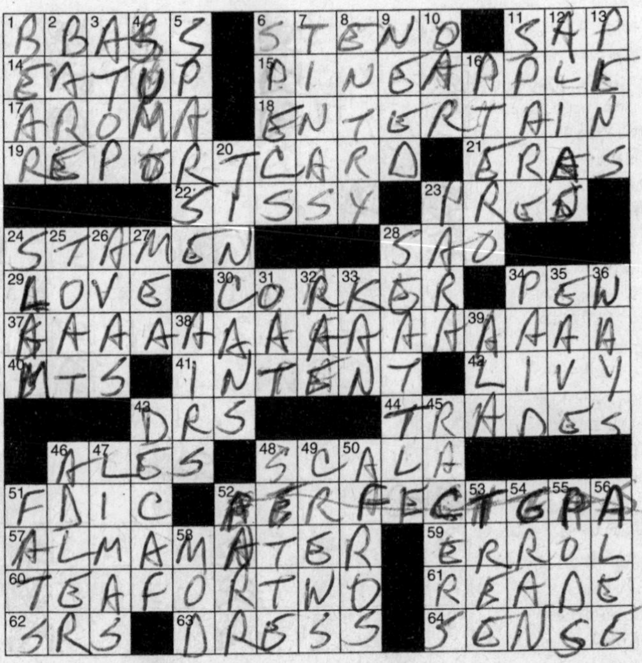

by Kevan Choset

44/59

ACROSS

1 Big blowout
5 Vehicles with meters
9 Like some committees
14 Charles Lamb's nom de plume
15 Cookie with creme inside
16 Takes a card from the pile
17 Where to order egg salad
18 Flintstone fellow
19 Designer Karan
20 Practically gives away
23 Whole lot
24 Restless
27 Bandleader Shaw
29 Big galoots
31 "Vive le ___!"
32 Faint from rapture
33 Waterless
34 Mulligatawny, for one
35 Starts telling a different story
38 Theme park attraction
39 Bringing up the rear
40 Magician's rods
41 Gallery display
42 One who's suckered
43 Voting districts
44 Pushed snow aside
46 Saucy
47 Prepares to be punished
53 Desperately want
55 Homeboy's turf
56 Hurry up
57 Macho guys
58 English princess
59 River in an Agatha Christie title
60 Apply, as pressure
61 Not the original color
62 Meal in a pot

DOWN

1 People retire to these spots
2 Toward the sheltered side
3 Window feature
4 Dangerous bit of precipitation
5 Morning eyeopener
6 Turn signal
7 Brewski
8 Word after baking or club
9 Extras
10 Speak in a monotone
11 Loiter
12 Part of B.Y.O.B.
13 Jefferson Davis org.
21 David's weapon, in the Bible
22 Soft leather
25 Pings and dings
26 "Holy mackerel!"
27 Spinning
28 Celebrity's upward path
29 Cropped up
30 Pub offering
32 Throw out
33 "On the double!"
34 Bravura performances
36 Escape the detection of
37 Bunch of bees
42 Not half bad
43 Pulled dandelions, say
45 Be indecisive
46 Give a buzz
48 Certain herring
49 Chichi
50 Clubs or hearts
51 Capri, for one
52 Enjoy some gum
53 Friend of Fidel
54 Mystery author Stout

by Nancy Salomon and Kendall Twigg

138

59/D

ACROSS

1 "60 Minutes" airer
4 Gator relative
8 Nyasaland, now
14 Stephen of "The Crying Game"
15 Quad building
16 Readied for print
17 Post-O.R. stop
18 Meat marking
19 Brings disgrace to
20 Knowing no more than before
23 Part of a Vandyke
24 Mangy mutt
25 Stitch up
28 Lanchester of film
29 Words after a rude encounter, maybe
33 "___ extra cost!"
34 Devious sorts
35 One pointing, as a gun
39 Feel awful
41 Secret meeting
42 Mazola competitor
44 Gets a gander of
46 F.B.I.'s prime quarries
48 Twofold
52 Dr. who handles otitis cases: Abbr.
53 Neolithic ___
54 Where Idi Amin ruled
56 Buffet deal
59 Positive aspect
62 Swarming pest
63 Bio stat
64 Gawks
65 Low-cal
66 D.C. V.I.P.
67 Lecherous goatmen
68 Divorcés
69 Sink trap's shape

DOWN

1 Shrink in fear
2 Act nonchalant
3 Steamy spots
4 Water park slide
5 Most reckless
6 Shoppe sign word
7 Lobster portion
8 Snafus
9 Followers
10 Pants-on-fire guy
11 20's dispenser, for short
12 Teeny
13 Driver's lic. and others
21 Airport info: Abbr.
22 Convenience store bagful
25 Neuter
26 Part of B.P.O.E.
27 All-star game team, maybe
30 ___ roll (winning)
31 Like tasty cake
32 Anthem contraction
33 Metal joiner
35 Very top
36 Mineral in spinach
37 Atomizer's release
38 N.Y. winter setting
40 General in gray
43 Like a rowboat that's adrift
45 Teach
47 Dissenting vote
48 Vice president Quayle
49 Apprehension
50 Almanac sayings
51 Nears midnight
55 Billionaire Bill
56 Open-roofed
57 Leer at
58 Operating system on many Internet servers
59 ___ Constitution
60 Sch. group
61 Warmed the bench

by Nancy Kavanaugh

14/35

ACROSS

1 Musical genre pioneered by Bill Haley and His Comets
5 Cove
10 Partner of ready and willing
14 Unattractive tropical fruit
15 Voting site
16 Hit with the fist
17 Sunbather's award?
19 Sandwich fish
20 Still
21 Before, in poetry
22 Interpret without hearing
24 1051 on monuments
25 Edward who wrote "The Owl and the Pussycat"
26 Temples in the Far East
30 Assassinating
33 Old-time actress Massey
34 Join, in woodworking
36 La Paz is its cap.
37 President after Tyler
38 Sun-bleached
39 "___ Ben Adhem," Leigh Hunt poem
40 Finish
41 Duelist Burr
42 Was bright, as the sun
43 Mark for misconduct
45 Gas ratings
47 Kuwaiti leader
48 Sun or planet
49 Depot baggage handlers
52 Actress Joanne
53 Next-to-last Greek letter
56 Wings: Lat.
57 Romantics' awards?
60 1/500 of the Indianapolis 500
61 Have a mad crush on
62 Colorful gem
63 [No bid]
64 Changed direction, as a ship
65 Actor Billy of "Titanic"

DOWN

1 Slippers' color in "The Wizard of Oz"
2 Shrek, for one
3 Blood problem
4 One of the same bloodline
5 Portugal and Spain together
6 Snout
7 Auction unit
8 List-ending abbr.
9 Tickled pink
10 Off course
11 Sad person's award?
12 Moon goddess
13 Old-time exclamation
18 Mrs. F. Scott Fitzgerald
23 Nectar source
24 Neurotic TV detective played by Tony Shalhoub
26 Spoke (up)
27 On one's own
28 Big recording artists' awards?
29 Brainy
30 Dictation taker
31 Nary a soul
32 Affixes (to)
35 Wedding 58-Down
38 Good sportsmanship
39 "Moby-Dick" captain
41 Song for a diva
42 Olympic gymnast Kerri
44 Roasts' hosts
46 ___ beef
49 Entrance to an expressway
50 Director Kazan
51 Scotch's partner
52 Dreadful
53 Insect stage
54 Go across
55 ___ of Man
58 See 35-Down
59 Family relation, for short

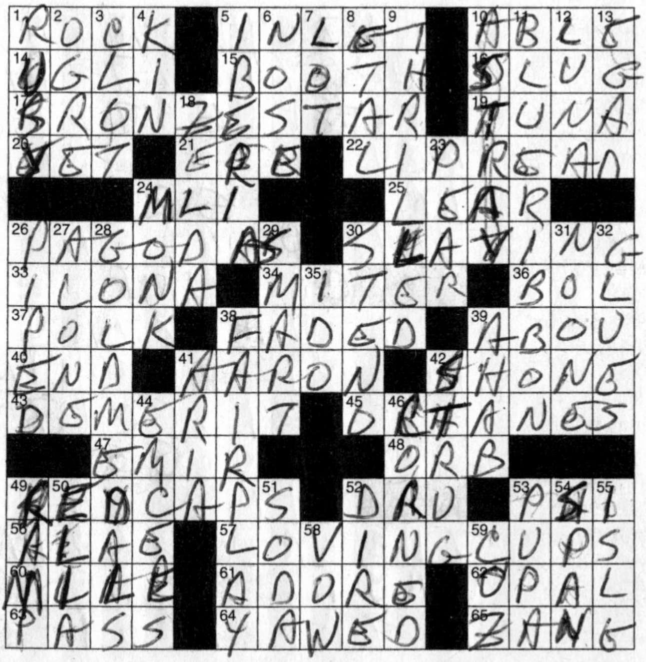

by Bernice Gordon

140

35/58

ACROSS

1 "If it ___ broke . . ."
5 "Guilty," e.g.
9 Clio winner
14 Most stuck-up
16 Poker ploy
17 "M.T.A." singers, 1959
19 Makes merry
20 Chart shape
21 "Bearded" flower
22 Mall binge
25 Murals and such
28 Dover's state: Abbr.
29 Rang out
31 Like gastric juice
32 40 winks
33 Group values
34 Paul Scott chronicles set in India
37 Weather map area
38 Have more troops than
39 Right on the map
40 Response to someone pointing
41 Actress Peeples
44 Take a gander at
45 Make ___ of (botch)
46 U.S.M.C. V.I.P.'s
47 German article
48 Is fearful of
50 Schubert chamber work
56 Fritter away
57 Unusual sort
58 Place for a kiss
59 Hatchling's home
60 Wagnerian earth goddess

DOWN

1 ___ Lindgren, Pippi Longstocking's creator
2 Naturally belong
3 It may be seen, heard or spoken, in a saying
4 Quick puffs
5 A.T.M. necessities
6 Trouser part
7 Pothook shape
8 J.D. holder: Abbr.
9 Golfer Palmer, to pals
10 See socially
11 Former Russian orbiter
12 "___ was saying . . ."
13 Prefix with natal
15 Up to, for short
18 Newspaper page
22 Home of the N.H.L.'s Sharks
23 Awards to be hung
24 Positions of esteem
25 Need liniment
26 Knee-slapper
27 Six-pointers, in brief
29 Hair-splitter?
30 LAX abbr.
31 Envelope abbr.
32 Gumball cost, once
33 The "E" in Q.E.D.
34 Cafeteria carrier
35 Vacuum feature
36 Buddy in Bordeaux
37 Lab charge
40 Mae West's "___ Angel"
41 Less cluttered
42 "You're so right!"
43 Courtroom fig.
45 Broadcaster
46 Sci-fi, for one
47 James of blues
48 The Everly Brothers, e.g.
49 Josh
50 Onetime Pan Am rival
51 Linden of "Barney Miller"
52 Body shop fig.
53 Java container
54 ___ kwon do
55 Football game divs.

by Len Elliott

ACROSS

1 Mall component
6 Genesis twin
10 Fly like an eagle
14 Hiker's path
15 Goatee's locale
16 Time for eggnog
17 Having no entryways?
19 A.A.A. recommendations: Abbr.
20 Left on a map
21 How some ham sandwiches are made
22 Letter after theta
23 Disney World attraction
25 Opposite of whole, milkwise
27 "French" dog
30 "I'm ready to leave"
32 Down Under bird
33 Britannica, for one: Abbr.
35 "Thanks, Pierre!"
38 Squeal (on)
39 ___ standstill (motionless)
40 City that Fred Astaire was "flying down to" in a 1933 hit
42 "Dear old" family member
43 Jogs
45 Looks sullen
47 Poetic palindrome
48 Tributary
50 Word before Nevada or Leone
52 Hold back
54 Give a benediction to
56 Ball field covering
57 Motionless
59 Campaign funders, for short
63 Buffalo's lake
64 Having no vision?
66 Submarine danger
67 Number between dos and cuatro
68 Weird
69 Habitual tipplers
70 Gumbo vegetable
71 Modify to particular conditions

DOWN

1 Put in the hold
2 "___ Grit" (John Wayne film)
3 Quaker ___
4 Ran amok
5 Santa's little helper
6 Commercial prefix with Lodge
7 In a moment
8 Bright and breezy
9 Still in the out-box, as mail
10 Injection selection
11 Having no commandment?
12 Prince Valiant's wife
13 Plopped down again
18 Museum guide
24 Delighted
26 Gradual absorption method
27 Saucy
28 Bradley or Sharif
29 Having no typeset letters?
31 Stocking shade
34 Where to watch whales in Massachusetts, with "the"
36 Writer John Dickson ___
37 Inkling
41 "The only thing we have to fear is fear ___": F.D.R.
44 Prairie homes
46 It goes around the world
49 Mississippi River explorer
51 Caught sight of
52 Agenda details
53 The first part missing in the author's name ___ Vargas ___
55 The second part missing in the author's name ___ Vargas ___
58 Istanbul resident
60 Taj Mahal locale
61 Intel product
62 Typesetting mark
65 Poseidon's domain

by Holden Baker

142

15

ACROSS

1 Sir, in India
6 Gounod production
11 Word with toll or roll
14 ___ acid
15 Cartoonist Kelly and others
16 Singer on half the 1984 album "Milk and Honey"
17 Hard-to-please labor protester?
19 Bird's beak
20 ¢¢¢
21 Unc's wife
23 Busta Rhymes rhymes
27 Like some of the Sahara
28 Flies off the handle
29 West Indian native
30 Mar. 17 figure, from 58-Across
31 Hooch
33 Punch in the stomach response
36 Shirts and blouses
37 Beetle Bailey's commander
38 ___'acte (intermission)
39 With 4-Down, modern printing fluid
40 Farm fence features
41 Prefix with -gon
42 A paramedic may look for one
44 Employ
45 Popular Ford
47 Skilled in reasoning
49 Eve's downfall
50 Lose at the bank?
51 Race unit
52 Cheap promotional trip?
58 See 30-Across
59 1973 #1 Rolling Stones hit
60 Bench site
61 Long-distance letters
62 Sailors' stories
63 Like a beach

DOWN

1 Doofus
2 Parisian pal
3 Drunk's utterance
4 See 39-Across
5 Political protest of sorts
6 Because of, with "to"
7 Successful negotiation results
8 The "E" of B.P.O.E.
9 Way to go: Abbr.
10 "Steps in Time" autobiographer
11 Pretty woman's hat?
12 Singer Bryant
13 ___ Smith, first female jockey to win a major race
18 Cross and Parker products
22 Where: Lat.
23 Musical breaks
24 ___-Detoo ("Star Wars" droid)
25 Plaything that yips?
26 Vacation spots
27 Loll
29 Gear teeth
31 Au naturel
32 Globe
34 Holy Roman emperor, 962–73
35 Swiss money
37 Talk back
38 Creepy: Var.
40 Toronto ballplayer
41 Multicar accidents
43 www.yahoo.com, e.g.
44 Pilgrimage to Mecca
45 Actress Shire
46 Besides, with "from"
47 Actor Alan
48 "The Highwayman" poet Alfred
50 Bridge builder, e.g.: Abbr.
53 Italian article
54 Actress Vardalos
55 "The Wizard of Oz" locale: Abbr.
56 Bitter ___
57 Slinky or boomerang

by Roy Leban

ACROSS

1 Pitches four balls to
6 Cain's brother
10 Insurrectionist Turner and others
14 Not reacting chemically
15 Muse of history
16 Monogram part: Abbr.
17 Pilfer
18 Kitchen gadget that turns
20 "Faster!"
22 No great ___
23 Iced tea flavoring
26 Full complement of fingers
27 Sob
30 Before, in poetry
31 Classic gas brand
34 Composer Rachmaninoff
36 Midsection muscles, for short
37 "Faster!"
40 Knight's title
41 Rat or squirrel
42 Dye containers
43 Western Indian
44 Linear, for short
45 Rope-a-dope boxer
47 Fixes
49 1960s–'70s space program
52 "Faster!"
57 Cramped space
59 Rich cake
60 Primer dog
61 Sharif of film
62 Gives an audience to
63 Band with the 1988 #1 hit "Need You Tonight"
64 Monthly payment
65 Birds by sea cliffs

DOWN

1 Bit of smoke
2 Contrarians
3 Bloodsucker
4 Volcano that famously erupted in 1883
5 Acts of the Apostles writer
6 Bank holdings: Abbr.
7 Dull
8 Mozart's "a"
9 Circle
10 Daughter of a sister, perhaps
11 Ben Stiller's mother
12 Bit of business attire
13 Narrow water passage: Abbr.
19 Washed-out
21 Money for retirement
24 What a satellite may be in
25 Digs with twigs?
27 Kennel club info
28 "Son of ___!"
29 Had a cow
31 ___ salts
32 Luxury hotel accommodations
33 Safe
35 Mahler's "Das Lied von der ___"
38 Snowman of song
39 Villain
46 Can't stand
48 Amounts in red numbers
49 Notify
50 Ship's navigation system
51 Weird
53 Norse thunder god
54 Terse directive to a chauffeur
55 Panache
56 "___ of the D'Urbervilles"
57 Popular TV police drama
58 The WB competitor

by M. Francis Vuolo

144

ACROSS

1 Home to Honolulu
5 Sticky stuff
9 Mends, as socks
14 "The Good Earth" mother
15 Good lot size
16 "The Waste Land" poet
17 Where to find a hammer, anvil and stirrup
19 Oro y ___ (Montana's motto)
20 Charlie Rose's network
21 An Arkin
22 Ease up
23 It may be found in front of a saloon
26 Tone-___ (rapper)
27 Strong hand cleaner
31 "Doe, ___ . . ." ("The Sound of Music" lyric)
34 Former Queens stadium
36 6 on a phone
37 Picture-filled item often seen in a living room
41 "C'___ la vie"
42 Missing the deadline
43 Bonkers
44 Hopelessness
47 What 20-Across lacks
48 Foyer
54 Former White House pooch
57 Private eyes
58 Romance
59 Seed coverings
60 International business mantra
62 Carnival show
63 Lends a hand
64 Valuable rocks
65 Odist to a nightingale
66 McCartney played it in the Beatles
67 Top ratings

DOWN

1 That certain "something"
2 It may be airtight
3 Verb with thou
4 Sturm ___ Drang
5 Irish dialect
6 Continental divide?
7 Big ape
8 ___ capita
9 Unseat
10 Apportions
11 Inlets
12 Post-it
13 Ollie's partner in old comedy
18 Capital of Punjab province
22 Faithful
24 Staff leader?
25 First-year West Pointer
28 Melville romance
29 Before long
30 Snaillike
31 Passed with flying colors
32 Teaspoonful, maybe
33 Young newts
34 Football legend Bart
35 Where a rabbit may be hidden
38 10-point type
39 First-born
40 Twaddle
45 Small shot
46 Liqueur flavorers
47 Admission
49 Courtyards
50 Must-haves
51 Vigilant
52 Waterproof wool used for coats
53 Silt deposit
54 Word that can follow the end of 17-, 23-, 37-, 48- or 60-Across
55 "Dies ___" (liturgical poem)
56 Old Italian coin
60 Groovy
61 Twaddle

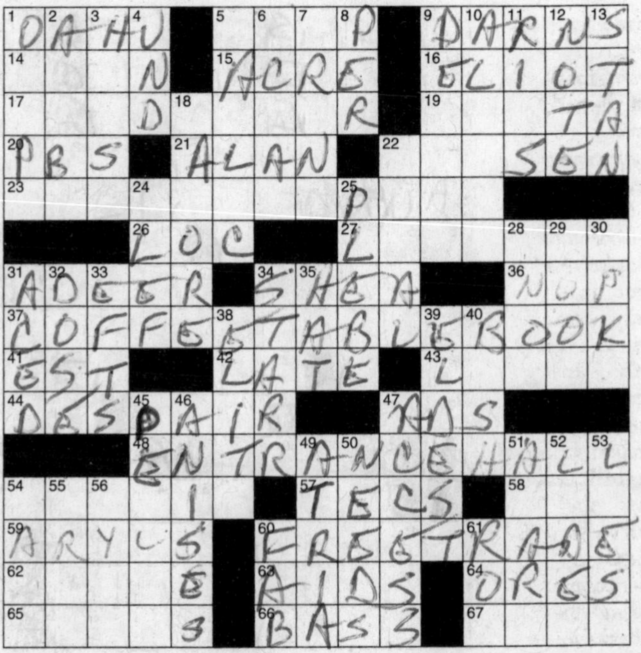

by Sarah Keller

145

ACROSS

1 Poi source
5 "The Thin Man" dog
9 Rum-soaked cakes
14 Stench
15 Where an honoree may sit
16 Friend, south of the border
17 Rocket scientist's employer
18 Prefix with potent
19 Alpine song
20 Not much
23 ___ glance (quickly)
24 Center of activity
25 Grammys, e.g.
29 Tip for a ballerina
31 Aide: Abbr.
35 Funnel-shaped
36 Craze
38 Hurry
39 Activities that generate no money
42 Surgery spots, for short
43 Indians of New York
44 Jack who ate no fat
45 Seeded loaves
47 Dog-tag wearers, briefly
48 Choirs may stand on them
49 Overly
51 Loser to D.D.E. twice
52 Boatswains, e.g.
59 R-rated, say
61 Poker payment
62 Confess
63 Tutu material
64 Rude look
65 Peru's capital
66 Back tooth
67 Slips
68 Fizzless, as a soft drink

DOWN

1 Cargo weights
2 Sandler of "Big Daddy"
3 Painter Bonheur
4 Face-to-face exam
5 Takes as one's own
6 Pago Pago's land
7 Salon application
8 Where Nepal is
9 Louisiana waterway
10 Microscopic organism
11 Bridge declarations
12 Questionnaire datum
13 Note after fa
21 Scottish beau
22 "A League of ___ Own" (1992 comedy)
25 Cast member
26 "What, me ___?"
27 Liqueur flavorer
28 Speed (up)
29 Blackmailer's evidence
30 Burden
32 English county
33 Ravi Shankar's instrument
34 Checkups
36 1052, in a proclamation
37 St. Francis' birthplace
40 Lingo
41 Raises
46 "A Streetcar Named Desire" woman
48 Directs (to)
50 Stream bank cavorter
51 "___ you" ("You go first")
52 Clout
53 Connecticut campus
54 Unique individual
55 Ranch newborn
56 Diabolical
57 Capital south of Venezia
58 Whack
59 Bank amenity, for short
60 Pair

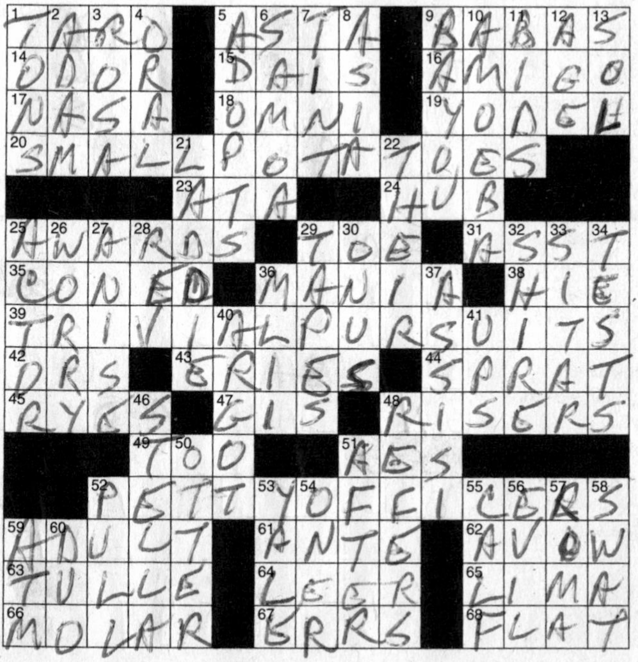

by Joy C. Frank

146

ACROSS

1 ___ the Red
5 Fragrant blossom
10 "Right on!"
14 Woodworking groove
15 Excitedly
16 Stack
17 He wrote "Utopia" in an ancient language
19 Yard sale tag
20 Partner of "ifs" and "ands"
21 Arterial trunks
23 Do a favor
26 Be charitable
28 Tilted
29 Oxidize
30 A.A.A. suggestion: Abbr.
33 Office stamp
34 Better halves
35 Disney Store item
36 "How Sweet ___"
37 Mocks
38 Something that shouldn't be left hanging
39 Twilight time to a poet
40 More immense
41 Rear
42 TV prog. with a different host each week
43 Cupid's counterpart
44 Author Lee
45 Inner circle member
47 Keats and others
48 Hogan dweller
50 Seed cover
51 Oscar winner Guinness
52 Blind poet who often wrote in an ancient language
58 Desertlike
59 Gladden
60 Dust Bowl refugee
61 Pianist Dame Myra
62 Dravidian language
63 ___ contendere

DOWN

1 Summer hrs. in N.J.
2 Cheer
3 Life-changing statement
4 Farm vehicles
5 Endured
6 Many PC's
7 London lav
8 Vacuum's lack
9 Purifies
10 Not close
11 He taught an ancient language in film
12 Old London Magazine essayist
13 Celebrated Prohibition-era lawman
18 Tool with a cross handle
22 Feedbag feed
23 "Golden" things
24 Vanquished
25 What 17- and 52-Across and 11-Down all were
26 Curtain
27 North Carolina's ___ Banks
31 Some china
32 Church V.I.P.'s
34 Myopic cartoon character
37 Certain Boeing
38 Church music maker
40 Muslim pilgrimage
41 Arm bones
44 Spam producer
46 Adds punch to, as punch
48 Bygone auto
49 Toward shelter
50 Not pro
53 Commercial suffix with Motor
54 Biblical ark passenger
55 Ref's decision
56 3-in-One product
57 "The Matrix" role

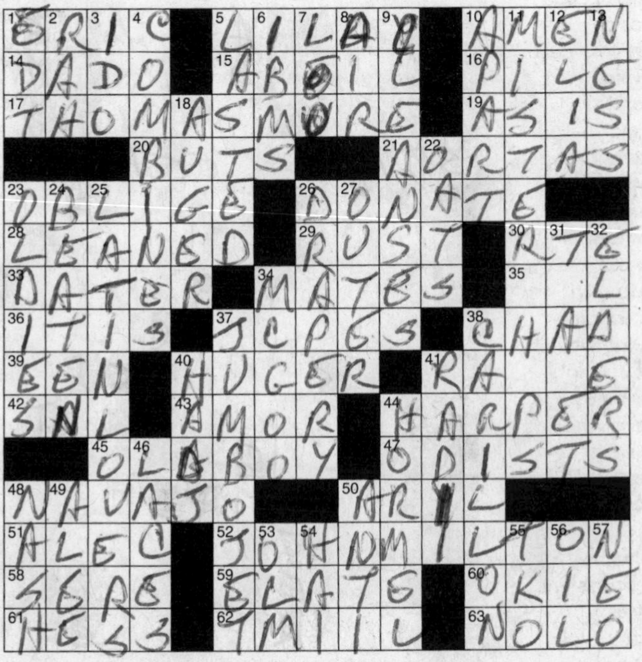

by Gene Newman

147

11/21

ACROSS

1 Tree that people carve their initials in
6 Pepper's partner
10 Author Dinesen
14 Stevenson of 1950s politics
15 Dunkable cookie
16 Plot parcel
17 "Dee-licious!"
19 Alum
20 Carson's predecessor on "The Tonight Show"
21 Surgeon's outfit
23 Play parts
26 Goes to sleep, with "off"
29 Skirt lines
30 Bangkok native
31 Like snow after a blizzard, perhaps
33 Corrosions
35 Eyelid problem
36 Spanish aunt
39 Crying
42 Evangeline or Anna Karenina, e.g.
44 What candles sometimes represent
45 "Very funny!"
47 Animal nose
48 Show biz parent
52 Go left or right
53 Petri dish filler
54 Where the Himalayas are
55 Not in port
56 Main arteries
58 Den
60 High spirits
61 "Dee-licious!"
67 Fanny
68 Certain woodwind
69 Pitcher Martínez
70 Painting and sculpting, e.g.
71 Yards advanced
72 Animal in a roundup

DOWN

1 San Francisco/Oakland separator
2 School's Web site address ender
3 Shade tree
4 Where a tent is pitched
5 "Howdy!"
6 Grow sick of
7 Quarterback's asset
8 Moon lander, for short
9 Santa's sackful
10 "Amen!"
11 "Dee-licious!"
12 Saudis and Iraqis
13 Classic sneakers
18 American, abroad
22 Bar "where everybody knows your name"
23 Skylit lobbies
24 Newswoman Connie
25 "Dee-licious!"
27 ___ Moines
28 Genesis son
32 Color, as an Easter egg
34 African desert
37 Get used (to)
38 MetLife competitor
40 Scandal sheet
41 Where the Mets could be met
43 Perfectly precise
46 Mornings, briefly
49 Spuds
50 Some Texas tycoons
51 "Just the facts, ___"
53 One who hears "You've got mail"
56 Taj Mahal site
57 Urban haze
59 Little devils
62 Entrepreneur's deg.
63 "Who, me?"
64 "___ to Joy"
65 Mine find
66 "Le Coq ___"

by Nancy Salomon and Kyle Mahowald

148

40/53

ACROSS

1 Sharp-eyed raptor
6 Kid's getaway
10 Military level
14 Lamebrain
15 Off base illegally
16 "Garfield" dog
17 "The Godfather" actor's reputation?
19 Umpteen
20 U.F.O. fliers
21 Novelist Zane
22 River under London Bridge, once
24 Alfalfa, Spanky and others
26 Tibia's place
27 Christian pop singer Grant
28 Camera-friendly events
32 Cheap jewelry
35 Rapunzel's abundance
36 Off-key, in a way
37 Garage occupant
38 "It ain't over till it's over" speaker
39 Gawk at
40 Beach sidler
41 New York City's ___ River
42 Comprehend
43 Arrange in columns
45 Old French coin
46 Rolling in the dough
47 Stops talking suddenly
51 Pants measure
54 Soccer success
55 Expert
56 Fan club's honoree
57 U2 singer's journey?
60 Indian tourist site
61 River to the Caspian
62 Lecture jottings
63 Posterior
64 Kittens' cries
65 Dress to kill, with "up"

DOWN

1 Fireplace glower
2 Line from the heart
3 Wimbledon court surface
4 Actor Chaney
5 Final stage, in chess
6 Yuletide sweets
7 On vacation
8 S.U.V. "chauffeur," maybe
9 Overabundance
10 Actor Ray's discussion group?
11 First mate?
12 "The Whole ___ Yards"
13 Florida islets
18 Air France destination
23 Chart topper
25 Roman statesman's thieving foe?
26 Tank top, e.g.
28 Analyze, as a sentence
29 Gymnast Korbut
30 Buddies
31 Put one's foot down?
32 Hostilities ender
33 Subtle glow
34 Attempt
35 Shrubby tract
38 Lauderdale loafer
42 Cooperate (with)
44 Soused
45 Pole or Bulgarian
47 Puts on ice
48 Petty quarrels
49 More than suggests
50 Metrical verse
51 Tall tale teller
52 Upper hand
53 Writer Ephron
54 Chew like a rat
58 Vein contents
59 "___ rang?"

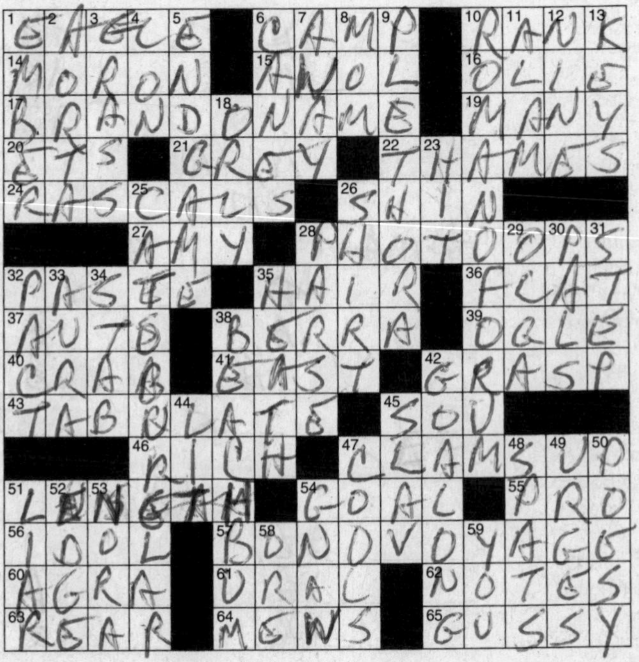

by Lynn Lempel

54/4

ACROSS

1 Tow
5 From County Clare, e.g.
10 ___ pet (onetime fad item)
14 "The Thin Man" pooch
15 Off-limits
16 "Crazy" bird
17 Manual transmission
19 "What've you been ___?"
20 Politely
21 High-spirited horse
23 Swap
24 From one side to the other
26 Shade of beige
28 Warwick who sang "Walk On By"
32 Tree branch
36 Makes a row in a garden, say
38 "Hasta la vista!"
39 Operatic solo
40 Academy Award
42 Fighting, often with "again"
43 Goes off on a mad tangent
45 With 22-Down, Korea's location
46 Bone-dry
47 Moose or mouse
49 Perlman of "Cheers"
51 Upstate New York city famous for silverware
53 Twinkie's filling
58 Versatile legume
61 Entraps
62 Jai ___
63 Lakeshore rental, perhaps
66 Lass
67 Between, en français
68 Taking a break from work
69 One of two wives of Henry VIII
70 Hem again
71 Loch ___ monster

DOWN

1 Lacks, quickly
2 Up and about
3 Ancient city NW of Carthage
4 Tied, as shoes
5 ___-bitsy
6 Shout from the bleachers
7 There: Lat.
8 Until now
9 Souped-up car
10 Standard drink mixers
11 Arizona tribe
12 Tiny amount
13 Shortly
18 Swiss artist Paul ___
22 See 45-Across
24 Came up
25 What a TV host reads from
27 Funnywoman Margaret
29 Evening, in ads
30 Dark film genre, informally
31 Villa d'___
32 "___ Croft Tomb Raider" (2001 film)
33 Tehran's land
34 Prefix with skirt or series
35 Transportation for the Dynamic Duo
37 Bird's name in "Peter and the Wolf"
41 Numbered rd.
44 Of sound mind
48 Frog, at times
50 Unappealing skin condition
52 Idiotic
54 1990s Israeli P.M.
55 Wear away
56 Breakfast, lunch and dinner
57 Kefauver of 1950s politics
58 The "Star Wars" trilogy, for one
59 Actress Lena
60 Folksy tale
61 Whole bunch
64 Alcoholic's woe
65 Rapper Dr. ___

by Jeffrey Harris

150

05/17

ACROSS

1 New stable arrival
5 Wrigley team
9 Beginning
14 Old Dodge model
15 Pronto!
16 Captain Nemo's creator
17 Jared of "Panic Room"
18 "A ___ formality!"
19 Chip away at
20 Winter accessory
23 Up to, in ads
24 Coll., e.g.
25 However, informally
28 Caffeine source for many
33 Learn about
35 The whole shebang
36 Forest canine
38 Sailing hazards
41 Geo. W. Bush has one
42 Artfully dodge
43 Simple door fastener
46 Price word
47 Black-and-orange songbird
48 Polite drivers, at merges
51 Columbia Univ. locale
52 Something to shuck
54 ___ de Cologne
55 What the ends of 20-, 36- and 43-Across suggest
61 Language of India
64 Actress Malone
65 Tea time, perhaps
66 French farewell
67 Wide-eyed
68 Book after II Chronicles
69 1692 witch trials city
70 Fine-tune
71 For fear that

DOWN

1 Arlo Guthrie's genre
2 Spilled salt, say
3 Pro's foe
4 Ray of "GoodFellas"
5 The Kennedy years, figuratively
6 Played for a sap
7 3 Musketeers units
8 Eyeglasses, informally
9 "Yoo-hoo!"
10 Soft ball material
11 Sellout indicator
12 Cut short
13 Pigskin prop
21 Part of three-in-a-row
22 Yearn (for)
25 Minstrel show group
26 Player in extra-point attempts
27 Job seekers' good news
28 Graphite element
29 Legendary Mrs. who owned a cow
30 Frock wearer
31 Arm or leg
32 Perth ___, N.J.
34 Piercing tool
37 Java neighbor
39 To's partner
40 Element #34
44 First wife of Jacob
45 Like many MTV viewers
49 Slip behind
50 Camper's bag
53 Indian prince
55 ___ fixe (obsession)
56 Toy block maker
57 Get ___ the ground floor
58 Gooey stuff
59 Sharer's word
60 "Dang!"
61 Is afflicted with
62 Actress Lupino
63 Zip

by Nancy Kavanaugh

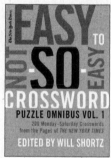

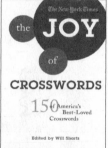

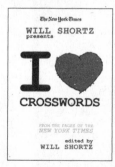

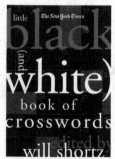

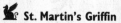

ANSWERS

1

A	M	I	N	■	T	A	M	P	A	■	A	S	P	S
C	A	N	T	■	A	L	I	A	S	■	S	A	L	E
H	I	G	H	C	H	U	R	C	H	■	S	P	I	N
E	N	O	■	A	I	M	■	■	■	D	U	P	E	D
D	E	T	E	C	T	■	S	P	E	E	C	H	■	■
■	■	■	W	H	I	C	H	I	S	W	H	I	C	H
T	H	R	E	E	■	H	E	N	S	■	■	R	O	O
B	O	O	S	T	■	A	A	A	■	I	D	E	A	L
A	B	A	■	■	M	I	T	T	■	N	A	S	T	Y
R	O	S	H	H	A	S	H	A	N	A	H	■	■	■
■	■	T	O	U	P	E	E	■	I	S	L	A	N	D
A	R	B	O	R	■	■	■	A	C	E	■	C	O	O
D	E	E	P	■	F	O	U	R	H	C	L	U	B	S
O	P	E	L	■	C	A	R	N	E	■	A	T	E	E
S	O	F	A	■	C	R	I	E	S	■	G	E	L	S

2

I	D	E	A	L	■	B	A	A	■	■	A	G	O	G
C	I	R	R	I	■	U	R	N	S	■	C	E	D	E
B	L	A	C	K	S	M	I	T	H	■	I	T	E	M
M	A	S	S	E	U	R	■	S	E	E	D	S	■	■
S	T	E	■	■	B	A	R	■	■	L	I	M	I	T
■	E	D	E	L	■	P	E	T	T	Y	C	A	S	H
■	■	■	M	I	T	■	C	O	O	S	■	R	I	O
■	U	N	I	T	E	D	A	R	T	I	S	T	S	■
F	D	A	■	H	A	I	R	■	E	A	T	■	■	■
Y	O	U	N	G	L	O	V	E	■	N	A	R	C	■
I	N	T	O	O	■	■	E	A	N	■	■	E	L	I
■	■	I	O	W	A	S	■	R	O	O	S	T	E	D
B	A	L	D	■	B	R	O	W	N	S	T	O	N	E
A	Z	U	L	■	S	A	R	A	■	L	O	R	C	A
N	O	S	E	■	■	S	A	X	■	O	A	T	H	S

3

T	O	M	B	S	■	P	S	S	T	■	■	J	I	M
A	M	O	R	Y	■	H	O	W	E	■	A	O	N	E
V	A	C	A	N	T	A	P	A	R	T	M	E	N	T
I	N	K	N	O	T	S	■	G	R	O	U	P	I	E
■	■	■	■	N	O	E	L	■	■	P	L	I	E	D
E	M	P	T	Y	P	R	O	M	I	S	E	S	■	■
R	E	A	I	M	■	■	W	A	V	Y	■	C	S	I
G	A	T	E	■	G	I	D	D	Y	■	G	O	A	S
O	T	C	■	F	I	D	O	■	■	A	M	P	U	P
■	■	H	O	L	L	O	W	V	I	C	T	O	R	Y
A	L	A	M	O	■	■	N	O	T	E	■	■	■	■
S	I	D	E	C	A	R	■	R	E	H	E	A	T	S
B	L	A	N	K	C	A	R	T	R	I	D	G	E	S
A	L	M	S	■	O	K	I	E	■	G	I	A	N	T
D	Y	S	■	■	G	E	N	X	■	H	E	R	D	S

4

P	L	O	W	■	B	L	A	B	■	C	E	A	S	E
H	O	B	O	■	L	A	T	E	■	O	R	D	E	R
D	O	E	R	■	O	R	E	G	■	R	I	D	E	R
S	T	Y	L	I	N	G	M	O	O	S	E	■	■	■
■	■	■	D	A	D	O	■	N	I	A	■	M	O	E
S	E	W	■	M	I	S	S	I	N	G	L	Y	N	X
U	N	E	A	S	E	■	T	A	K	E	A	N	A	P
I	R	E	D	■	■	B	U	S	■	■	N	A	P	A
S	A	L	E	S	M	A	N	■	O	L	D	H	A	T
S	P	A	N	K	I	N	G	G	N	U	■	S	R	S
E	T	D	■	I	C	I	■	R	E	N	T	■	■	■
■	■	■	C	R	A	S	H	I	N	G	B	O	A	R
B	A	Y	O	U	■	T	A	L	E	■	I	D	L	E
O	C	E	A	N	■	E	L	L	S	■	R	O	S	A
B	E	A	T	S	■	R	O	E	S	■	D	R	O	P

5

A	C	T	O	R	■	O	P	A	L	■	B	O	Z	O
S	A	R	D	I	■	P	A	V	E	■	L	I	A	R
K	N	E	E	B	R	A	C	E	S	■	A	N	N	E
S	E	X	■	C	O	R	E	■	S	I	S	K	E	L
■	■	■	T	A	U	T	■	G	E	N	T	■	■	■
C	H	A	R	G	E	■	D	E	N	T	I	S	T	S
A	E	R	I	E	■	P	O	N	E	■	N	O	A	H
L	I	M	P	■	D	A	V	I	D	■	G	A	T	E
I	D	O	L	■	A	L	E	E	■	S	C	R	U	B
F	I	R	E	A	R	M	S	■	M	I	A	S	M	A
■	■	■	C	A	K	E	■	S	U	M	P	■	■	■
Z	E	B	R	A	S	■	J	O	N	I	■	T	I	S
A	B	O	O	■	P	I	E	F	I	L	L	I	N	G
C	R	A	W	■	O	S	S	A	■	E	B	E	R	T
H	O	R	N	■	T	H	U	R	■	S	O	R	E	S

6

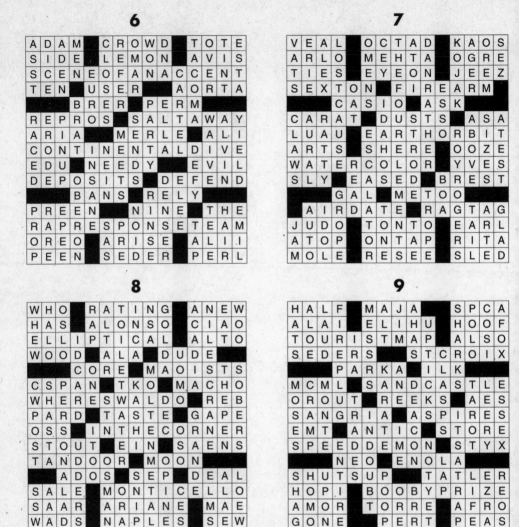

A	D	A	M		C	R	O	W	D		T	O	T	E
S	I	D	E		L	E	M	O	N		A	V	I	S
S	C	E	N	E	O	F	A	N	A	C	C	E	N	T
T	E	N		U	S	E	R			A	O	R	T	A
			B	R	E	R		P	E	R	M			
R	E	P	R	O	S		S	A	L	T	A	W	A	Y
A	R	I	A			M	E	R	L	E		A	L	I
C	O	N	T	I	N	E	N	T	A	L	D	I	V	E
E	D	U		N	E	E	D	Y			E	V	I	L
D	E	P	O	S	I	T	S		D	E	F	E	N	D
			B	A	N	S		R	E	L	Y			
P	R	E	E	N			N	I	N	E		T	H	E
R	A	P	R	E	S	P	O	N	S	E	T	E	A	M
O	R	E	O		A	R	I	S	E		A	L	I	I
P	E	E	N		S	E	D	E	R		P	E	R	L

7

V	E	A	L		O	C	T	A	D		K	A	O	S
A	R	L	O		M	E	H	T	A		O	G	R	E
T	I	E	S		E	Y	E	O	N		J	E	E	Z
S	E	X	T	O	N		F	I	R	E	A	R	M	
			C	A	S	I	O		A	S	K			
C	A	R	A	T		D	U	S	T	S		A	S	A
L	U	A	U		E	A	R	T	H	O	R	B	I	T
A	R	T	S		S	H	E	R	E		O	O	Z	E
W	A	T	E	R	C	O	L	O	R		Y	V	E	S
S	L	Y		E	A	S	E	D		B	R	E	S	T
			G	A	L		M	E	T	O	O			
	A	I	R	D	A	T	E		R	A	G	T	A	G
J	U	D	O		T	O	N	T	O		E	A	R	L
A	T	O	P		O	N	T	A	P		R	I	T	A
M	O	L	E		R	E	S	E	E		S	L	E	D

8

W	H	O		R	A	T	I	N	G		A	N	E	W
H	A	S		A	L	O	N	S	O		C	I	A	O
E	L	L	I	P	T	I	C	A	L		A	L	T	O
W	O	O	D		A	L	A		D	U	D	E		
			C	O	R	E		M	A	O	I	S	T	S
C	S	P	A	N		T	K	O		M	A	C	H	O
W	H	E	R	E	S	W	A	L	D	O		R	E	B
P	A	R	D		T	A	S	T	E		G	A	P	E
O	S	S		I	N	T	H	E	C	O	R	N	E	R
S	T	O	U	T		E	I	N		S	A	E	N	S
T	A	N	D	O	O	R		M	O	O	N			
		A	D	O	S		S	E	P		D	E	A	L
S	A	L	E		M	O	N	T	I	C	E	L	L	O
S	A	A	R		A	R	I	A	N	E		M	A	E
W	A	D	S		N	A	P	L	E	S		S	E	W

9

H	A	L	F		M	A	J	A			S	P	C	A
A	L	A	I		E	L	I	H	U		H	O	O	F
T	O	U	R	I	S	T	M	A	P		A	L	S	O
S	E	D	E	R	S			S	T	C	R	O	I	X
			P	A	R	K	A		I	L	K			
M	C	M	L		S	A	N	D	C	A	S	T	L	E
O	R	O	U	T		R	E	E	K	S		A	E	S
S	A	N	G	R	I	A		A	S	P	I	R	E	S
E	M	T		A	N	T	I	C		S	T	O	R	E
S	P	E	E	D	D	E	M	O	N		S	T	Y	X
			N	E	O		E	N	O	L	A			
S	H	U	T	S	U	P			T	A	T	L	E	R
H	O	P	I		B	O	O	B	Y	P	R	I	Z	E
A	M	O	R		T	O	R	R	E		A	F	R	O
G	O	N	E			P	E	R	T		P	E	A	S

10

M	V	P		W	A	I	T	S	O	N		S	P	A
O	O	H		A	L	T	O	O	N	A		Q	E	D
O	T	O		R	O	C	O	C	O	S	T	Y	L	E
D	E	E	D		N	H	L			T	I	D	E	S
		B	A	E	Z			I	T	A	L			
	D	E	L	M	O	N	I	C	O	S	T	E	A	K
M	O	S	E	S		O	S	A	G	E		X	K	E
O	W	N	S		T	R	A	N	S		S	P	I	N
E	S	O		T	A	D	A	S		P	L	A	T	O
N	E	W	M	E	X	I	C	O	S	T	A	T	E	
			E	R	I	C			U	S	S	R		
E	N	I	A	C			J	A	B		H	I	C	K
H	I	D	D	E	N	C	O	S	T	S		A	R	I
U	K	E		L	O	O	S	E	L	Y		T	A	N
D	E	A		S	T	P	E	T	E	R		E	G	G

11

A	D	O	S		B	A	L	S	A		N	E	S	T
R	O	T	H		O	C	E	A	N		I	T	C	H
A	L	T	O		S	T	A	L	K		T	H	O	U
B	L	O	W	I	N	I	N	T	H	E	W	I	N	D
			C	O	I	N	S			D	I	C	E	S
A	R	C	A	N	A			B	A	I	T			
C	E	O	S			S	L	A	N	T		A	C	E
H	E	R	E	C	O	M	E	S	T	H	E	S	U	N
E	L	K		A	V	O	W	S			G	I	R	D
			S	T	A	G			S	T	O	A	T	S
A	S	P	I	C			A	S	C	O	T			
R	H	Y	T	H	M	O	F	T	H	E	R	A	I	N
S	A	R	I		A	R	I	E	L		I	S	L	A
O	M	E	N		C	A	R	R	E		P	E	L	T
N	E	S	S		S	L	E	E	P		S	A	S	S

12

M	R	S		G	O	T	I	T		S	P	A	T	E
E	O	N		O	P	I	N	E		A	L	L	A	Y
A	L	A		D	I	N	N	E	R	T	A	B	L	E
D	E	F		S	E	E	S	T	O		Y	A	K	S
E	X	U	D	E				H	O	P	S			
			O	N	S	E	T		K	I	T	S	C	H
C	L	O	U	D	O	V	E	R		T	A	H	O	E
H	E	R	B		P	E	N	A	L		T	I	D	E
A	G	I	L	E		N	O	S	E	D	I	V	E	D
R	O	G	E	T	S		R	H	I	N	O			
			A	C	H	E				A	N	G	S	T
S	M	U	G		I	N	S	P	O	T		A	T	E
D	A	T	E	A	N	D	T	I	M	E		T	E	N
A	G	I	N	G		O	A	S	I	S		O	A	T
K	I	L	T	S		W	Y	A	T	T		R	M	S

13

S	A	N	T	A		P	A	C	E		A	C	M	E
A	L	I	E	N		I	B	E	T		B	L	I	P
W	I	N	S	O	M	E	L	O	S	E	S	O	M	E
S	T	A	T		I	R	E	S		B	O	G	I	E
			T	I	N				H	E	R			
	Y	O	U	D	I	D	Y	O	U	R	B	E	S	T
S	A	M	B	A		R	O	U	S	T		R	H	O
K	L	E	E		W	I	D	T	H		P	A	A	R
E	I	N		R	I	L	E	D		E	A	T	M	E
W	E	S	T	I	L	L	L	O	V	E	Y	O	U	
			E	N	D				E	L	S			
S	A	G	A	S		H	E	A	T		L	E	N	T
C	L	O	S	E	B	U	T	N	O	C	I	G	A	R
A	I	R	E		A	R	N	O		U	P	O	N	E
B	E	E	T		A	L	A	N		E	S	S	A	Y

14

W	A	R	N		I	D	I	O		A	M	A	T	I
E	T	A	T		W	O	M	B		G	A	B	O	N
B	A	T	H	T	O	W	E	L		O	R	B	I	T
T	R	E		C	U	R	T	A	I	N	C	A	L	L
V	I	S	I	B	L	Y			D	I	I			
			C	Y	D		A	M	A	Z	E	D	A	T
B	E	S	O			A	M	O	R	E		A	P	E
B	L	A	N	K	E	X	P	R	E	S	S	I	O	N
Q	E	D		E	M	I	L	E			E	S	P	N
S	E	R	E	N	E	L	Y		P	A	M			
			A	T	E			P	E	T	I	T	E	S
P	I	C	T	U	R	E	S	H	O	W		U	L	T
A	D	H	O	C		G	U	N	P	O	W	D	E	R
A	N	O	U	K		G	E	O	L		A	O	N	E
R	O	O	T	Y		O	R	M	E		D	R	A	W

15

P	R	E	K		B	E	N	C	H		C	A	L	L
H	O	N	E		E	C	O	L	I		O	R	E	O
D	U	R	A	N	D	U	R	A	N		S	T	E	W
S	T	A	T	U	S			S	D	I		U	R	I
		G	O	D		M	O	S	U	L	I	R	A	Q
I	T	I	N	E	R	A	R	Y		L	O	O	T	S
S	A	N			E	N	D		S	E	T			
H	I	G	H	W	A	Y	E	N	T	R	A	N	C	E
			T	I	P		R	C	A			A	H	A
S	P	I	T	Z		T	E	A	T	A	S	T	E	R
G	R	A	P	E	S	O	D	A		H	O	I		
T	A	G		N	I	B			D	E	N	O	T	E
M	I	R	O		F	O	U	N	D	M	O	N	E	Y
A	S	E	A		T	O	S	C	A		R	A	R	E
J	E	E	R		S	T	O	R	Y		A	L	M	S

16

A	V	I	L	A		T	E	L	E		R	D	A	S
V	I	D	A	L		A	X	E	L		A	E	R	O
A	R	E	S	T	I	N	G	O	F	F	I	C	E	R
S	T	A	T		D	A	I	S		E	L	K		
T	U	L	S	A	O	K			E	B	B	E	T	S
				B	L	A	R	E	D		I	D	Y	L
	H	I	H	O			I	V	Y		R	O	P	Y
	A	C	O	U	N	T	P	A	S	T	D	U	E	
E	L	E	M		E	S	O			A	S	T	A	
R	O	S	E		S	O	N	I	C	S				
A	S	H	P	I	T			T	A	K	E	A	I	M
		E	L	L		P	E	C	S		E	L	O	I
A	P	E	A	L	T	O	T	H	E	C	R	O	W	D
M	A	T	T		A	D	U	E		S	I	N	A	I
P	O	S	E		P	S	I	S		T	E	E	N	S

17

S	I	N	A	I		S	T	L	O		P	O	R	E
A	N	A	I	S		E	R	O	S		E	N	O	S
P	A	T	R	I	O	T	A	C	T		S	H	O	T
			S	T	I	T	C	H	I	N	T	I	M	E
R	E	P	T	I	L	E			N	O	O	G	I	E
O	V	E	R		Y	E	S	M	A	N		H	E	M
B	E	R	E	A			H	I	T	A	T			
		M	A	R	I	S	A	T	O	M	E	I		
			M	I	N	O	R			E	N	D	U	P
R	E	Q		S	T	U	P	I	D		O	L	L	A
E	X	A	C	T	A			S	U	R	R	E	A	L
P	E	N	N	A	N	T	R	A	C	E	S			
O	T	T	O		D	E	B	I	T	H	O	M	A	S
S	E	A	T		E	L	I	A		A	L	I	B	I
E	R	S	E		M	E	S	H		B	O	X	E	R

18

	G	E	D		G	A	B	S		E	D	S	E	L
P	O	U	R		A	U	R	A		D	O	U	S	E
A	I	R	J	O	R	D	A	N		I	N	B	E	D
S	T	A		F	B	I			S	T	O	P		
H	E	I	R	T	O	T	H	E	T	H	R	O	N	E
A	R	L	O			S	O	N	Y		S	E	E	R
			A	L	T		N	O	L	O		N	O	R
		E	R	E	I	S	A	W	E	L	B	A		
I	Q	S		W	A	H	L		S	E	A			
R	U	T	S		R	U	E	S			E	Z	R	A
A	I	R	E	D	A	L	E	T	E	R	R	I	E	R
		A	X	I	S			A	L	B		N	C	O
M	O	N	T	E		A	E	R	L	I	N	G	U	S
A	R	G	O	T		D	O	V	E		S	E	S	E
C	O	E	N	S		O	N	E	S		A	R	E	

19

D	E	L	H	I		C	A	P	E		I	B	E	T
I	V	I	E	D		A	L	E	E		C	O	D	A
F	E	N	W	A	Y	P	A	R	K		E	G	G	O
			S	H	A	R	I	F		J	A	D	E	S
A	I	M		O	R	I		O	M	E	G	A		
S	T	A	T	E	N		P	R	E	T	E	N	D	S
P	A	R	E	S		B	R	A	S	S		O	M	E
E	L	S	E		K	E	A	T	S		O	V	I	D
N	I	H		A	L	L	Y	E		T	W	I	N	E
S	C	A	N	D	A	L	S		R	A	N	C	O	R
		M	O	U	N	T		A	U	K		H	R	S
S	H	A	N	E		O	N	S	P	E	C			
L	O	S	E		S	W	A	M	P	S	C	O	T	T
A	L	O	E		G	E	N	A		T	U	D	O	R
W	A	N	D		T	R	O	D		O	P	E	R	A

20

R	A	G	A		V	O	I	L	A		F	A	Z	E
E	R	A	S		A	R	R	A	U		O	N	I	T
P	E	R	K		M	E	A	N	S		R	A	P	S
O	N	C	E	U	P	O	N	A	T	I	M	E		
S	A	I	D	H	I			I	R	S		R	A	I
E	S	A		U	R	I	S		I	M	C	O	L	D
			W	H	E	N	I	W	A	S	A	B	O	Y
A	L	S	O			I	K	E			R	E	E	L
B	A	C	K	I	N	T	H	E	D	A	Y			
C	R	I	S	T	O		S	P	E	C		U	T	A
S	A	M		S	S	W			I	R	O	N	O	N
		I	N	Y	E	A	R	S	G	O	N	E	B	Y
J	E	T	E		O	R	I	O	N		E	V	A	H
A	G	A	R		U	N	C	L	E		L	E	G	O
W	O	R	D		T	S	K	E	D		S	N	O	W

21

H	A	F	T	S		W	A	G	E		A	D	Z	E
A	R	L	E	N		O	V	A	L		I	R	O	N
J	O	Y	E	U	X	N	O	E	L		R	E	O	S
I	M	B	I	B	E		C	A	S	A	B	A		
	A	Y	N		N	R	A			L	A	M	P	S
		G	L	A	E	D	E	L	I	G	J	U	L	
A	R	G	U	E		D	O	S	O			O	R	U
B	I	O	P	I	C	S		P	L	U	M	B	E	R
A	D	D			N	E	E	R		M	U	S	E	S
F	E	L	I	Z	N	A	V	I	D	A	D			
T	R	I	N	I			E	T	A		B	A	M	
		N	E	T	M	E	N		R	E	A	P	E	D
E	L	E	V		B	U	O	N	N	A	T	A	L	E
D	O	S	E		A	R	F	S		S	H	R	E	K
U	S	S	R		S	O	F	A		E	S	T	E	E

22

J	A	M	B	S		I	M	P	E	I		B	O	X
A	W	A	I	T		N	A	I	L	S		O	H	M
P	A	R	T	Y	A	N	I	M	A	L		R	I	A
A	R	I	S	E	N		T	E	L		A	N	O	N
N	E	O			D	E	A	N		H	S	T		
			C	R	E	D	I	T	R	E	P	O	R	T
R	A	P	P	E	R	S		O	E	R		R	E	O
A	C	R	O	S	S				S	E	G	U	E	S
I	T	O		H	E	S		A	T	T	E	N	D	S
L	I	F	E	I	N	P	R	I	S	O	N			
		E	S	P		L	O	T	T			P	D	A
L	O	S	T		P	I	C		O	S	I	R	I	S
I	R	S		P	I	C	K	U	P	T	R	U	C	K
N	C	O		A	T	E	I	N		D	O	N	E	E
E	A	R		W	A	R	N	S		S	N	E	R	D

23

J	E	S	T		J	A	C	O	B		S	C	A	M
A	C	N	E		U	N	I	T	E		T	A	R	O
W	H	O	C	A	N	I	T	B	E		E	L	E	V
S	O	B		D	K	N	Y		P	R	A	I	S	E
			S	A	Y			F	E	E	L	F	O	R
W	H	A	T	M	A	T	T	E	R	S				
O	O	N	A		R	B	I	S		A	P	S	O	S
W	H	E	R	E	D	O	E	S	I	T	H	U	R	T
S	O	W	E	D		N	O	U	S		A	R	E	A
				W	H	E	N	P	I	G	S	F	L	Y
S	T	U	D	I	O	S			T	R	E			
T	O	R	E	N	T		L	I	S	A		F	I	G
A	M	B	I		W	H	Y	P	A	Y	M	O	R	E
I	M	A	C		A	I	R	O	F		O	X	E	N
D	Y	N	E		R	E	E	S	E		M	Y	S	T

24

A	L	M	A		I	B	A	R		S	I	D	E	B
M	U	O	N		R	I	L	E		P	R	A	D	A
S	A	R	A	T	O	G	A	S	P	R	I	N	G	S
O	U	T	L	A	N	D	S		R	A	S	C	A	L
		G	O	T	O			N	O	W	H	E	R	E
N	I	A	G	A	R	A	F	A	L	L	S			
O	R	G		R	E	L	I	N	E		E	S	A	U
M	E	E	T	S		T	E	T		S	A	I	L	S
E	S	S	O		T	E	R	E	S	A		L	A	P
			L	A	R	R	Y	S	U	M	M	E	R	S
C	A	M	E	R	A	S			L	O	A	N		
A	D	O	R	E	S		A	T	L	A	N	T	I	S
J	O	N	A	T	H	A	N	W	I	N	T	E	R	S
U	S	O	N	E		O	K	I	E		A	R	A	T
N	E	S	T	S		L	A	G	S		S	A	N	S

25

L	A	C	Y		A	D	M	I	T		D	I	K	E
O	B	I	E		R	E	I	N	S		E	R	L	E
B	U	T	T	H	A	T	S	N	O	T	F	A	I	R
E	T	E		A	R	E	S			O	A	T	E	S
			C	H	A	R		N	U	T	M	E	G	
O	L	D	H	A	T		B	A	S	I	E			
M	O	R	E			A	R	D	E	N		V	I	A
E	V	E	R	Y	O	N	E	I	S	G	O	I	N	G
N	E	W		O	R	D	E	R			W	E	R	E
			G	U	A	R	D		S	P	E	W	E	D
	L	I	A	B	L	E		B	A	L	D			
L	O	R	R	E			H	I	Y	A		D	U	O
I	C	A	N	T	D	O	A	N	Y	T	H	I	N	G
P	A	N	E		S	U	R	G	E		E	M	I	R
S	L	I	T		L	I	M	O	S		P	E	T	E

26

W	A	L	S	H			K	E	N		P	S	S	T
A	T	A	R	I		A	R	C	H		A	L	T	O
S	P	R	I	N	G	R	O	L	L		D	I	A	N
H	A	G		T	O	S	C	A		S	U	N	N	Y
	R	O	T	A	T	E		I	D	T	A	G		
			S	T	I	N	G	R	A	Y		S	P	A
E	L	S	A		T	A	R		M	E	S	H	E	S
D	O	W	R	Y		L	E	A		S	T	O	R	K
A	R	I	S	E	S		G	U	M		A	T	M	S
M	E	N		S	I	N	G	S	O	N	G			
		G	E	E	S	E		T	R	U	S	T	S	
D	I	V	A	S		S	C	R	O	D		W	P	A
A	M	O	S		S	T	R	I	N	G	B	E	A	N
D	A	T	E		P	L	E	A		E	R	E	C	T
A	X	E	D		Y	E	W			D	A	N	E	S

27

S	H	A	R	P		C	A	V	E	D		P	A	T
E	A	G	E	R		A	L	E	R	O		O	L	E
C	L	O	S	E	F	R	I	E	N	D		P	A	M
				N	E	V	E	R		G	R	U	M	P
	O	B	T	U	S	E			Z	E	A	L	O	T
J	U	L	E	P	S		D	H	A	R	M	A		
O	T	O	E	S		H	O	O	P	S		R	B	I
K	I	S	S		C	A	R	B	S		T	B	A	R
Y	E	S		F	O	L	I	O		M	A	R	L	A
		O	L	I	V	E	S		S	A	T	E	E	N
E	R	M	I	N	E			M	A	C	A	W	S	
M	I	T	Z	I		O	H	A	R	A				
E	L	O		C	O	M	I	C	A	B	B	O	T	T
N	E	B		K	N	A	C	K		R	E	T	R	O
D	Y	E		Y	A	N	K	S		E	A	T	U	P

The missing clue: Bud

28

A	T	O	M		E	C	O	N		C	O	L	A	S
L	I	M	O		M	O	L	E		O	R	A	L	S
A	L	A	N		I	A	G	O		E	G	R	E	T
S	T	R	O	N	G	L	A	N	G	U	A	G	E	
			L	A	R	S		L	O	R	N	E		
D	O	T	I	M	E		L	I	N		S	P	U	R
E	V	I	T	A		R	A	G	E	S		R	T	E
M	I	G	H	T	Y	A	P	H	R	O	D	I	T	E
O	N	E		H	E	I	S	T		N	I	N	E	S
B	E	R	G		A	N	E		S	A	R	T	R	E
		W	E	A	R	S		M	I	T	T			
	P	O	T	E	N	T	P	O	T	A	B	L	E	S
R	O	O	S	T		O	L	L	A		I	O	N	A
O	L	D	E	N		R	E	A	R		K	N	O	W
Z	E	S	T	A		M	A	R	S		E	E	L	S

29

O	W	I	N	G		I	C	U			P	O	T	S
R	O	D	E	O		R	I	N	D		O	M	E	N
A	V	E	R	S		O	R	Z	O		L	E	N	O
L	E	A	D	P	E	N	C	I	L		I	G	O	R
				E	X	S		P	E	A	S	A	N	T
D	O	U	B	L	E	T	S		D	U	H			
E	D	N	A		C	O	O	P		F	J	O	R	D
N	O	T	S		S	N	A	R	L		O	U	S	E
G	R	O	S	S		E	P	E	E		K	I	T	E
			G	A	P		S	C	A	R	E	S	U	P
V	A	C	U	O	U	S		L	S	U				
A	G	R	I		M	I	N	U	T	E	M	A	I	D
L	O	O	T		P	L	O	D		F	A	R	S	I
I	N	C	A		S	O	R	E		U	N	C	L	E
D	Y	E	R			S	A	D		L	O	S	E	S

30

G	A	R	B		B	R	O	W		A	P	P	L	E
O	R	E	O		O	E	N	O		F	R	I	E	S
H	A	C	K	Y	S	A	C	K		L	A	P	S	E
O	B	E		A	C	R	E		L	A	N	E	S	
M	I	S	S	Y	O	U		H	E	C	K	L	E	R
E	A	S	Y			P	L	U	G		S	I	N	K
			N	A	G		A	B	U	T		N	E	O
	H	I	C	K	O	R	Y	S	M	O	K	E	D	
R	O	D		A	L	O	T		E	G	O			
A	L	E	S		D	R	O	P			L	A	W	S
H	O	C	K	N	E	Y		R	O	M	A	N	I	A
	G	L	E	A	N		R	I	S	E		G	P	S
B	R	A	I	N		H	U	C	K	A	B	E	E	S
E	A	R	N	A		A	S	E	A		B	L	U	E
A	M	E	S	S		T	E	R	R		S	A	P	S

31

H	O	F	F	A		S	K	I		V	I	B	E	S
A	B	D	U	L		P	A	L		U	S	U	R	P
G	I	A	N	T	B	I	L	L		L	A	I	N	E
			N	O	I	R	E		A	C	A	C	I	A
E	B	A	Y		C	O	L	T	P	A	C	K	E	R
D	A	L	L	A	S			R	I	N				
I	B	E	A	M		S	E	A	S		M	A	Y	O
C	A	R	D	I	N	A	L	C	H	A	R	G	E	R
T	R	O	Y		O	U	S	T		L	O	R	N	E
				X	I	N			E	T	C	E	T	C
C	H	I	E	F	S	A	I	N	T		T	E	A	K
R	O	N	N	I	E		L	O	T	T	O			
A	W	F	U	L		S	U	P	E	R	B	O	W	L
S	T	O	R	E		O	V	A		A	E	R	I	E
S	O	R	E	S		B	U	R		P	R	E	G	O

32

W	I	S	P		C	R	I	P	E	S		T	I	M
A	L	O	E		D	E	N	A	L	I		O	N	E
F	I	F	T	H	C	O	L	U	M	N		P	A	L
T	E	T	R	A			E	L	I		V	I	L	E
		T	O	I	L	E	T	A	R	T	I	C	L	E
T	R	O	L	L	E	D			A	V	A			
I	O	U		S	A	G	E	S		A	L	I	B	I
L	O	C	H		P	A	P	E	R		S	N	U	B
E	T	H	A	N		R	A	D	I	O		T	R	I
			I	F	S			G	O	P	H	E	R	S
S	C	A	R	L	E	T	L	E	T	T	E	R		
M	A	N	Y		R	O	E			I	S	L	A	M
I	N	N		B	E	S	T	P	I	C	T	U	R	E
T	O	E		U	N	C	O	O	L		O	D	I	E
H	E	X		B	E	A	N	I	E		N	E	A	T

33

A	T	M	O		R	A	T	E	D		B	O	O	M
B	R	I	S		A	G	A	P	E		E	R	M	A
C	U	S	S		D	E	N	I	M		A	D	E	N
	S	H	O	W	I	N	G	C	O	N	C	E	R	N
A	T	M		O	U	T				I	H	A	T	E
L	E	A	S	E	S		J	O	E	S		L	A	D
P	E	S	T			V	A	R	L	E	T			
		H	O	L	D	I	N	G	F	I	R	M		
			P	A	U	L	E	Y			E	A	T	S
A	L	T		N	E	A	T		I	B	E	R	I	A
S	O	U	S	A				S	N	O		I	N	D
P	A	R	T	I	N	G	C	O	M	P	A	N	Y	
E	T	N	A		O	M	A	N	I		R	A	T	S
C	H	I	N		M	E	G	A	N		T	R	I	O
T	E	N	D		S	N	E	R	D		Y	A	M	S

34

B	O	S	C		P	I	G	S	T	Y		G	R	A	S
A	N	K	A		E	N	A	M	O	R		L	A	S	T
D	R	I	V	I	N	G	M	I	S	S	D	A	I	S	Y
M	E	T		S	T	O	U	T	S		A	N	S	E	L
O	P	T		M	A	T	T	E		E	N	C	O	R	E
V	O	I	C	E	D				C	L	I	E	N	T	S
E	R	S	E			P	A	T	O	I	S				
	T	H	E	B	L	A	C	K	D	A	H	L	I	A	
				R	O	D	E	O	S			E	S	P	N
V	A	S	S	A	L	S				T	R	O	U	P	E
A	R	E	T	H	A		M	E	D	I	A		P	E	T
S	C	R	A	M		P	O	L	I	T	Y		P	A	Z
T	H	E	N	A	M	E	O	F	T	H	E	R	O	S	E
L	I	N	D		O	N	S	I	T	E		U	S	E	R
Y	E	A	S		S	T	E	N	O	S		N	E	R	O

35

L	O	F	T		E	B	O	L	A		O	M	S	K
I	D	I	O		N	O	R	A	D		M	U	N	I
F	I	V	E	S	T	A	R	G	E	N	E	R	A	L
T	E	E	T	E	R					A	L	A	I	N
		C	O	E		F	I	V	E	B	E	L	L	S
S	T	E	T	S		A	F	I	R	S	T			
H	A	N	O	I		T	S	A	R			G	A	D
E	X	T	E	N	T				S	I	C	I	L	Y
D	I	S			G	U	L	F		N	O	M	D	E
			T	A	I	P	E	I		P	U	M	A	S
T	A	K	E	S	F	I	V	E		O	N	E		
O	D	E	T	S					A	R	T	F	U	L
Q	U	A	R	T	E	R	P	A	S	T	F	I	V	E
U	L	N	A		R	A	B	B	I		O	V	E	N
E	T	E	S		A	T	S	E	A		R	E	A	D

36

P	A	T	T	I	■	R	I	F	F	■	A	S	E	A
A	V	I	A	N	■	O	M	A	R	■	P	A	T	S
J	A	L	F	R	E	D	P	R	U	F	R	O	C	K
A	L	L	T	I	M	E	■	■	G	O	O	P	■	■
M	O	E	■	■	T	O	S	S	■	O	N	A	I	R
A	N	D	I	E	■	■	A	W	E	D	■	U	R	I
■	■	■	P	I	L	S	N	E	R	■	U	L	A	N
■	J	J	O	N	A	H	J	A	M	E	S	O	N	■
P	I	E	D	■	L	E	O	T	A	R	D	■	■	■
A	M	T	■	B	A	A	S	■	■	R	A	F	T	S
Z	I	P	P	O	■	F	E	A	R	■	■	R	I	P
■	■	L	O	F	T	■	■	S	E	R	R	A	T	E
J	D	A	N	F	O	R	T	H	Q	U	A	Y	L	E
L	A	N	D	■	O	B	O	E	■	S	T	E	E	D
O	D	E	S	■	N	I	P	S	■	T	E	D	D	Y

37

A	C	M	E	■	R	A	N	O	N	■	F	U	R	Y
B	I	A	S	■	I	R	A	T	E	■	O	N	E	A
C	O	C	A	■	P	A	N	I	C	■	C	A	P	P
■	■	H	U	M	P	B	A	C	K	W	A	I	L	■
A	V	E	■	A	L	I	■	■	■	O	L	D	E	R
B	A	T	T	L	E	C	R	E	A	K	■	E	T	E
A	L	E	U	T	■	■	E	R	G	■	I	D	E	A
■	■	■	F	A	R	M	G	R	O	A	N	■	■	■
S	E	C	T	■	A	A	A	■	■	R	C	P	T	S
O	A	R	■	B	E	L	L	A	N	D	H	O	W	L
P	R	O	S	Y	■	■	■	T	O	E	■	B	O	Y
■	M	A	K	E	S	A	B	O	O	B	O	O	■	■
H	A	T	E	■	E	L	A	N	D	■	A	X	L	E
E	R	I	E	■	R	U	R	A	L	■	H	E	E	L
S	K	A	T	■	A	M	B	L	E	■	U	S	A	F

38

L	I	T	U	P	■	M	A	S	T	■	F	A	N	S
A	R	O	S	E	■	O	K	R	A	■	O	V	A	L
G	E	N	E	R	A	T	I	O	N	■	R	O	S	A
E	N	G	■	■	W	O	N	■	L	E	E	W	A	Y
R	E	A	C	T	O	R	■	H	I	T	S	■	■	■
■	■	■	A	W	L	■	P	A	N	A	T	E	L	A
T	E	T	R	A	■	L	I	V	E	S	A	L	I	E
A	T	O	B	■	S	E	X	E	S	■	T	I	E	R
M	A	J	O	R	E	D	I	N	■	P	I	A	N	O
S	T	O	N	E	A	G	E	■	R	E	O	■	■	■
■	■	■	A	S	H	E	■	S	E	A	N	C	E	S
B	L	O	T	T	O	■	A	P	E	■	■	O	V	O
R	A	V	I	■	R	E	V	E	L	A	T	I	O	N
O	R	E	O	■	S	P	I	N	■	S	A	N	K	A
W	A	R	N	■	E	A	S	T	■	P	O	S	E	R

39

S	T	A	G	E	■	T	A	N	G	O	■	H	I	T
A	R	I	E	S	■	I	C	E	A	X	■	U	F	O
C	U	R	T	A	I	N	C	A	L	L	■	M	O	P
■	■	■	B	U	S	H	■	■	■	I	N	A	R	T
B	A	B	Y	■	B	A	T	H	S	P	O	N	G	E
U	N	O	■	A	N	T	E	U	P	■	D	C	O	N
G	O	B	A	D	■	■	A	N	A	■	S	O	T	S
■	■	B	L	O	O	D	S	T	R	E	A	M	■	■
J	A	Y	E	■	M	I	I	■	■	S	T	E	R	N
I	L	K	A	■	N	O	N	F	A	T	■	D	A	B
G	U	N	S	L	I	N	G	E	R	■	S	Y	N	C
S	M	I	T	E	■	■	■	I	M	A	C	■	■	■
A	N	G	■	T	H	I	N	G	S	D	R	A	W	N
W	A	H	■	B	A	C	O	N	■	Z	A	I	R	E
S	E	T	■	E	D	I	T	S	■	E	M	M	Y	S

40

A	D	D	S	■	■	D	O	W	N	■	B	O	B	S
D	I	R	T	■	M	A	C	H	O	■	L	A	R	K
U	V	E	A	■	A	C	H	E	S	■	O	K	A	Y
L	A	W	R	E	N	C	E	W	E	L	K	■	■	■
T	N	T	■	L	I	A	R	■	J	E	E	R	A	T
■	■	H	U	L	A	■	■	G	O	D	■	A	C	E
R	T	E	S	■	C	L	A	M	B	I	S	Q	U	E
A	R	L	E	S	■	O	S	E	■	N	A	U	R	U
F	A	I	R	A	M	O	U	N	T	■	H	E	A	P
T	I	N	■	L	E	T	■	■	H	I	L	L	■	■
S	L	E	E	T	S	■	F	L	E	D	■	W	P	A
■	■	■	L	I	T	T	L	E	B	O	P	E	E	P
M	A	U	I	■	I	R	A	T	E	■	A	L	A	S
R	A	Z	Z	■	Z	E	R	O	S	■	A	C	R	E
S	H	I	A	■	O	X	E	N	■	■	R	H	Y	S

41

F	U	M	E		S	E	M	I		B	A	S	I	N
U	N	I	V		A	X	E	D		A	C	H	O	O
S	I	D	E		L	I	M	E		S	T	E	W	S
S	T	A	N	D	A	T	E	A	S	E		D	A	Y
Y	E	S	S	I	R			S	A	M	B	A		
			O	B	I	E	S		P	A	R	T	E	D
I	C	U		S	E	V	E	N		N	E	E	D	Y
L	A	P	D		D	A	T	E	S		W	A	G	E
S	M	A	R	T		C	O	A	L	S		R	E	D
A	E	N	E	A	S		F	R	I	T	O			
		D	I	X	O	N			M	O	P	T	O	P
B	A	A		F	L	O	R	I	D	A	T	E	C	H
A	S	T	R	O		W	A	C	O		S	R	T	A
S	T	E	E	R		A	N	E	W		I	R	E	S
H	I	M	O	M		Y	A	R	N		N	A	T	E

42

S	T	O	I	C		N	E	A	R		C	O	A	T
H	O	N	D	A		U	R	G	E		O	A	T	H
E	A	T	I	N	G	C	R	O	W		I	S	E	E
A	D	O		C	U	L		G	R	A	N	T	E	E
			R	E	N	E	E		I	R	E			
		T	A	L	K	I	N	G	T	U	R	K	E	Y
J	O	E	Y	S			C	O	E	N		A	R	E
E	R	T	E		C	A	R	T	S		I	S	I	N
E	A	R		T	O	N	Y			A	M	E	N	S
P	L	A	Y	I	N	G	P	O	S	S	U	M		
			A	N	D		T	R	E	S	S			
D	E	F	R	A	U	D		G	A	I		B	A	A
O	V	E	R		C	R	Y	I	N	G	W	O	L	F
C	A	T	O		T	I	M	E		N	O	R	M	A
K	N	E	W		S	P	A	S		S	W	E	A	R

43

S	E	Z		U	T	T	E	R		R	A	N	D	B
I	L	E		N	O	O	S	E		A	D	O	R	E
T	I	R	E	S	O	M	E	W	I	N	D	B	A	G
A	H	O	L	E				I	N	S		I	T	S
T	U	S	K	E	D	W	A	R	T	H	O	G		
			S	N	O	O	Z	E		O	L	D	I	E
J	A	M			L	E	O		P	R	I	E	S	T
P	R	O	M	P	T	S		P	E	T	N	A	M	E
E	M	B	E	R	S		R	E	T			L	E	S
G	E	S	S	O		H	E	A	R	S	T			
		C	A	P	E	A	F	R	I	K	A	N	E	R
E	R	E		O	T	T				E	L	E	N	A
D	A	N	I	S	H	P	H	Y	S	I	C	I	S	T
G	R	E	T	A		I	M	E	A	N		G	U	T
E	A	S	E	L		N	O	N	O	S		H	E	Y

44

W	A	G	S		A	D	D	U	P		E	L	S	E
I	D	E	A		L	O	O	S	E		N	O	U	N
G	O	L	D	F	I	N	G	E	R		O	W	E	D
			D	I	S	S				R	U	S	T	S
L	A	M	E	N	T		S	H	R	U	G			
E	R	A	S	E		S	T	E	E	L	H	E	A	D
T	O	R	T		E	T	E	R	N	E		R	H	O
H	U	T		C	L	A	R	E	T	S		R	O	W
A	S	H		A	D	L	I	B	S		B	A	R	N
L	E	A	D	B	E	L	L	Y		S	E	N	S	E
			V	E	R	S	E		G	O	A	D	E	D
A	C	T	O	R				E	L	A	N			
R	O	A	R		S	I	L	V	E	R	B	A	C	K
A	L	G	A		P	R	E	E	N		A	L	O	E
B	A	S	K		Y	E	A	R	N		G	A	N	G

45

S	A	M	I	A	M		A	L	A			T	A	O
A	G	E	N	D	A		W	E	N	T	S	O	L	O
P	E	R	S	O	N	A	L	I	T	Y	Q	U	I	Z
S	E	E			I	F	S			P	U	T	T	Y
			I	S	L	A		S	P	E	E			
P	R	O	Q	U	A	R	T	E	R	B	A	C	K	
L	A	P	S	E			O	R	O		L	A	N	A
E	N	E		D	A	R	K	A	G	E		P	E	T
A	U	R	A		C	O	Y			S	H	R	E	W
	P	A	T	C	H	W	O	R	K	Q	U	I	L	T
			O	L	E	S		S	A	S	H			
M	T	I	D	A			O	V	I			E	E	E
M	I	N	D	Y	O	U	R	P	S	A	N	D	Q	S
E	M	I	S	S	A	R	Y		E	V	E	N	U	P
S	E	T			K	I	X		R	E	T	A	I	N

46

B	E	T	■	E	F	F	U	S	E	■	M	A	Y	S
U	Z	I	■	F	O	R	A	L	L	■	A	L	O	E
N	R	C	■	F	L	O	R	I	D	A	K	E	Y	S
T	A	K	E	A	I	M	■	M	E	D	I	C	O	S
■	■	E	N	C	A	M	P	■	S	O	N	■	■	■
T	A	R	G	E	T	■	I	N	T	L	■	J	A	S
A	S	T	A	■	E	D	G	E	■	P	L	U	N	K
S	T	A	G	E	■	O	P	T	■	H	I	N	D	I
T	O	P	E	R	■	D	E	S	I	■	O	K	I	E
E	R	E	■	O	D	O	N	■	M	I	N	D	E	D
■	■	■	A	D	O	■	S	I	M	M	E	R	■	■
S	I	N	C	E	R	E	■	S	E	A	L	A	N	T
T	H	I	R	D	S	T	R	I	N	G	■	W	A	R
L	O	C	I	■	A	T	E	A	S	E	■	E	M	I
O	P	E	D	■	L	A	S	H	E	S	■	R	E	X

47

A	D	A	M	S	■	S	O	F	A	■	I	N	G	E
B	A	D	A	T	■	A	W	E	S	■	N	E	O	N
A	N	D	C	R	O	W	N	T	H	Y	G	O	O	D
S	I	S	■	I	L	O	■	A	T	O	M	■	■	■
E	S	T	■	D	E	F	S	■	R	R	A	T	E	D
■	H	O	M	E	O	F	T	H	E	B	R	A	V	E
■	■	■	A	S	S	■	R	H	E	A	■	D	E	B
B	A	A	S	■	■	H	A	H	■	■	P	A	N	T
A	R	T	■	O	L	I	N	■	I	P	O	■	■	■
L	E	T	F	R	E	E	D	O	M	R	I	N	G	■
M	A	N	I	A	C	■	S	U	M	O	■	A	A	S
■	■	■	S	L	A	B	■	G	I	G	■	B	T	U
W	I	T	H	B	R	O	T	H	E	R	H	O	O	D
O	D	I	E	■	R	A	N	T	■	A	B	B	R	S
W	A	N	D	■	E	T	T	A	■	M	O	S	S	Y

48

T	R	E	K	S	■	T	A	C	K	■	S	E	C	T
E	A	G	L	E	■	O	B	O	E	■	I	N	R	E
A	N	G	E	R	■	U	L	N	A	■	X	D	I	N
■	■	S	E	A	N	P	E	N	N	S	P	E	N	S
N	A	H	■	■	T	E	R	I	■	I	M	A	G	E
B	R	E	A	T	H	E	■	V	I	M	■	R	E	D
C	E	L	L	O	■	■	D	E	N	I	M	■	■	■
■	A	L	A	N	L	A	D	D	S	L	A	D	S	■
■	■	■	S	E	E	D	S	■	■	A	R	R	A	Y
D	A	D	■	D	I	M	■	P	E	R	S	O	N	A
A	E	I	O	U	■	I	M	A	X	■	■	P	E	W
B	R	A	D	P	I	T	T	S	P	I	T	S	■	■
S	A	L	E	■	B	O	W	S	■	T	A	H	O	E
A	T	I	T	■	A	N	T	E	■	S	T	O	R	M
T	E	N	S	■	R	E	F	S	■	Y	A	T	E	S

49

A	L	P	S	■	S	P	E	C	K	■	V	A	S	E
S	E	R	A	■	W	I	L	L	A	■	E	L	A	N
H	A	I	L	C	A	E	S	A	R	■	L	A	I	D
E	S	C	O	R	T	■	■	W	E	E	V	I	L	S
S	T	E	N	O	■	T	W	E	L	V	E	■	■	■
■	■	■	■	C	R	E	E	D	■	A	T	L	A	S
A	T	M	S	■	I	R	A	■	I	N	F	A	N	T
V	E	I	L	■	T	I	T	A	N	■	O	N	T	O
E	X	C	U	S	E	■	H	U	T	■	G	A	S	P
S	T	A	S	H	■	M	E	L	O	N	■	■	■	■
■	■	■	H	A	Z	A	R	D	■	A	F	T	E	R
H	O	F	F	M	A	N	■	■	E	T	O	I	L	E
A	C	L	U	■	P	U	R	P	L	E	R	A	I	N
S	T	A	N	■	P	A	I	R	S	■	T	R	O	T
P	O	N	D	■	A	L	B	E	E	■	E	A	T	S

50

D	O	C	S	■	S	T	U	M	P	■	S	T	A	R
U	R	A	L	■	R	I	G	O	R	■	O	H	I	O
F	I	N	E	W	I	T	H	M	E	■	W	A	R	Y
F	O	N	D	A	■	■	■	M	E	A	N	T	■	■
E	L	O	■	L	I	P	S	Y	N	C	■	S	D	I
L	E	T	S	D	O	I	T	■	S	T	P	A	U	L
■	■	■	C	O	N	T	A	C	■	S	E	G	A	L
M	O	O	R	■	S	H	R	U	B	■	P	O	L	S
A	S	K	E	W	■	S	E	R	I	F	S	■	■	■
T	H	E	W	H	O	■	A	L	L	R	I	G	H	T
H	A	Y	■	I	N	S	T	Y	L	E	■	M	I	A
■	■	D	A	M	U	P	■	■	■	S	K	I	D	S
T	A	O	S	■	S	U	R	E	W	H	Y	N	O	T
O	N	K	P	■	E	R	I	C	A	■	R	O	U	E
E	Y	E	S	■	S	T	O	O	D	■	A	R	T	S

51

H	O	G	S		I	S	N	T		L	A	P	P	S
A	L	E	E		S	E	A	R		A	T	E	U	P
G	L	O	W		R	E	D	O		N	O	R	M	A
A	I	R		M	A	R	A	T	H	O	N	M	A	N
R	E	G	G	A	E			S	O	L	E			
		Y	E	L	L	O	W		L	I	S	B	O	N
A	N	G	L	E		M	A	V	E	N		O	N	O
L	O	I	S		V	I	V	I	D		W	R	I	T
E	R	R		G	A	T	E	S		C	A	S	T	E
C	A	L	M	E	D		R	E	C	A	N	T		
			O	N	E	A			R	E	T	A	R	D
W	O	N	D	E	R	W	O	M	A	N		L	E	O
A	R	I	E	S		A	M	E	N		A	B	E	L
H	E	N	R	I		R	E	N	E		C	O	V	E
L	O	A	N	S		E	N	D	S		E	Y	E	S

52

F	A	S	T		B	I	T	E		D	I	T	C	H
L	U	K	E		I	D	O	L		E	N	O	L	A
O	D	I	N		G	L	O	M		F	A	T	A	L
W	I	N	S	O	M	E	L	O	S	E	S	O	M	E
			I	D	A				O	N	E			
	G	O	O	D	C	O	P	B	A	D	C	O	P	
B	A	R	N	S		P	A	I	R	S		M	A	T
I	R	A	S		S	T	I	R	S		S	A	V	E
O	T	T		S	C	E	N	T		A	N	N	E	X
	H	E	S	A	I	D	S	H	E	S	A	I	D	
			A	R	F				F	I	G			
O	N	A	G	A	I	N	O	F	F	A	G	A	I	N
M	O	T	E	L		A	R	L	O		I	R	M	A
N	O	R	S	E		B	A	E	R		N	E	A	T
I	R	A	T	E		S	L	A	T		G	A	M	E

53

J	I	B	E		S	H	A	R	I		E	K	E	D
U	S	E	S		T	O	X	I	N		D	E	L	E
S	W	E	P	T	A	S	I	D	E		A	P	S	E
T	E	T		A	G	E	S		P	E	S	T	E	R
S	A	L	M	O	N				T	U	N	A		
O	R	E	O		A	V	I	D		R	E	T	R	O
			B	O	T	A	N	Y		E	R	I	C	A
U	P	S		P	E	P	T	A	L	K		T	A	R
P	A	T	T	I		O	R	D	E	A	L			
C	L	A	R	A		R	O	S	A		E	A	C	H
		M	I	T	T				R	A	T	T	L	E
R	I	P	L	E	Y		M	A	N	X		T	A	D
O	N	T	O		P	T	A	M	E	E	T	I	N	G
B	R	A	G		E	A	G	E	R		U	R	G	E
S	E	X	Y		S	P	I	N	S		B	E	S	S

54

B	L	O	G	S		T	A	F	F	Y		C	I	A
R	O	M	E	O		A	L	I	C	E		A	M	S
O	N	E	T	W	O	P	U	N	C	H		R	P	I
W	I	N	S		T	I	M			U	M	P	E	D
			M	O	O	N		T	A	D	P	O	L	E
I	M	P	A	L	E	S		I	N	I	G	O		
M	E	A	R	A			T	K	O			L	A	B
P	A	R	T	N	E	R	S	I	N	C	R	I	M	E
S	N	L			V	E	E			R	A	N	I	N
		O	W	N	E	D		S	N	A	G	G	E	D
F	O	R	W	A	R	D		T	E	M	P			
L	O	G	I	C			A	M	O		A	R	I	A
I	M	A		H	U	F	F	A	N	D	P	U	F	F
R	P	M		O	G	L	E	R		D	E	L	F	T
T	H	E		S	H	O	W	Y		T	R	E	Y	S

55

B	R	A	T	S		B	A	S	K	S		A	S	I
A	D	O	R	E		O	R	O	N	O		N	H	L
M	A	K	E	A	N	O	F	F	E	R		D	E	L
			S	N	A	G		T	E	E	T	H	E	S
P	A	W	S		P	I	E	S			O	O	N	A
O	R	E		M	E	E	T	H	A	L	F	W	A	Y
M	E	D	E	A			S	O	N	O	F			
P	A	S	T	D	U	E		E	G	G	E	D	O	N
			C	A	N	N	Y			E	E	R	I	E
C	O	M	E	T	O	T	E	R	M	S		N	N	W
A	B	I	T			R	A	R	E		R	O	K	S
C	O	N	C	I	S	E		A	S	T	A			
T	I	C		S	E	A	L	T	H	E	D	E	A	L
U	S	E		A	R	T	I	E		M	A	G	N	A
S	T	D		K	E	Y	E	D		P	R	O	N	G

56

S	T	R	A	P		D	A	N	E		K	A	L	E
T	H	E	M	E		O	R	A	L		A	X	I	S
A	R	I	E	L		G	E	R	I		H	O	S	T
R	U	N	N	I	N	G	A	C	C	O	U	N	T	
				C	I	I			I	A	N			
P	R	I	V	A	T	E	E	N	T	R	A	N	C	E
L	I	N	E	N			M	O	E	S		A	O	L
A	C	N	E		H	E	A	R	D		L	O	C	I
I	C	E		S	I	M	I			S	A	M	O	A
D	I	R	T	Y	P	O	L	I	T	I	C	I	A	N
			R	N	S			N	I	A				
	P	R	A	C	T	I	C	A	L	M	A	G	I	C
L	O	O	N		E	D	E	N		E	L	I	Z	A
B	L	O	C		R	O	B	E		S	E	N	O	R
J	O	K	E		S	L	U	R		E	G	A	D	S

57

H	A	T	S		V	I	L	A		R	O	P	E	S
I	L	I	E		A	X	E	L		A	L	L	A	H
F	A	L	A		S	N	I	T		G	E	E	S	E
I	S	T	H	A	T	A	F	A	C	T		A	Y	E
			A	B	L	Y		R	O	A	R	S	A	T
A	N	Y	W	A	Y		B	R	O	G	U	E		
H	O	O	K	S		S	E	A	R		E	G	G	S
A	P	U		H	I	T	L	I	S	T		O	A	T
B	E	D	S		S	I	L	L		B	O	O	Z	E
		O	R	A	L	L	Y		S	O	N	N	E	T
M	I	N	I	M	A	L		X	E	N	A			
E	D	T		I	M	L	I	S	T	E	N	I	N	G
N	O	S	E	D		I	G	O	T		D	O	E	R
S	L	A	Y	S		F	O	U	L		O	N	E	A
A	S	Y	E	T		E	R	T	E		N	A	R	Y

58

J	I	V	E		S	P	L	I	C	E		B	I	C
I	N	I	T		A	L	A	N	O	N		E	S	O
B	R	E	A	D	B	A	S	K	E	T		L	T	R
S	E	S	S	I	O	N	S		R	E	T	T	O	N
				M	T	S		S	C	R	U	B		
S	U	D	S	E	S		Q	U	I	E	T	U	D	E
C	L	O	T	S		R	A	Z	O	R		C	A	L
A	N	G	E		F	I	T	I	N		S	K	I	M
L	A	B		S	E	T	A	E		B	A	L	S	A
P	R	I	S	O	N	E	R		B	O	L	E	Y	N
		S	L	U	G	S		S	A	X				
R	E	C	A	P	S		T	A	K	E	C	A	R	E
E	A	U		C	H	O	W	D	E	R	H	E	A	D
M	R	I		A	U	P	A	I	R		U	R	G	E
O	P	T		N	I	P	S	E	Y		M	O	E	N

59

E	M	I	R			M	O	D	E	M		A	B	C
M	I	S	E	R		A	B	O	V	E		T	O	O
U	N	E	M	O	T	I	O	N	A	L		L	O	P
S	T	E	A	M	Y		E	S	S		M	A	Z	E
			P	E	S	O	S		I	R	I	S	E	S
A	S	H		R	O	D		A	V	E	R			
M	N	E	M	O	N	I	C	D	E	V	I	C	E	S
M	A	M	A			O	O	H			A	R	I	A
O	P	P	O	R	T	U	N	E	M	O	M	E	N	T
			R	Y	E	S		R	A	N		W	E	E
S	P	H	I	N	X		K	E	Y	E	D			
H	O	E	S		T	A	U		A	D	O	R	E	D
A	K	A		F	I	N	D	I	N	G	N	E	M	O
R	E	D		E	L	T	O	N		E	U	B	I	E
P	R	Y		W	E	I	S	S			T	A	T	S

60

T	U	B	A		B	E	D	S		P	A	T	S	Y
U	R	A	L		O	M	A	N		A	D	I	E	U
G	I	S	T		T	A	R	A		S	L	E	E	K
	S	H	O	O	T	I	N	G	S	T	A	R	R	
				I	L	L			A	R	I			
T	R	I	P	L	E		M	A	N	Y		S	I	S
E	E	R	I	E		P	A	C	T		E	T	N	A
N	E	A	N	D	E	R	T	H	A	L	M	A	N	N
E	S	T	E		N	O	T	E		A	I	R	E	D
T	E	E		A	D	D	S		A	L	T	E	R	S
			O	R	E			A	V	A				
	W	O	R	L	D	W	I	D	E	W	E	B	B	
G	E	N	I	E		O	D	O	R		V	A	I	L
A	N	T	O	N		R	E	P	S		E	R	T	E
S	T	O	N	E		K	A	T	E		N	E	E	D

61

Z	A	P	P	A		P	A	S	H	A		J	E	T
E	T	H	A	N		I	S	L	E	T		O	R	E
B	E	A	T	T	H	E	H	E	A	T		S	I	N
R	U	S	H	E	E			W	R	I	T	H	E	D
A	P	E	S		R	C	A		T	R	I			
				S	E	A	L	T	H	E	D	E	A	L
P	L	U	M	E		S	I	R	S		B	A	R	E
R	E	R	U	N		T	B	A		S	I	R	E	N
O	V	A	L		S	L	A	G		A	T	L	A	S
F	I	L	L	T	H	E	B	I	L	L				
			A	H	A		A	C	E		M	A	Y	S
A	F	G	H	A	N	S			C	L	I	Q	U	E
F	L	U		T	A	K	E	T	H	E	C	A	K	E
R	E	F		I	N	A	W	E		A	R	B	O	R
O	A	F		S	A	T	E	D		R	O	A	N	S

62

F	L	E	C	K		T	E	E	S		A	H	A	B
S	A	T	I	E		A	X	L	E		L	O	L	A
T	R	A	V	E	L	V	I	S	A		B	R	E	T
O	V	I		P	O	E	T		L	A	U	N	C	H
P	A	L	O	M	A	R		P	E	R	M	S		
			T	U	N	N	E	L	V	I	S	I	O	N
	S	L	I	M			L	I	E	D		N	B	A
B	O	A	S		H	O	V	E	L		H	O	O	P
A	H	S		B	A	L	I			G	E	N	E	
H	O	T	E	L	V	I	S	I	T	O	R			
		P	R	E	E	N		N	O	T	A	B	I	T
S	A	L	A	D	A		S	L	O	E		A	R	E
E	R	A	S		S	T	E	E	L	V	I	S	O	R
R	A	C	E		A	R	A	T		E	D	E	N	S
F	L	E	D		Y	A	M	S		N	O	R	S	E

63

C	O	R	P	S		P	O	L	L		S	T	O	P
O	F	A	R	C		A	P	I	A		H	A	R	I
M	A	Y	O	R		G	E	N	T	L	E	M	A	N
			P	A	T	O	N	T	H	E	B	A	C	K
S	T	O	O	P	E	D				V	A	L	L	I
P	E	T	S	E	M	A	T	A	R	Y		E	E	E
A	D	I	E	U			U	P	N					
S	S	S		P	I	T	B	O	S	S		M	I	T
					T	O	E			U	S	E	N	O
E	M	T		P	O	T	S	T	A	R	T	E	R	S
S	O	A	M	I				S	P	R	I	T	E	S
P	U	T	O	N	E	O	V	E	R	O	N			
I	N	T	R	A	N	S	I	T		U	G	L	I	S
E	D	E	N		O	H	O	S		N	E	E	D	Y
S	S	R	S		W	A	L	E		D	R	I	E	R

64

R	A	B	B	I		T	O	T	O		P	H	A	T
E	L	L	E	N		A	P	E	X		A	E	R	O
E	L	A	N	D		K	E	N	O		R	A	C	Y
S	A	R	D	I	N	E	C	A	N	A	R	D		
E	Y	E		R	E	F		N	I	N		B	A	A
			T	A	X	I	S	T	A	N	D	A	R	D
G	A	I	A		T	V	A		N	A	R	N	I	A
L	I	N	T			E	N	D			O	D	E	R
A	M	O	E	B	A		T	O	T		I	S	L	E
S	A	C	R	E	D	C	O	W	A	R	D			
S	T	U		E	V	A		N	B	A		T	W	A
		L	A	T	E	S	T	B	U	Z	Z	A	R	D
S	P	A	M		R	H	E	E		O	H	G	O	D
P	E	T	E		S	E	R	A		R	O	U	T	E
A	P	E	S		E	D	I	T		S	U	P	E	R

65

S	H	A	Q		S	H	I	P	S		G	A	B	S
P	E	R	U		P	E	R	O	T		O	P	A	L
A	N	T	E		A	R	M	O	R		M	E	N	U
			B	A	R	B	A	R	A	B	O	X	E	R
E	T	H	E	L				E	W	E	R			
J	O	E	C	O	C	K	E	R		D	R	A	M	S
E	R	A		T	A	I	L		D	E	A	D	O	N
C	E	R	F		S	N	I	P	E		H	A	T	E
T	U	T	O	R	S		Z	A	S	U		G	E	E
S	P	Y	R	I		M	A	R	K	S	P	I	T	Z
			S	N	C	C				A	R	O	S	E
I	T	S	A	D	O	G	S	L	I	F	E			
T	A	C	K		D	R	A	I	N		P	R	A	M
C	L	U	E		A	A	R	O	N		P	O	L	O
H	E	M	S		S	W	A	N	S		Y	E	L	P

66

C	H	E	V	Y		S	H	A	Q		S	P	O	T
A	E	R	I	E		T	O	F	U		T	E	A	R
P	R	I	V	A	T	E	P	R	O	P	E	R	T	Y
O	R	C	A		O	R	S	O		A	P	S	E	S
			L	Y	O	N			A	R	D	E	N	T
H	I	D	D	E	N	A	G	E	N	D	A			
A	V	A	I	L			A	R	K		D	E	J	A
W	A	R		P	A	N	G	R	A	M		C	U	B
K	N	E	E		R	O	N			E	P	O	D	E
			S	E	C	R	E	T	B	A	L	L	O	T
C	A	R	O	M	S			A	L	D	A			
A	L	I	B	I		Z	U	L	U		T	Y	C	O
C	O	V	E	R	T	O	P	E	R	A	T	I	O	N
T	O	E	S		A	N	O	N		S	E	P	A	L
I	F	S	O		G	E	N	T		P	R	E	X	Y

67

R	A	J			S	P	E	W		S	A	G	A	S
S	P	U	R		P	O	R	E		T	R	A	M	P
V	A	L	E		A	O	N	E		R	A	Z	O	R
P	R	E	F	E	R	R	E	D	S	A	L	A	R	Y
S	T	P	E	T	E			Y	O	W				
			R	A	K	E	S		S	H	I	P	T	O
A	T	M	E		E	L	L	A		A	N	E	A	R
T	H	A	N	K	Y	O	U	L	E	T	T	E	R	S
T	R	I	C	E		N	E	I	N		E	S	S	O
N	O	N	E	E	D		S	A	T	Y	R			
				P	I	P			R	E	V	S	U	P
J	O	B	A	P	P	L	I	C	A	T	I	O	N	S
A	R	O	M	A		U	N	P	C		E	L	B	A
M	A	N	I	C		S	T	A	T		W	A	I	T
B	L	A	D	E		H	O	S	E			R	D	S

68

A	R	C	O		D	E	L	F	T		N	E	M	O
S	A	H	L		E	M	I	L	E		O	X	E	N
S	H	E	L		S	O	L	A	R		N	I	N	E
	R	E	A	L	I	T	Y	B	I	T	E	S		
N	A	T		I	R	E				E	T	T	A	S
C	H	A	R	L	E	S	T	O	N	C	H	E	W	S
O	S	H	E	A			U	K	E		I	D	L	E
			A	C	R	O	B	A	T	I	C			
D	I	A	L		E	W	E			L	A	P	A	Z
A	F	R	I	C	A	N	S	W	A	L	L	O	W	S
M	I	T	Z	I				H	U	B		N	E	A
		D	A	I	L	Y	D	I	G	E	S	T	S	
L	O	E	B		S	A	U	T	E		S	O	O	T
E	C	C	L		A	L	D	E	R		T	O	M	E
O	T	O	E		T	E	E	N	S		S	N	E	E

69

T	G	I	F		R	I	P	E		A	D	A	P	T
R	A	N	I		E	M	I	L		L	O	N	E	R
A	T	T	N		M	A	S	H		T	I	N	N	Y
M	O	O	G	O	O	G	A	I	P	A	N			
	S	W	E	R	V	E			O	R	G	A	N	S
			R	A	E		D	I	P		S	W	A	P
E	G	R	E	T		R	I	G	I	D		A	N	A
V	O	O	D	O	O	E	C	O	N	O	M	I	C	S
A	F	T		R	U	D	E	R		T	O	T	E	M
D	O	O	M		T	O	Y		N	C	R			
E	R	R	A	N	D			H	O	O	P	L	A	
			Y	O	O	H	O	O	I	M	H	O	M	E
I	D	A	H	O		O	B	I	S		I	S	I	S
T	O	T	E	S		W	I	S	E		N	E	G	S
S	H	A	M	E		L	E	T	S		E	R	O	O

70

A	U	N	T		B	A	S	S		Y	A	W	N	S
S	N	E	E		A	R	L	O		E	T	H	O	S
T	R	A	P		I	C	E	R		S	H	A	R	E
H	E	R	E	S	T	H	E	R	E	M	O	T	E	
M	A	B	E	L			T	O	Y		S	S	T	S
A	L	Y		A	H	S		W	E	B		N	U	N
			E	M	B	E	D			A	L	E	R	O
	I	L	L	M	O	W	T	H	E	L	A	W	N	
S	N	A	K	E			S	U	R	L	Y			
I	S	R		R	O	W		B	A	A		L	B	J
R	U	G	S		R	O	T			S	P	I	R	E
	L	E	T	S	G	O	O	U	T	T	O	E	A	T
H	A	S	A	T		D	A	R	E		P	S	I	S
I	T	S	M	E		E	D	I	T		U	T	N	E
S	E	E	P	S		N	Y	S	E		P	O	S	T

71

L	O	F	T	S	■	C	A	P	E	■	B	R	A	G
T	U	L	I	P	■	A	L	E	X	■	L	E	T	O
D	R	A	M	A	■	L	O	C	H	■	A	L	O	E
■	■	R	O	C	K	M	U	S	I	C	I	A	N	S
S	T	E	R	E	O	■	■	■	B	A	R	T	A	B
C	O	D	■	S	P	A	S	T	I	C	■	E	L	Y
I	O	U	S	■	■	G	R	O	T	T	O	■	■	■
■	■	P	A	P	E	R	T	R	A	I	L	S	■	■
■	■	■	D	I	N	E	A	T	■	■	D	O	L	L
G	A	P	■	P	R	E	S	E	T	S	■	A	Y	E
O	R	O	M	E	O	■	■	■	R	A	S	P	E	D
S	C	I	S	S	O	R	S	K	I	C	K	S	■	■
S	A	N	D	■	T	O	W	N	■	H	A	T	E	S
I	N	T	O	■	E	L	I	E	■	E	T	A	T	S
P	A	Y	S	■	D	O	M	E	■	T	E	R	S	E

72

A	L	C	O	A	■	A	E	S	O	P	■	G	A	S
J	I	H	A	D	■	D	I	A	N	E	■	O	N	T
O	V	A	T	E	■	E	N	R	O	N	L	O	G	O
B	E	N	■	S	A	L	S	■	■	N	I	G	E	L
■	B	U	M	■	L	E	T	T	S	■	E	L	L	A
T	A	K	E	S	T	H	E	V	A	L	U	E	O	F
R	I	A	T	A	■	■	I	A	T	E	■	■	■	■
A	T	H	O	U	S	A	N	D	I	N	R	O	M	E
■	■	■	■	R	O	L	F	■	■	Y	A	H	O	O
S	Y	M	B	O	L	F	O	R	C	A	R	B	O	N
P	E	E	R	■	D	A	R	E	D	■	A	O	N	■
A	M	N	I	O	■	■	M	A	S	K	■	T	R	U
S	E	T	T	L	E	D	U	P	■	N	O	H	I	T
M	N	O	■	E	X	I	L	E	■	O	B	E	S	E
S	I	R	■	G	O	M	A	D	■	T	I	R	E	S

73

A	C	M	E	■	A	E	R	■	T	S	E	T	S	E
N	O	I	R	■	J	L	O	■	O	P	E	R	A	S
D	O	N	A	D	A	M	S	■	R	O	G	E	R	S
R	E	D	S	O	X	■	S	P	A	R	■	A	D	E
E	D	S	E	L	■	E	I	G	H	T	Y	S	I	X
■	■	■	S	L	U	R	■	A	S	Y	O	U	■	■
T	N	T	■	E	E	N	Y	■	■	■	G	R	I	T
W	O	U	L	D	Y	O	U	B	E	L	I	E	V	E
A	W	R	Y	■	■	■	M	O	N	A	■	R	Y	E
■	■	B	R	U	S	H	■	R	O	S	A	■	■	■
S	H	O	E	P	H	O	N	E	■	S	N	I	F	F
T	A	J	■	L	A	N	E	■	S	O	I	R	E	E
O	N	E	C	A	R	■	G	E	T	S	M	A	R	T
R	O	T	A	T	E	■	E	L	O	■	A	T	M	E
M	I	S	T	E	R	■	V	F	W	■	L	E	I	S

74

C	U	R	S	■	A	M	B	E	R	■	A	W	A	Y
O	L	E	O	■	W	I	L	M	A	■	F	E	T	A
S	C	R	O	L	L	L	O	C	K	■	F	L	O	W
M	E	A	N	Y	■	K	N	E	E	■	A	L	P	S
O	R	N	E	R	Y	■	D	E	R	A	I	L	■	■
■	■	■	S	E	E	S	■	■	■	B	R	I	N	E
J	E	S	T	■	A	P	A	C	H	E	■	K	E	G
O	N	T	■	T	R	I	P	L	E	L	■	E	R	G
L	V	I	■	A	N	N	E	A	L	■	O	D	D	S
T	Y	L	E	R	■	■	■	M	E	S	H	■	■	■
■	■	L	A	P	S	E	S	■	N	O	M	O	R	E
P	A	L	S	■	A	S	A	P	■	I	S	L	A	M
E	X	I	T	■	S	Q	U	A	L	L	L	I	N	E
R	I	F	E	■	S	U	N	N	I	■	A	V	O	N
U	S	E	R	■	Y	E	A	S	T	■	W	E	N	D

75

L	A	P	S	■	L	O	O	S	E	■	H	A	V	E
A	R	E	A	■	O	M	A	H	A	■	A	R	A	L
S	T	A	N	■	R	E	S	E	T	■	D	E	L	I
■	■	■	D	E	N	N	I	S	S	I	N	N	E	D
O	T	T	■	L	E	S	S	■	■	S	T	A	T	E
D	R	U	M	S	■	■	■	C	P	L	■	S	S	S
D	A	N	I	E	L	N	A	I	L	E	D	■	■	■
S	P	A	N	■	S	A	N	T	A	■	O	S	L	O
■	■	■	D	W	A	Y	N	E	Y	A	W	N	E	D
M	P	G	■	E	T	S	■	■	■	I	N	A	N	E
C	R	A	W	L	■	■	A	C	I	D	■	G	A	S
G	E	R	A	L	D	G	L	A	R	E	D	■	■	■
I	V	A	N	■	O	R	O	N	O	■	A	L	F	A
L	U	G	E	■	P	I	N	O	N	■	S	O	I	L
L	E	E	S	■	E	P	E	E	S	■	H	U	G	E

76

C	U	R	T	I	N			R	E	A	D	S	T	O
O	P	E	N	B	A	R		A	Y	K	R	O	Y	D
P	I	A	N	I	S	T		D	E	C	O	D	E	D
S	N	L		S	T	E	R	N	O		P	A	S	S
			R	E	Y		E	E	N					
J	A	D	E	S		I	S	R		C	H	A	S	E
U	N	I	S		O	D	E		W	O	E	F	U	L
L	I	V	E	F	R	O	M	N	E	W	Y	O	R	K
E	M	E	E	R	S		B	A	T		D	O	G	E
P	A	R	D	O		M	L	B		F	A	T	E	S
					H	O	E		B	E	Y			
R	O	T	C		O	R	D	E	A	L		N	B	C
I	N	E	R	R	O	R		T	R	I	B	O	R	O
B	E	L	U	S	H	I		H	O	N	O	R	E	R
S	I	E	S	T	A	S			N	E	W	M	A	N

77

F	R	A	Y		R	A	I	L		R	I	F	T	S
Y	U	L	E		E	T	R	E		E	M	A	I	L
I	T	S	A		C	L	A	N		F	A	N	N	Y
	H	O	R	S	E	A	N	D	B	U	G	G	Y	
			N	O	D	S			L	E	E			
G	I	S		R	E	T	R	I	A	L		A	S	A
A	D	M	I	T			I	D	S		P	L	U	S
M	E	A	T	A	N	D	P	O	T	A	T	O	E	S
M	A	L	T		O	N	E			M	A	U	D	E
A	L	L		G	R	A	N	I	T	E		D	E	T
			S	O	S			G	O	N	G			
	N	I	C	K	E	L	A	N	D	D	I	M	E	
C	O	B	R	A		A	R	O	D		V	I	S	E
A	D	E	E	R		C	A	R	L		E	S	P	Y
N	E	T	W	T		E	P	E	E		N	O	N	E

78

E	R	I	N		S	R	T	A	S		N	A	M	E
S	O	S	A		C	O	A	C	H		E	V	A	N
Q	U	I	T	D	A	Y	D	R	E	A	M	I	N	G
S	E	N	H	O	R	A	S			L	E	V	E	R
			A	G	A	L		M	O	M	S			
	D	O	N	T	B	E	S	O	N	A	I	V	E	
M	E	N	S	A			E	V	E		S	E	V	E
E	L	I		G	E	T	R	E	A	L		X	E	R
A	V	O	N		G	A	T			I	S	E	R	E
	E	N	O	U	G	H	A	L	R	E	A	D	Y	
			U	S	S	R		A	I	N	T			
S	L	A	V	E			S	O	B	E	R	E	S	T
C	O	M	E	D	O	W	N	T	O	E	A	R	T	H
A	L	I	A		W	E	I	S	S		P	L	E	A
B	L	E	U		E	S	T	E	E		S	E	M	I

79

C	L	U	B		S	H	E	L	F		E	L	K	S
L	I	N	E		H	O	M	E	R		L	E	A	K
E	L	I	E		A	L	I	V	E		F	A	Z	E
F	I	T	T	O	B	E	T	I	E	D		S	O	W
			R	U	B	S			P	A	T	H	O	S
C	H	E	E	R	Y		E	R	A	S	E			
H	O	L	D	S		C	R	A	S	H	D	I	E	T
E	P	A			D	O	W	N	S			H	A	H
F	I	N	A	L	E	D	I	T		A	B	O	V	E
			L	I	N	E	N		U	S	O	P	E	N
T	H	R	I	F	T			O	S	H	A			
A	A	A		T	U	R	N	T	H	E	T	I	D	E
G	I	Z	A		R	O	U	T	E		M	A	I	D
U	K	E	S		E	L	D	E	R		A	G	E	D
P	U	S	H		S	E	E	R	S		N	O	S	Y

80

S	A	T		K	R	I	L	L		T	I	L	T	S
P	E	R		I	N	D	I	A		I	C	A	H	N
I	R	E		L	A	S	T	S	A	M	U	R	A	I
E	I	E	I	O			H	E	R	B		A	N	T
L	E	S	T	W	E	F	O	R	G	E	T			
			S	A	B	E			O	R	A	N	G	E
C	H	A		T	R	A	I	T			C	O	E	D
L	I	S	T	T	O	S	T	A	R	B	O	A	R	D
A	R	I	A			T	O	N	E	R		H	E	Y
D	E	S	I	R	E			T	A	U	S			
			L	O	S	T	H	E	R	S	H	E	E	P
S	T	A		O	S	H	A			S	A	R	G	E
L	U	S	T	F	O	R	L	I	F	E		O	R	E
A	B	A	S	E		E	A	S	E	L		D	E	L
P	A	P	E	R		E	S	T	E	S		E	T	S

81

H	A	N	G		E	P	S	O	M		I	H	O	P
O	N	E	A		P	O	P	P	A		G	U	L	L
S	T	A	R		I	C	E	I	N		U	R	G	E
S	I	T	B	A	C	K	A	N	D	R	E	L	A	X
			L	P	S		K	E	Y	E	S			
M	I	M	E	O		P	O	D		L	S	A	T	S
E	W	E			R	E	F		M	I	S	C	U	E
D	O	W	N	F	O	R	T	H	E	C	O	U	N	T
I	N	L	A	I	D		H	A	G			R	E	A
A	T	S	I	X		R	E	D		B	L	A	S	T
			L	I	M	E	D		O	O	O			
C	O	M	E	T	O	T	E	R	M	S	W	I	T	H
A	X	E	D		L	I	V	E	N		E	D	A	M
S	E	M	I		T	R	I	N	I		N	I	N	O
K	N	O	T		S	E	L	E	S		D	O	G	S

82

L	E	N	O		D	F	L	A	T		A	S	T	I
E	V	I	L		A	R	O	M	A		M	E	I	R
S	A	G	E		M	E	T	E	R		B	R	A	E
		H	O	U	S	E	T	R	A	I	L	E	R	S
A	C	T		R	E	O				M	E	N	A	T
F	A	C	I	A	L	F	E	A	T	U	R	E	S	
A	T	A	L	L			R	U	B	S				
R	O	P	E		P	A	R	K	S		A	T	R	A
				E	A	S	E			S	T	R	E	P
	C	A	R	T	R	I	D	G	E	C	L	I	P	S
T	R	E	A	T				O	V	A		E	S	O
B	E	R	M	U	D	A	S	H	O	R	T	S		
S	W	A	M		E	B	O	O	K		O	O	P	S
P	E	T	E		F	L	U	M	E		G	U	R	U
S	L	E	D		T	Y	P	E	D		A	T	O	P

83

S	P	A	T		S	A	I	L		M	I	R	E	D
I	O	T	A		E	B	R	O		Y	O	U	R	E
N	U	T	C	R	A	C	K	E	R	S	U	I	T	E
A	N	Y	H	O	W		S	W	A	T		N	E	D
I	D	S		W	A	C		S	P	I	T			
			A	S	T	R	O		S	Q	U	A	T	S
A	M	A	T		E	E	L	S		U	R	I	A	H
B	O	L	T	F	R	O	M	T	H	E	B	L	U	E
R	A	T	I	O		N	O	R	A		A	S	T	A
A	T	O	L	L	S		S	A	T	I	N			
			A	L	A	S		Y	R	S		A	C	C
A	S	A		O	A	T	S		A	N	I	M	A	L
S	C	R	E	W	B	A	L	L	C	O	M	E	D	Y
P	A	N	A	M		R	O	O	K		A	B	E	D
S	N	O	R	E		E	G	O	S		M	A	T	E

84

S	U	M	A	C	S		C	B	S		S	T	A	T
A	T	O	N	A	L		O	L	E		L	E	A	R
W	I	N	D	T	U	N	N	E	L		E	S	A	U
I	C	E	R		S	E	A	N		S	E	T		
N	A	T	E		H	A	N	D	P	U	P	P	E	T
			T	R	Y				U	P	S	I	Z	E
A	G	A	T	E		G	R	A	S	P		L	I	N
F	I	N	I	S	H	I	N	G	S	E	C	O	N	D
R	A	T		P	A	S	S	E		R	O	T	E	S
O	N	E	T	O	N				E	S	P			
S	T	R	I	N	G	B	E	A	N		A	D	A	M
		O	D	D		L	A	R	D		P	E	L	E
B	L	O	B		B	E	S	T	S	E	L	L	E	R
M	I	M	I		R	A	Y		U	S	E	F	U	L
W	E	S	T		A	K	A		P	L	A	T	T	E

85

A	G	O	G		U	P	S	E	T		N	E	W	T
L	O	B	E		G	O	T	T	I		I	S	E	E
P	R	O	A	T	H	L	E	T	E		G	A	P	E
O	P	E	R	A		S	M	A	S	H	H	I	T	S
			U	R	L				O	U	T			
	S	U	P	P	O	R	T	I	N	G	C	A	S	T
S	H	H		S	C	O	R	N		S	A	N	T	A
A	A	H	S		H	O	U	N	D		P	I	E	D
A	M	U	C	K		S	T	I	E	S		S	E	A
B	E	H	I	N	D	T	H	E	W	H	E	E	L	
			S	I	R				Y	O	N			
C	A	B	S	T	A	N	D	S		V	A	L	U	E
O	S	L	O		F	O	R	T	H	E	B	E	S	T
S	T	I	R		T	O	N	E	R		L	E	N	A
T	O	P	S		S	N	O	W	S		E	R	A	S

86

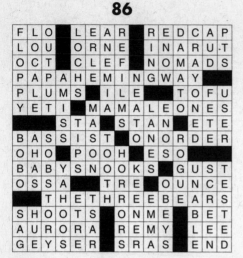

F	L	O	■	L	E	A	R	■	R	E	D	C	A	P
L	O	U	■	O	R	N	E	■	I	N	A	R	U	T
O	C	T	■	C	L	E	F	■	N	O	M	A	D	S
P	A	P	A	H	E	M	I	N	G	W	A	Y	■	■
P	L	U	M	S	■	I	L	E	■	■	T	O	F	U
Y	E	T	I	■	M	A	M	A	L	E	O	N	E	S
■	■	■	S	T	A	■	S	T	A	N	■	E	T	E
B	A	S	S	I	S	T	■	O	N	O	R	D	E	R
O	H	O	■	P	O	O	H	■	E	S	O	■	■	■
B	A	B	Y	S	N	O	O	K	S	■	G	U	S	T
O	S	S	A	■	■	T	R	E	■	O	U	N	C	E
■	■	T	H	E	T	H	R	E	E	B	E	A	R	S
S	H	O	O	T	S	■	O	N	M	E	■	B	E	T
A	U	R	O	R	A	■	R	E	M	Y	■	L	E	E
G	E	Y	S	E	R	■	S	R	A	S	■	E	N	D

87

P	A	N	G	■	D	E	B	T	■	C	H	I	M	E
O	B	O	E	■	E	L	I	E	■	R	I	D	E	R
K	I	L	T	■	A	L	L	S	■	A	L	E	R	T
E	D	A	M	■	F	A	L	L	I	N	L	O	V	E
R	E	N	A	M	E	■	S	A	V	E	■	■	■	■
■	■	■	R	A	N	D	■	■	A	S	S	I	S	I
S	N	A	R	L	■	O	M	A	N	■	E	D	E	N
L	I	M	I	T	■	P	O	P	■	S	T	E	A	D
A	L	I	E	■	D	E	M	S	■	I	T	A	L	Y
M	E	D	D	L	E	■	■	E	A	R	L	■	■	■
■	■	■	■	A	N	T	I	■	D	E	E	P	E	R
G	E	T	E	N	G	A	G	E	D	■	D	A	S	H
I	L	I	A	D	■	L	I	V	E	■	O	T	T	O
R	I	N	S	E	■	O	V	E	N	■	W	I	E	N
L	A	T	E	R	■	N	E	R	D	■	N	O	S	E

88

H	O	B	B	Y	■	M	A	R	C	■	S	T	A	G
O	P	E	R	A	■	O	L	E	O	■	H	E	R	R
T	A	D	A	S	■	J	O	A	N	■	A	N	N	E
■	H	O	W	S	H	O	U	L	D	I	K	N	O	W
■	■	F	L	E	E	■	■	M	O	D	E	■	■	■
S	L	R	■	R	A	M	P	■	S	T	I	F	L	E
W	O	O	S	■	D	O	I	N	■	A	T	R	I	A
I	T	S	A	N	Y	O	N	E	S	G	U	E	S	S
S	T	E	V	E	■	D	E	C	K	■	P	E	L	E
H	O	S	E	R	S	■	S	K	I	D	■	F	E	D
■	■	■	S	T	E	M	■	■	E	U	R	O	■	■
C	A	N	T	S	A	Y	F	O	R	S	U	R	E	■
A	U	D	I	■	L	E	A	P	■	T	B	A	L	L
P	R	A	M	■	E	Y	R	E	■	E	L	L	I	S
S	A	K	E	■	D	E	E	D	■	D	E	L	E	D

89

G	R	A	S	P	■	S	A	C	S	■	I	M	S	O
R	I	G	O	R	■	O	M	O	O	■	N	O	O	K
A	B	E	L	I	N	C	O	L	N	■	L	O	B	S
S	E	N	I	O	R	C	I	T	I	Z	E	N	S	■
S	Y	D	■	R	A	E	■	■	A	S	T	U	T	E
Y	E	A	R	■	■	R	A	M	■	A	S	N	O	T
■	■	■	E	O	N	■	D	I	T	Z	■	I	R	S
■	J	U	N	I	O	R	V	A	R	S	I	T	Y	■
T	A	R	■	L	I	L	I	■	I	A	N	■	■	■
O	N	E	A	L	■	S	L	R	■	■	E	S	P	Y
N	I	T	R	I	C	■	■	E	L	K	■	T	O	V
■	T	H	E	T	H	I	R	D	E	S	T	A	T	E
R	O	A	N	■	I	N	C	O	N	T	E	M	P	T
D	R	N	O	■	P	L	A	N	■	A	T	E	I	T
A	S	E	T	■	S	A	S	E	■	R	E	N	E	E

90

A	S	H	C	A	N	■	S	H	U	T	■	E	S	Q
C	L	A	U	D	E	■	M	A	H	I	■	T	H	U
R	U	N	J	E	S	S	E	R	U	N	■	H	O	I
E	R	G	O	■	S	Y	L	P	H	■	B	A	E	Z
■	■	■	■	J	I	L	L	S	■	R	O	N	■	■
E	M	A	N	U	E	L	■	■	R	E	X	A	L	L
M	U	L	A	N	■	A	O	R	T	A	■	L	E	O
B	L	O	W	G	A	B	R	I	E	L	B	L	O	W
E	T	H	■	L	A	I	R	S	■	I	R	E	N	E
D	I	A	L	E	R	■	■	O	C	T	A	N	E	S
■	■	S	I	S	■	R	E	T	R	Y	■	■	■	■
H	D	T	V	■	S	O	R	T	A	■	O	A	S	T
I	D	A	■	F	L	Y	R	O	B	I	N	F	L	Y
V	A	T	■	Y	O	K	O	■	B	A	Z	A	A	R
E	Y	E	■	I	G	O	R	■	E	M	E	R	G	E

91

H	A	R	S	H		I	C	A	N		L	O	L	A
A	L	I	C	E		N	A	T	O		I	B	I	S
N	A	D	I	R		C	R	O	C		N	O	A	H
G	R	E	E	N	B	A	Y	P	A	C	K	E	R	
	M	A	N	I	A				R	I	A			
			C	A	R	P	E	T	B	A	G	G	E	R
M	I	L	E		T	E	X	A	S		E	L	L	E
E	T	A				T	U	N				U	S	A
S	E	M	I		M	E	R	G	E		D	E	E	M
A	M	A	T	E	U	R	B	O	X	E	R			
			A	T	T				E	G	E	S	T	
	V	O	L	C	A	N	I	C	C	R	A	T	E	R
M	A	G	I		N	O	V	A		E	M	O	T	E
O	L	L	A		T	S	A	R		T	O	R	R	E
P	E	E	N		S	Y	N	E		S	N	E	A	K

92

H	A	R	P		P	L	A	N		P	A	D	R	E
O	L	E	O		R	O	M	A		O	B	O	E	S
B	E	F	O	R	E	Y	O	U	K	N	O	W	I	T
B	U	R	L	A	P		I	S	I	T		N	N	E
S	T	Y		G	P	S		E	D	I	T	S		
			Q	U	I	C	K	A	S	A	W	I	N	K
	M	S	U		N	A	M			C	O	Z	E	N
R	O	T	I		G	R	A	B	S		B	E	R	T
B	E	E	C	H			R	A	P		I	D	O	
I	N	A	H	E	A	R	T	B	E	A	T			
		D	E	R	M	A		E	E	G		A	B	C
A	L	Y		B	A	T	S		D	E	A	R	I	E
R	I	G	H	T	T	H	I	S	S	E	C	O	N	D
C	L	I	M	E		E	T	T	U		R	A	G	E
S	I	G	M	A		R	E	A	P		E	R	O	S

93

S	T	U	T	Z		I	M	A	M		P	A	V	E
P	O	L	E	S		G	I	N	O		U	S	E	R
O	N	C	E	A	M	O	N	T	H		R	H	E	A
I	K	E		Z	E	R	O		A	L	P	E	R	T
L	A	R	O	S	A		T	R	I	A	L			
			R	A	G	A		O	R	D	E	A	L	S
I	R	M	A		E	G	G	O		S	H	R	E	K
M	O	A	N		R	H	Y	M	E		E	B	A	Y
A	M	I	G	O		A	M	E	X		A	S	K	S
C	A	M	E	R	A	S		R	O	A	R			
			J	E	S	T	S		D	I	T	T	O	S
T	H	R	U	S	T		P	L	U	M		A	B	O
M	A	U	I		H	I	Y	O	S	I	L	V	E	R
A	L	E	C		M	O	O	G		N	O	I	S	E
N	O	S	E		A	N	N	E		G	A	S	E	S

94

S	M	O	G		S	T	A	G	E		M	E	S	A
L	A	V	A		H	O	V	E	R		U	S	P	S
A	X	E	R		O	R	I	O	N		E	S	A	U
G	I	N	G	E	R	R	O	G	E	R	S			
			O	F	T	E	N			A	L	P	E	N
P	A	P	Y	R	U	S		G	A	L	I	L	E	O
A	M	I	L	E			O	M	S			A	L	T
R	O	S	E	M	A	R	Y	C	L	O	O	N	E	Y
R	E	C			N	F	L			S	P	A	R	E
O	B	E	L	I	S	K		A	M	H	E	R	S	T
T	A	S	E	R			G	O	R	E	N			
			P	E	P	P	E	R	M	A	R	T	I	N
B	O	D	E		A	I	R	T	O		O	U	Z	O
M	U	I	R		S	T	R	A	T		A	T	O	P
W	I	N	S		S	A	Y	S	O		D	U	D	E

95

C	A	D	G	E		D	E	A	N		A	R	C	H
A	C	O	R	N		R	E	N	O		L	U	A	U
G	R	E	A	T		E	R	O	S		I	N	C	A
Y	E	S	V	I	R	G	I	N	I	A		I	A	N
			E	R	A	S	E		E	G	G	N	O	G
T	I	N	S	E	L			D	R	N	O			
R	O	O	T		P	L	I	E		E	B	B	E	D
I	T	I		T	H	E	R	E	I	S		A	A	R
P	A	R	S	E		A	E	R	O		A	L	V	A
			A	S	A	P			N	U	T	M	E	G
C	A	R	O	L	S		S	E	I	N	E			
A	B	A		A	S	A	N	T	A	C	L	A	U	S
D	I	V	A		U	H	O	H		L	I	L	L	E
I	T	E	M		M	O	R	E		A	E	T	N	A
Z	E	N	O		E	Y	E	R		D	R	E	A	M

96

H	E	E	L		F	I	E	F		H	A	M	E	L
A	L	A	I		O	N	T	O		A	M	U	L	E
H	M	S	B	O	U	N	T	Y		S	O	F	I	A
A	S	T	R	A	L		A	T	T	H	E	T	O	P
			E	R	S	T			H	A	B	I	T	S
D	O	L	T	S		E	S	P	A	N	A			
A	L	I	T		P	A	P	A	Y	A		F	U	R
F	A	M	O	U	S	R	A	C	E	H	O	R	S	E
T	V	A		N	E	A	R	E	R		N	A	M	E
			N	E	U	T	E	R		P	E	N	A	L
E	N	N	E	A	D			S	E	R	F			
M	A	I	L	R	O	O	M		L	A	I	D	U	P
I	D	E	S	T		J	E	L	L	Y	F	I	S	H
R	I	C	O	H		A	L	O	E		T	R	E	Y
S	A	E	N	S		I	S	B	N		H	E	R	S

97

B	A	R		A	E	T	N	A		D	E	G	A	S
A	T	O		S	Q	U	A	T		E	N	O	L	A
S	O	B		P	U	L	P	F	I	C	T	I	O	N
S	P	E	C	I	A	L			D	A	R	N	E	D
			R	U	N	T		T	E	L	L	Y		
M	A	T	T		O	Z	O	N	E		F	E	S	T
A	L	P		T	R	A	P	S		S	E	A	T	O
T	E	E	T	H		P	S	I		R	E	S	I	N
E	V	E	R	Y		A	E	G	I	S		T	N	T
S	E	L	A		S	T	E	N	S		L	O	G	O
			S	T	E	A	D		O	M	A	R		
A	R	C	H	I	E			S	T	E	W	A	R	D
J	U	I	C	E	N	E	W	T	O	N		N	O	R
A	L	T	A	R		S	H	O	P	S		G	T	O
R	E	I	N	S		T	Y	P	E	A		E	S	P

98

M	A	G	I		T	E	L	L		A	R	M	O	R
A	M	E	N		E	X	I	T		D	O	O	N	E
J	O	E	J	E	T	T	E	R		L	O	T	S	A
			A	F	R	O	S		D	I	T	H	E	R
A	D	M	I	R	A	L		S	O	B		E	T	S
D	O	Y	L	E			C	E	N	S	O	R		
O	R	S		M	I	N	U	E	T		A	J	A	R
B	A	T	S		S	O	F	T	G		F	U	S	E
E	L	E	C		O	N	F	O	O	T		I	S	A
		R	I	F	L	E	S			A	R	C	E	D
B	E	Y		A	D	S		A	N	X	I	E	T	Y
I	N	J	O	K	E		T	R	E	E	S			
B	R	E	V	E		J	U	N	E	S	Q	U	A	D
L	O	S	E	R		A	T	A	D		U	R	G	E
E	N	T	R	Y		S	U	Z	Y		E	L	A	N

99

U	S	D	A		P	L	O	P		A	S	C	A	P
L	E	E	R		C	A	V	S		S	C	A	L	E
T	O	M	B	O	S	L	E	Y		P	O	K	E	S
R	U	M	O	R		A	R	C	H	I	T	E	C	T
A	L	E	R	T				H	A	R	T			
				H	A	L	F		W	E	B	C	A	M
R	O	N	H	O	W	A	R	D		R	A	M	B	O
A	S	E	A		E	N	E	R	O		I	D	B	E
F	L	A	P	S		E	R	I	N	M	O	R	A	N
T	O	P	P	L	E		E	P	E	E				
			Y	O	U	R				C	A	N	A	L
D	E	A	D	W	R	O	N	G		C	R	A	N	E
A	D	L	A	I		M	I	L	W	A	U	K	E	E
B	A	B	Y	S		P	L	E	A		B	E	N	D
S	M	A	S	H		S	E	E	D		A	D	D	S

100

S	T	E	A	M		T	N	O	T	E		B	A	R
C	R	A	V	E		R	O	W	E	D		A	M	O
H	E	R	E	S	J	O	H	N	N	Y		G	P	A
E	M	T		S	U	P				S	O	B	E	R
M	O	H	S		D	E	N	S			F	O	R	E
E	L	E	A		O	Z	O	N	E	L	A	Y	E	R
D	O	N	A	S			S	E	R	A		S	S	S
			B	I	G	C	H	E	E	S	E			
A	B	O		M	A	H	I			S	N	A	G	S
B	A	T	H	S	P	O	N	G	E		O	M	A	N
A	T	T	A			O	G	O	D		S	I	L	O
S	T	O	I	C				V	A	N		A	I	R
H	E	M		A	L	I	C	E	M	A	R	B	L	E
E	R	A		K	I	N	E	R		V	I	L	E	R
S	Y	N		E	P	S	O	N		Y	O	Y	O	S

101

L	O	W	S		W	A	S	P	S		A	M	P	S
O	A	H	U		A	L	L	I	N		D	O	L	E
I	T	O	L	D	Y	O	U	S	O		A	L	E	X
S	H	A	K	E	S	P	E	A	R	E	P	L	A	Y
			S	C	I			N	E	S	T			
A	S	H		A	D	A	M			S	A	L	S	A
T	H	E	I	D	E	S	O	F	MAR.		B	E	L	L
W	O	R	S	E		O	V	I		B	L	O	O	P
A	V	O	N		MAR.	F	I	F	T	E	E	N	T	H
R	E	N	T	S			N	E	E	D		A	H	A
			S	T	A	G			E	E	K			
F	A	M	O	U	S	L	A	S	T	W	O	R	D	S
I	B	A	R		S	O	O	T	H	S	A	Y	E	R
J	E	E	R		A	R	N	I	E		L	E	F	T
I	T	S	Y		D	Y	E	R	S		A	S	T	A

102

D	R	A	W	L		L	I	Z	A		E	G	G	O
R	O	M	E	O		A	D	A	M		S	O	I	L
A	S	P	I	C		P	A	N	E		S	A	M	E
P	I	E	R	O	F	T	H	E	R	E	A	L	M	
E	E	R			O	O	O			W	Y	L	I	E
D	R	E	A	M	U	P		A	S	E		O	C	T
			T	A	L		S	A	W		D	U	K	E
	Q	U	A	Y	T	O	T	H	E	C	I	T	Y	
F	U	N	D		I	V	Y		E	A	R			
D	I	S		S	P	A		A	T	L	E	A	S	T
A	B	E	T	S			A	D	O			S	T	U
	B	E	R	T	H	O	F	A	N	A	T	I	O	N
A	L	M	A		I	H	O	P		B	E	T	O	N
R	E	L	Y		R	I	O	T		B	E	I	G	E
E	D	Y	S		T	O	T	S		A	N	S	E	L

103

L	I	L	I		E	W	E	R		D	W	A	R	F
E	D	E	N		V	I	C	E		O	N	C	U	E
G	O	N	E	W	I	T	H	T	H	E	W	I	N	D
O	L	D	P	A	L		O	R	E	S		D	T	S
			T	I	T	O		O	A	T	S			
B	A	M		T	W	A	S		T	I	M	B	E	R
A	L	O	E		I	S	E	E		M	O	O	L	A
S	I	N	G	I	N	I	N	T	H	E	R	A	I	N
E	V	E	R	T		S	O	H	O		E	T	T	A
D	E	T	E	S	T		R	O	T	H		S	E	T
			T	A	I	L		S	W	A	P			
A	O	L		D	E	E	M		A	G	E	N	D	A
T	H	E	P	E	R	F	E	C	T	S	T	O	R	M
T	I	A	R	A		T	A	P	E		T	R	E	E
Y	O	D	E	L		S	L	U	R		Y	A	W	N

104

J	U	L	E	P		P	L	A	N	B		G	S	A
A	R	O	A	R		R	O	S	S	I		O	M	S
B	E	W	R	I	T	E	B	A	C	K		N	U	S
			S	E	A	S	O	N		I	N	E	R	T
R	A	W		S	T	S			S	N	I	F	F	S
O	D	E	T	T	A		D	O	M	I	N	I		
T	A	R	A	S		P	A	L	E		N	S	E	C
O	L	E	G		M	A	R	I	E		I	S	N	O
R	E	C	S		O	V	E	N		H	E	I	S	T
		L	A	S	S	E	R		H	A	S	O	U	T
V	I	O	L	A	S			P	E	R		N	E	A
E	N	T	E	R		A	U	R	A	T	E			
I	S	H		O	U	T	T	O	L	A	U	N	C	H
N	E	E		N	A	M	E	S		C	R	E	P	E
S	T	D		G	R	O	P	E		K	O	O	L	S

105

M	A	C	S		H	O	U	R		H	A	Z	E	L
U	G	L	Y		E	S	S	E		A	V	E	R	Y
N	O	O	N		A	H	E	M		M	O	U	S	E
C	R	U	C	I	V	E	R	B	A	L	I	S	T	
H	A	D		T	E	A		R	U	E	D			
			B	E	N		M	A	R	T		J	A	B
A	X	I	O	M		B	O	N	A		C	O	L	A
C	R	O	S	S	W	O	R	D	E	D	I	T	O	R
H	A	W	N		H	O	S	T		I	N	S	E	T
E	Y	E		P	E	K	E		U	T	E			
			F	I	L	M		T	N	T		D	I	S
	E	N	I	G	M	A	T	O	L	O	G	I	S	T
G	L	E	N	S		K	A	T	E		R	O	L	E
U	B	O	A	T		E	X	E	S		I	D	E	A
M	A	N	L	Y		R	I	M	S		D	E	S	K

106

S	C	E	N	I	C		S	E	C		E	B	A	N
T	U	X	E	D	O		A	R	R		L	A	N	E
A	R	E	O	L	A		B	R	O		D	U	D	S
F	I	R		E	X	T	R	A	C	R	E	D	I	T
F	E	T	E			R	I	N	S	E	S			
			R	E	S	A	N	D		S	T	R	O	M
J	O	H	N	N	Y	C	A	S	H			O	P	A
U	N	I	S	O	N				E	M	O	T	E	S
S	T	E			C	L	A	I	M	C	H	E	C	K
T	O	R	A	H		A	T	T	A	I	N			
			N	E	S	T	E	A			O	A	R	S
D	E	P	T	H	C	H	A	R	G	E		D	I	E
O	R	A	L		R	E	L		I	M	P	U	G	N
L	I	V	E		O	R	O		S	M	I	L	E	S
L	E	E	R		D	S	T		T	A	T	T	L	E

107

J	A	M	S		M	A	Y	O	R		S	E	L	F
O	B	O	E		A	R	E	W	E		T	R	I	O
T	E	N	C	O	M	M	A	N	D	M	E	N	T	S
S	T	O	O	L	I	E			D	A	V	I	E	S
			N	E	E	D	E	D		R	E	E	S	E
E	G	A	D	S			X	E	D	I	N			
C	L	U	E		P	A	P	U	A	N		M	B	A
H	U	N	D	R	E	D	A	C	R	E	W	O	O	D
O	T	T		U	S	E	N	E	T		H	A	Z	E
			G	L	O	P	S			H	I	T	O	N
F	A	I	R	E		T	E	A	M	U	P			
A	C	C	O	R	D			G	A	L	L	O	P	S
T	H	O	U	S	A	N	D	I	S	L	A	N	D	S
E	O	N	S		F	E	I	N	T		S	C	A	T
D	O	S	E		T	O	N	G	S		H	E	S	S

108

W	A	S	P		F	D	A			P	E	T	I	T
A	R	I	A		R	I	C	A		O	X	I	D	E
N	E	X	T		A	S	H	E		L	A	T	E	R
		T	H	E	C	H	E	R	R	Y	M	O	O	N
D	A	Y		N	A	Y		O	O	P	S			
I	N	S	E	T	S		U	S	P	S		S	R	O
S	T	E	V	E		A	N	T	E		A	W	A	Y
C	O	V	E	R	O	F	D	A	R	K	N	E	S	S
O	N	E	S		S	T	E	R		L	E	A	S	T
S	Y	N		A	L	E	R		H	U	S	T	L	E
			S	T	I	R		D	A	T		S	E	R
N	E	W	M	A	N	A	G	E	M	E	N	T		
O	C	H	E	R		L	U	L	L		E	A	T	S
S	T	O	L	I		L	A	V	E		M	I	R	A
H	O	S	T	S			M	E	T		O	N	I	T

109

P	A	S	T	E	L		T	B	A	R		A	L	T
E	L	O	I	S	E		I	A	G	O		L	E	A
C	O	U	N	T	R	Y	C	L	U	B		B	A	N
S	T	L		E	N	O		D	E	E	P	E	N	D
		M	O	S	E	Y	S				A	R	T	E
M	C	A	N		R	O	C	K	B	O	T	T	O	M
P	U	T	T	S			H	O	Y	L	E			
H	E	E	H	A	W	S		P	E	E	R	S	A	T
			E	M	A	I	L			S	N	A	C	K
R	A	P	S	E	S	S	I	O	N		A	L	T	O
O	V	A	L				P	R	O	W	L	S		
L	I	L	Y	P	A	D		I	T	O		A	E	R
L	A	M		S	W	I	N	G	B	R	I	D	G	E
E	T	E		S	A	S	E		A	S	S	I	G	N
R	E	D		T	Y	K	E		D	E	S	P	O	T

110

A	B	E	T		L	A	U	D	S		M	E	A	T
L	U	L	U		O	N	S	E	T		E	R	G	O
G	R	A	N	D	P	A	N	J	A	N	D	R	U	M
A	G	L	A	R	E			A	R	O	U	S	E	S
			F	I	R	E	S		E	T	S			
	C	L	I	P		D	U	D		C	A	G	E	D
T	R	E	S		F	I	N	I	S	H		A	M	I
H	I	G	H	M	U	C	K	E	T	Y	M	U	C	K
A	B	A		E	N	T	I	T	Y		A	G	E	E
I	S	L	E	D		S	S	E		K	N	E	E	
			D	I	M		T	R	A	I	T			
E	T	H	I	C	A	L			S	W	I	V	E	L
T	H	E	B	I	G	E	N	C	H	I	L	A	D	A
C	E	L	L		I	N	U	R	E		L	I	E	N
H	Y	D	E		C	A	N	T	S		A	N	N	E

111

L	O	B	O	■	N	A	D	I	A	■	I	M	P	S
A	L	U	M	■	U	S	E	R	S	■	N	A	R	C
M	E	R	E	■	D	I	N	E	S	■	B	R	I	E
B	O	R	N	A	G	A	I	N	■	S	E	D	A	N
■	■	■	S	K	I	■	M	E	A	L	T	I	M	E
B	T	U	■	I	N	C	■	■	S	O	W	■	■	■
L	I	V	I	N	G	O	N	T	H	E	E	D	G	E
E	D	E	N	■	■	M	E	R	■	■	E	I	R	E
D	E	A	D	A	S	A	D	O	O	R	N	A	I	L
■	■	■	I	W	O	■	■	N	Y	E	■	L	P	S
R	E	V	E	R	S	E	S	■	S	P	A	■	■	■
E	D	I	F	Y	■	T	H	A	T	S	L	I	F	E
U	G	L	I	■	O	H	A	R	E	■	A	L	E	X
S	E	L	L	■	L	E	V	E	R	■	M	I	L	E
E	D	A	M	■	D	R	E	S	S	■	O	A	T	S

112

B	U	R	P	■	V	O	C	E	■	B	E	B	O	P
A	V	E	R	■	I	B	E	T	■	A	L	O	N	E
R	E	N	O	■	B	E	A	U	■	R	I	N	S	O
B	A	T	T	E	R	Y	S	I	Z	E	■	D	E	N
■	■	■	E	R	A	S	E	■	A	L	E	R	T	S
C	O	M	M	O	N	■	■	P	H	Y	L	A	■	■
O	H	O	■	S	T	J	O	H	N	■	S	T	O	W
B	I	T	T	E	■	A	A	A	■	S	E	I	N	E
B	O	O	R	■	A	M	T	R	A	K	■	N	E	V
■	■	R	I	F	T	S	■	■	T	A	N	G	L	E
D	A	G	G	E	R	■	S	P	A	T	E	■	■	■
E	R	R	■	M	I	N	O	R	L	E	A	G	U	E
B	I	O	T	A	■	A	N	N	O	■	R	A	N	K
U	S	U	A	L	■	R	I	D	S	■	B	L	U	E
T	E	P	E	E	■	C	A	L	S	■	Y	A	M	S

113

F	A	R	O	■	A	R	R	O	W	■	O	P	U	S
O	L	A	F	■	U	H	H	U	H	■	M	E	T	A
W	A	I	F	■	G	O	O	S	E	■	S	T	U	B
L	I	L	Y	M	U	N	S	T	E	R	■	U	R	L
■	■	■	E	A	S	E	■	■	D	I	A	N	N	E
D	E	P	A	R	T	■	B	I	L	O	X	I	■	■
O	Z	A	R	K	■	J	I	B	E	■	E	A	T	S
U	R	N	■	S	L	A	K	E	R	S	■	P	O	T
P	A	S	T	■	A	P	E	X	■	H	A	I	T	I
■	■	Y	A	W	N	E	R	■	D	O	D	G	E	R
H	E	Y	D	A	Y	■	■	B	E	A	D	■	■	■
E	L	O	■	D	A	I	S	Y	C	L	O	V	E	R
M	I	K	E	■	R	H	I	N	O	■	N	O	P	E
A	Z	U	R	■	D	O	N	O	R	■	T	I	E	D
N	A	M	E	■	S	P	E	W	S	■	O	D	E	S

114

S	P	E	C	■	E	B	A	Y	■	C	O	M	B	O
H	I	L	L	■	D	E	L	I	■	O	N	I	O	N
A	Q	U	A	■	I	D	L	E	■	G	L	A	Z	E
N	U	D	I	S	T	C	O	L	O	N	Y	■	■	■
D	E	E	R	E	■	H	Y	D	R	A	■	S	R	I
Y	T	D	■	D	I	E	■	S	E	C	T	I	O	N
■	■	■	L	A	R	C	H	■	■	■	I	S	B	N
B	A	R	E	N	A	K	E	D	L	A	D	I	E	S
A	V	O	N	■	■	■	P	R	E	X	Y	■	■	■
J	O	U	S	T	E	D	■	I	D	I	■	P	A	L
A	W	E	■	S	W	E	L	L	■	O	P	E	R	A
■	■	■	T	H	E	F	U	L	L	M	O	N	T	Y
H	A	N	O	I	■	I	N	R	I	■	S	C	U	M
A	R	B	O	R	■	L	A	I	D	■	S	I	R	E
S	C	A	N	T	■	E	R	G	O	■	E	L	O	N

115

S	W	A	M	■	R	A	S	H	■	D	A	I	S	Y
O	H	N	O	■	E	S	T	A	■	O	L	D	I	E
N	E	A	T	■	E	S	A	U	■	A	G	E	N	T
G	E	T	T	O	F	I	R	S	T	B	A	S	E	■
■	■	■	O	N	E	S	■	■	O	L	E	■	■	■
E	S	S	■	T	R	I	R	E	M	E	■	F	I	T
L	O	T	T	O	■	■	A	L	E	■	H	I	D	E
B	A	L	L	P	A	R	K	F	I	G	U	R	E	S
O	P	E	C	■	S	U	E	■	■	C	H	E	A	T
W	Y	O	■	T	H	E	R	M	A	L	■	S	L	Y
■	■	■	S	H	E	■	■	U	T	E	S	■	■	■
■	O	U	T	I	N	L	E	F	T	F	I	E	L	D
R	U	N	O	N	■	S	A	F	E	■	X	I	I	I
O	R	I	N	G	■	A	S	I	S	■	T	R	E	E
E	S	T	E	S	■	T	E	N	T	■	Y	E	N	S

116

I	B	E	R	I	A			J	A	I		S	T	A
D	A	N	A	N	G		C	U	T	S	H	O	R	T
O	N	E	D	G	E		A	L	L	E	Y	C	A	T
L	E	S	I	O	N		T	I	A		P	K	W	Y
			A	D	D		C	A	R	P	O	O	L	S
G	O	A	T		A	S	H		G	A	S			
A	C	C	E	S	S	C	O	D	E	S		F	A	B
L	H	A	S	A		A	F	R		T	A	L	I	A
S	O	D		F	O	R	T	U	N	A	T	E	L	Y
			F	E	R		H	M	O		L	E	S	S
C	A	M	I	S	O	L	E		N	S	A			
O	L	I	N		T	E	D		S	A	N	T	A	S
A	L	L	E	L	U	I	A		T	U	T	O	R	S
T	E	N	D	E	N	C	Y		O	N	A	P	A	R
S	S	E		I	D	A			P	A	N	E	L	S

117

A	P	T		C	H	I	L	I		G	O	R	E	N
D	A	Y		L	U	R	I	D		A	N	I	S	E
H	U	P	M	O	B	I	L	E		Z	A	P	P	A
O	L	E	I	N		S	Y	S	T	E	M			
C	A	S	S	I	S				A	B	A	S	E	D
			O	N	E	L	U	M	P	O	R	T	W	O
M	A	D		G	R	E	T	A		S	C	R	E	W
A	L	I	E		B	A	T	O	N		H	A	R	E
S	P	A	Y	S		P	E	R	I	L		Y	S	L
T	H	R	E	E	S	T	R	I	K	E	S			
S	A	Y	S	N	O				E	V	E	N	E	D
			L	O	W	E	R	S		I	R	A	Q	I
O	U	T	E	R		P	E	T	I	T	F	O	U	R
K	N	I	F	E		I	N	A	N	E		M	A	T
S	A	L	T	S		C	O	R	D	S		I	L	S

118

S	P	A	R	E		O	F	F	E	R		J	A	M
A	L	L	A	N		H	A	L	V	E		U	R	I
N	O	V	I	C	E	S	Q	U	A	D		N	I	L
S	W	A	N		M	U	S	E		T	O	K	E	N
			F	A	I	R			S	A	D	D	L	E
N	O	T	A	B	L	E	H	O	P	P	E	R		
U	V	U	L	A			A	C	R	E		A	I	R
D	A	N	L		P	A	R	T	Y		Y	W	C	A
E	L	I		T	E	M	P			C	O	E	U	R
		N	O	Y	E	S	O	F	C	O	U	R	S	E
A	R	G	Y	L	L			R	A	N	G			
R	I	F	L	E		O	B	I	S		O	O	N	A
G	T	O		N	O	M	A	D	H	A	T	T	E	R
O	E	R		O	R	A	N	G		S	M	O	R	E
T	S	K		L	A	R	G	E		S	E	E	D	S

119

J	E	T	S		I	M	A		A	R	E	T	O	O
U	P	R	O	O	T	E	D		B	A	S	I	N	S
T	H	U	R	G	O	O	D		A	Z	T	E	C	S
			B	R	O	W	N	V	B	O	A	R	D	
S	P	R	E	E				E	A	R				
H	U	I	T		A	N	N	E		E	E	L	E	D
O	L	D		A	S	E	A		O	D	D	I	T	Y
P	L	E	S	S	Y	V	F	E	R	G	U	S	O	N
P	I	R	A	T	E		T	R	E	E		T	I	A
E	N	S	O	R		E	A	R	L		T	E	L	S
				O	P	T				B	I	N	E	T
	O	F	E	D	U	C	A	T	I	O	N			
P	A	R	L	O	R		M	A	R	S	H	A	L	L
A	T	E	A	M	S		P	R	E	S	A	G	E	S
C	H	E	N	E	Y		S	T	S		T	O	D	D

120

L	A	Y	S		P	H	O	N	Y		A	W	A	Y
O	R	E	O		R	A	D	I	O		R	I	M	S
G	O	A	L		E	L	E	G	Y		E	T	A	L
J	U	S	T	A	S	I	T	H	O	U	G	H	T	
A	N	T	I	C		T	O	T		H	O	M	E	R
M	D	S		T	E	E		C	B	S		A	U	K
			M	I	A		W	A	R		N	Y	R	O
	U	P	R	I	G	H	T	P	I	A	N	O	S	
A	P	E	X		E	O	S		A	W	E			
B	L	T		A	R	T		S	R	A		I	F	S
S	I	N	A	I		C	E	L		R	A	D	I	I
	F	A	I	R	T	O	M	I	D	D	L	I	N	G
A	T	M	S		I	C	I	E	R		A	D	I	N
R	E	E	L		L	O	T	S	A		N	I	T	E
M	D	S	E		T	A	S	T	Y		S	T	E	T

121

D	I	R	E		T	R	A	M	P		C	A	S	A
I	D	O	L		R	E	C	U	R		A	V	O	N
R	E	D	S	K	Y	A	T	M	O	R	N	I	N	G
T	S	E		H	I	P	S			A	V	A	I	L
			B	A	N	S		F	I	N	A	N	C	E
S	P	R	A	N	G		S	O	A	K	S			
I	R	A	N			K	I	N	T	E		T	W	O
D	O	G	D	A	Y	A	F	T	E	R	N	O	O	N
E	W	E		R	E	N	T	S			O	G	R	E
			S	N	A	G	S		D	R	E	A	M	S
T	E	M	P	E	R	A		H	E	A	L			
A	L	O	E	S			S	O	L	I		A	C	E
B	L	U	E	S	I	N	T	H	E	N	I	G	H	T
L	E	N	D		B	E	A	U	T		R	E	I	N
E	N	D	S		N	O	T	M	E		E	D	N	A

122

N	O	D		A	F	T	E	R		P	O	P	U	P
A	L	E		D	O	N	N	E		E	L	E	N	A
R	E	T		D	U	T	C	H	T	R	E	A	T	Y
C	O	H	E	I	R		L	E	E	S		C	I	E
		R	A	N	T	S		A	N	O	T	H	E	R
W	R	O	U	G	H	T	I	R	O	N	Y			
E	O	N			S	O	S		R	A	R	I	N	G
E	V	E	R	T		A	S	S		L	O	S	E	R
D	E	S	I	R	E		U	A	R			V	E	E
			F	U	D	G	E	F	A	C	T	O	R	Y
C	O	R	T	E	G	E		E	C	L	A	T		
E	R	O		P	A	T	S		E	O	C	E	N	E
C	O	L	L	A	R	S	T	U	D	Y		D	O	E
I	N	L	E	T		O	L	L	I	E		I	L	L
L	O	A	T	H		N	O	E	N	D		N	O	S

123

M	O	L	L		D	E	J	A		P	O	S	I	T
E	D	I	E		E	R	O	S		A	L	I	C	E
S	O	S	O		V	E	N	I		N	I	L	E	S
A	R	T	I	F	I	C	I	A	L	T	O	O	T	H
			V	A	S	T			I	R	S			
L	A	C		T	E	S	T	I	F	Y		G	T	O
A	R	U	B	A			A	R	E		W	R	A	P
P	O	P	U	L	A	R	C	A	R	D	G	A	M	E
E	M	I	T		R	F	K			U	N	D	E	R
L	A	D		R	E	D	S	T	A	R		E	R	A
			T	E	N			A	G	E	S			
H	I	G	H	W	A	Y	O	V	E	R	P	A	S	S
A	G	O	R	A		A	M	E	N		R	U	L	E
T	O	N	E	R		P	O	R	T		A	R	E	A
S	T	E	E	D		S	O	N	S		Y	A	W	N

124

T	A	B	U		K	E	E	L	S		A	S	C	H
A	V	E	S		A	U	D	I	E		R	O	L	E
P	A	T	E	N	T	R	I	T	E		T	R	U	E
A	S	T	R	A	Y		F	E	S	T	E	R	E	D
S	T	E	I	N		C	Y	R		A	M	Y		
			D	A	D	A				R	I	S	E	R
H	I	S	S		I	M	A	M		A	S	I	D	E
A	S	H		T	E	E	T	E	R	S		T	I	E
S	P	I	T	E		L	E	N	O		S	E	E	K
H	Y	P	E	R				S	E	C	T			
		W	A	R		S	P	A		H	I	C	K	S
P	E	R	M	E	A	T	E		C	A	L	L	I	T
I	T	I	S		B	A	C	K	U	P	L	I	T	E
E	T	T	U		A	L	A	I	N		E	V	E	R
S	E	E	P		B	E	N	N	Y		D	E	R	N

125

L	O	Y	A	L		C	A	P	S		K	I	S	S
I	R	E	N	E		A	S	H	E		A	C	M	E
D	E	L	T	A		M	E	A	N		T	O	O	T
S	O	L	I	D	R	E	A	S	O	N	I	N	G	
				P	E	R		E	R	I	E			
L	I	Q	U	I	D	A	S	S	E	T		S	A	Y
U	S	U	R	P	S		H	I	S		Y	A	L	E
C	A	I	N	E		F	I	N		H	O	W	L	S
C	A	T	S		H	I	P		H	O	G	T	I	E
I	C	E		G	A	S	S	T	A	T	I	O	N	S
			P	O	S	H		I	M	P				
	W	H	A	T	S	T	H	E	M	A	T	T	E	R
J	A	I	L		L	A	I	R		N	A	I	V	E
I	D	L	E		E	I	R	E		T	U	N	E	S
M	E	T	S		S	L	E	D		S	T	A	R	T

126

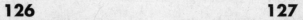

R	A	C	E		G	U	I	L	E		B	O	A	S
U	L	A	N		I	N	D	I	A		A	P	S	E
D	I	S	C	O	N	T	E	N	T	I	S	T	H	E
E	T	H	A	N		E	E	K		R	I	S	E	N
			P	I	E	S		U	F	O	S			
F	I	R	S	T	S	T	E	P	I	N		O	P	A
E	S	A	U		S	E	Q		N	I	C	H	E	S
T	E	L	L	A		D	U	B		C	H	A	O	S
O	R	L	E	S	S		I	A	M		A	R	N	E
R	E	Y		T	H	E	P	R	O	G	R	E	S	S
			C	H	O	U		C	O	I	L			
M	A	D	A	M		R	A	H		N	O	R	M	A
O	F	A	M	A	N	O	R	A	N	A	T	I	O	N
T	R	I	P		O	P	E	R	A		T	O	R	T
T	O	S	S		D	E	A	T	H		E	T	E	S

127

S	A	U	L		T	H	I	N		C	H	A	N	T
W	I	N	E		R	O	S	E		O	I	L	E	R
A	R	E	A		A	L	E	E		I	N	L	A	Y
R	O	A	D	S	I	D	E	D	I	N	E	R		
M	U	S	S	E	L	S			C	A	S	I	N	O
S	T	Y		M	E	T		M	E	G		G	E	N
			F	I	R	E	S	I	D	E	C	H	A	T
A	L	S	O			A	H	S			O	T	T	O
R	I	N	G	S	I	D	E	S	E	A	T			
T	E	A		P	R	Y		T	N	N		P	B	S
Y	U	P	P	I	E			H	A	N	G	O	U	T
		B	E	D	S	I	D	E	M	A	N	N	E	R
C	R	E	T	E		L	O	C	O		A	C	N	E
O	N	A	I	R		S	O	U	R		S	H	O	W
W	A	N	T	S		A	M	T	S		H	O	S	S

128

C	R	A	G		G	O	A	D		P	A	V	E	D
L	U	L	U		E	R	N	E		A	G	I	L	E
A	D	O	S		T	A	T	S		L	E	A	F	Y
N	E	U	T	R	A	L	Z	O	N	E				
			A	U	G			T	O	R	T	O	L	A
	R	E	V	E	R	S	E	O	S	M	O	S	I	S
H	E	Y		D	I	A	L			O	N	T	O	P
E	W	E	R		P	L	E	B	E		G	E	N	E
D	O	L	O	R			C	A	M	S		A	E	R
D	R	I	V	E	U	P	T	H	E	W	A	L	L	
A	D	D	E	D	T	O			R	A	N			
				P	A	R	K	R	A	N	G	E	R	S
A	T	A	R	I		T	E	A	L		O	K	I	E
L	O	G	O	N		E	N	I	D		R	E	S	T
B	O	O	Z	E		R	O	D	S		A	S	K	S

129

T	G	I	F		B	R	E	W	S		A	S	A	N
A	R	L	O		M	A	R	I	A		L	E	G	O
P	I	L	L	O	W	T	A	L	K		L	O	R	I
S	P	O	I	L	S			M	I	S	C	U	E	S
		G	O	D		S	E	A		A	L	L	E	Y
A	S	I	S		P	I	N		A	T	E			
B	I	C		S	O	F	A		D	E	A	C	O	N
B	L	A	N	K	E	T	C	O	V	E	R	A	G	E
A	L	L	O	Y	S		T	W	I	N		M	R	S
			F	L	Y		E	E	L		D	E	E	T
L	A	U	R	A		A	D	D		S	U	R		
E	X	H	I	B	I	T			S	A	L	A	D	A
D	I	A	L		S	H	E	E	T	M	U	S	I	C
G	A	U	L		L	O	R	N	A		T	H	E	M
E	L	L	S		E	L	E	C	T		H	Y	D	E

130

U	K	E	S		E	M	M	E		C	O	M	F	Y
S	E	X	Y		N	E	A	L		A	D	O	R	E
E	M	I	R		Z	A	G	S		D	E	L	I	A
R	O	T	A	R	Y	D	I	A	L		S	T	E	T
			C	U	M	E			A	S	S	E	S	S
I	N	J	U	N	E		B	E	M	O	A	N		
S	E	A	S		S	K	E	W	E	R		L	I	P
N	A	M	E	S		A	G	E		T	R	A	D	E
T	R	E		A	R	T	U	R	O		A	V	O	W
		S	A	L	O	O	N		A	P	P	A	L	S
C	R	I	M	E	A			S	K	I	S			
R	A	V	E		M	U	S	C	L	E	T	O	N	E
O	Z	O	N	E		N	O	R	A		A	R	C	A
F	O	R	D	S		I	S	O	N		R	E	A	R
T	R	Y	S	T		T	O	D	D		S	O	A	P

131

G	R	I	D		D	A	T	E		S	T	A	L	E
A	E	R	O		O	M	A	R		T	I	M	E	X
B	L	O	C		R	A	V	I		R	E	E	V	E
S	Y	N	T	H	E	T	I	C	F	A	B	R	I	C
			R	A	M				O	N	A			
A	R	T	I	F	I	C	I	A	L	G	R	A	S	S
M	O	U	N	T		A	N	N	I	E		L	E	E
A	R	T	E		O	P	T	I	C		M	E	N	D
T	E	T		B	U	R	R	O		L	O	U	S	E
I	M	I	T	A	T	I	O	N	B	U	T	T	E	R
			A	R	R				A	S	H			
C	O	U	N	T	E	R	F	E	I	T	B	I	L	L
H	O	R	D	E		E	A	R	L		A	L	O	E
U	N	S	E	R		E	R	I	E		L	I	N	T
M	A	A	M	S		L	E	N	D		L	A	G	S

132

A	T	B	A	T		G	O	L	F	S		I	C	E
M	O	O	L	A		A	W	E	E	K		S	O	D
B	R	A	I	N	F	R	E	E	Z	E		O	L	D
E	S	T		G	I	R	D	S		T	O	S	A	Y
R	O	S	E	L	L	E			A	C	D	C		
			M	E	L	T	E	D	C	H	E	E	S	E
W	H	A	M	S			A	I	R	Y		L	I	D
R	O	B	E		M	A	S	S	E		D	E	L	I
A	U	S		S	A	L	E			A	I	S	L	E
P	R	E	T	T	Y	P	L	E	A	S	E			
		N	O	R	A			S	C	H	M	E	A	R
G	O	T	T	A		T	O	P	I	C		L	S	U
A	P	E		F	L	O	R	I	D	A	K	E	Y	S
Z	E	E		E	A	G	L	E		N	O	N	E	T
E	L	S		S	T	A	Y	S		S	P	A	T	S

133

W	A	V	E		F	A	R	M		M	A	R	K	S
A	U	E	R		A	R	E	A		I	N	A	L	L
X	X	X	R	A	T	I	N	G		R	A	D	I	O
			A	R	C		E	N	G	A	G	I	N	G
S	C	O	T	I	A		W	A	R	C	R	I	E	S
P	A	P	I	S	T	S			I	L	A			
O	N	I	C	E		A	A	A	M	E	M	B	E	R
R	A	N				B	B	B				R	N	A
E	L	E	V	E	N	E	E	E		A	M	A	S	S
			A	X	E			T	A	P	E	S	U	P
S	T	E	N	C	I	L	S		R	I	N	S	E	S
P	E	N	D	U	L	U	M		A	N	D			
A	N	D	Y	S		G	E	O	R	G	E	I	I	I
S	T	O	K	E		E	L	L	A		R	O	A	N
M	O	R	E	S		S	T	E	T		S	U	N	K

134

A	S	F	A	R		L	S	A	T	S		F	I	G
L	A	R	G	O		E	P	C	O	T		I	R	A
K	I	E	R	K	E	G	A	A	R	D		N	O	R
A	N	S	E		T	A	R	D	E		D	E	N	Y
	T	H	E	A	C	T			I	S	N	T		
			S	C	H	O	P	E	N	H	A	U	E	R
S	M	O	T	E			R	O	T	E		N	C	O
H	A	L	O		D	R	A	N	O		R	E	O	S
A	M	Y		F	I	N	N			S	A	D	L	Y
H	A	M	M	A	R	S	K	J	O	L	D			
		P	E	N	T			E	R	R	A	T	A	
T	W	I	N		P	L	A	T	S		R	A	R	E
E	R	A		M	O	U	S	S	O	R	G	S	K	Y
R	A	D		G	O	A	P	E		O	U	T	I	E
M	P	S		T	R	U	S	T		O	N	E	N	D

135

T	A	S	T	E		S	W	A	M	P		T	I	L
A	N	T	E	S		P	A	N	E	L		O	N	E
B	Y	Y	E	S	T	E	R	D	A	Y		U	T	E
				E	R	A	S			W	A	T	E	R
S	P	O	O	N	E	R		P	R	O	U	D	L	Y
H	E	N	L	E	Y		C	H	O	O	S	E		
R	A	T	E	S		R	O	A	L	D		S	U	N
E	C	H	O		P	U	R	S	E		T	U	N	E
W	E	E		M	E	L	E	E		B	R	I	D	E
		D	O	O	L	E	Y		L	O	O	T	E	D
A	M	O	U	N	T	S		F	I	N	D	E	R	S
B	O	U	T	S			A	L	O	E				
O	R	B		T	H	I	S	I	N	S	T	A	N	T
M	E	L		E	E	R	I	E		U	R	I	A	H
B	Y	E		R	E	E	F	S		P	A	R	T	Y

136

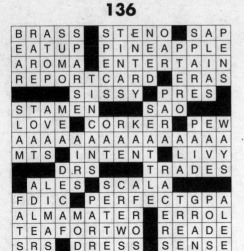

B	R	A	S	S	■	S	T	E	N	O	■	S	A	P
E	A	T	U	P	■	P	I	N	E	A	P	P	L	E
A	R	O	M	A	■	E	N	T	E	R	T	A	I	N
R	E	P	O	R	T	C	A	R	D	■	E	R	A	S
■	■	■	■	S	I	S	S	Y	■	P	R	E	S	■
S	T	A	M	E	N	■	■	■	S	A	O	■	■	■
L	O	V	E	■	C	O	R	K	E	R	■	P	E	W
A	A	A	A	A	A	A	A	A	A	A	A	A	A	A
M	T	S	■	I	N	T	E	N	T	■	L	I	V	Y
■	■	■	D	R	S	■	■	■	T	R	A	D	E	S
■	A	L	E	S	■	S	C	A	L	A	■	■	■	■
F	D	I	C	■	P	E	R	F	E	C	T	G	P	A
A	L	M	A	M	A	T	E	R	■	E	R	R	O	L
T	E	A	F	O	R	T	W	O	■	R	E	A	D	E
S	R	S	■	D	R	E	S	S	■	S	E	N	S	E

137

B	A	S	H	■	C	A	B	S	■	A	D	H	O	C
E	L	I	A	■	O	R	E	O	■	D	R	A	W	S
D	E	L	I	■	F	R	E	D	■	D	O	N	N	A
S	E	L	L	S	F	O	R	A	S	O	N	G	■	■
■	■	■	S	L	E	W	■	■	U	N	E	A	S	Y
■	A	R	T	I	E	■	A	P	E	S	■	R	O	I
S	W	O	O	N	■	A	R	I	D	■	S	O	U	P
C	H	A	N	G	E	S	O	N	E	S	T	U	N	E
R	I	D	E	■	L	A	S	T	■	W	A	N	D	S
A	R	T	■	D	U	P	E	■	W	A	R	D	S	■
P	L	O	W	E	D	■	■	P	E	R	T	■	■	■
■	■	F	A	C	E	S	T	H	E	M	U	S	I	C
C	R	A	V	E	■	H	O	O	D	■	R	U	S	H
H	E	M	E	N	■	A	N	N	E	■	N	I	L	E
E	X	E	R	T	■	D	Y	E	D	■	S	T	E	W

138

C	B	S	■	C	R	O	C	■	M	A	L	A	W	I
R	E	A	■	H	A	L	L	■	E	D	I	T	E	D
I	C	U	■	U	S	D	A	■	S	H	A	M	E	S
N	O	N	E	T	H	E	W	I	S	E	R	■	■	■
G	O	A	T	E	E	■	■	C	U	R	■	S	E	W
E	L	S	A	■	S	O	M	E	P	E	O	P	L	E
■	■	■	■	A	T	N	O	■	S	N	E	A	K	S
A	I	M	E	R	■	A	I	L	■	T	R	Y	S	T
C	R	I	S	C	O	■	S	E	E	S	■	■	■	■
M	O	S	T	W	A	N	T	E	D	■	D	U	A	L
E	N	T	■	E	R	A	■	■	U	G	A	N	D	A
■	■	■	A	L	L	Y	O	U	C	A	N	E	A	T
U	P	S	I	D	E	■	G	N	A	T	■	A	G	E
S	T	A	R	E	S	■	L	I	T	E	■	S	E	N
S	A	T	Y	R	S	■	E	X	E	S	■	E	S	S

139

R	O	C	K	■	I	N	L	E	T	■	A	B	L	E
U	G	L	I	■	B	O	O	T	H	■	S	L	U	G
B	R	O	N	Z	E	S	T	A	R	■	T	U	N	A
Y	E	T	■	E	R	E	■	L	I	P	R	E	A	D
■	■	■	M	L	I	■	■	■	L	E	A	R	■	■
P	A	G	O	D	A	S	■	S	L	A	Y	I	N	G
I	L	O	N	A	■	M	I	T	E	R	■	B	O	L
P	O	L	K	■	F	A	D	E	D	■	A	B	O	U
E	N	D	■	A	A	R	O	N	■	S	H	O	N	E
D	E	M	E	R	I	T	■	O	C	T	A	N	E	S
■	■	E	M	I	R	■	■	■	O	R	B	■	■	■
R	E	D	C	A	P	S	■	D	R	U	■	P	S	I
A	L	A	E	■	L	O	V	I	N	G	C	U	P	S
M	I	L	E	■	A	D	O	R	E	■	O	P	A	L
P	A	S	S	■	Y	A	W	E	D	■	Z	A	N	E

140

A	I	N	T	■	P	L	E	A	■	A	D	M	A	N
S	N	O	O	T	I	E	S	T	■	R	A	I	S	E
T	H	E	K	I	N	G	S	T	O	N	T	R	I	O
R	E	V	E	L	S	■	■	■	P	I	E	■	■	■
I	R	I	S	■	■	S	P	R	E	E	■	A	R	T
D	E	L	■	P	E	A	L	E	D	■	A	C	I	D
■	■	■	C	A	T	N	A	P	■	E	T	H	O	S
■	T	H	E	R	A	J	Q	U	A	R	T	E	T	■
F	R	O	N	T	■	O	U	T	M	A	N	■	■	■
E	A	S	T	■	I	S	E	E	I	T	■	N	I	A
E	Y	E	■	A	M	E	S	S	■	■	G	E	N	S
■	■	■	E	I	N	■	■	■	D	R	E	A	D	S
T	H	E	T	R	O	U	T	Q	U	I	N	T	E	T
W	A	S	T	E	■	R	A	R	E	B	R	E	E	D
A	L	T	A	R	■	N	E	S	T	■	E	R	D	A

141

S	T	O	R	E	■	E	S	A	U	■	S	O	A	R
T	R	A	I	L	■	C	H	I	N	■	Y	U	L	E
O	U	T	O	F	D	O	O	R	S	■	R	T	E	S
W	E	S	T	■	O	N	R	Y	E	■	I	O	T	A
■	■	■	E	P	C	O	T	■	N	O	N	F	A	T
P	O	O	D	L	E	■	L	E	T	S	G	O	■	■
E	M	U	■	E	N	C	Y	C	■	M	E	R	C	I
R	A	T	■	A	T	A	■	R	I	O	■	D	A	D
T	R	O	T	S	■	P	O	U	T	S	■	E	R	E
■	■	F	E	E	D	E	R	■	S	I	E	R	R	A
I	M	P	E	D	E	■	B	L	E	S	S	■	■	■
T	A	R	P	■	S	T	I	L	L	■	P	A	C	S
E	R	I	E	■	O	U	T	O	F	S	I	G	H	T
M	I	N	E	■	T	R	E	S	■	E	E	R	I	E
S	O	T	S	■	O	K	R	A	■	A	D	A	P	T

142

S	A	H	I	B	■	O	P	E	R	A	■	B	A	R
A	M	I	N	O	■	W	A	L	T	S	■	O	N	O
P	I	C	K	Y	P	I	C	K	E	T	■	N	I	B
■	■	■	■	C	E	N	T	S	■	A	U	N	T	Y
R	A	P	S	O	N	G	S	■	L	I	B	Y	A	N
E	R	U	P	T	S	■	■	C	A	R	I	B	■	■
S	T	P	A	T	■	B	O	O	Z	E	■	O	O	F
T	O	P	S	■	S	A	R	G	E	■	E	N	T	R
S	O	Y	■	B	A	R	B	S	■	P	E	N	T	A
■	■	P	U	L	S	E	■	■	H	I	R	E	O	N
T	A	U	R	U	S	■	A	N	A	L	Y	T	I	C
A	P	P	L	E	■	E	R	O	D	E	■	■	■	■
L	A	P	■	J	U	N	K	Y	J	U	N	K	E	T
I	R	E	■	A	N	G	I	E	■	P	I	A	N	O
A	T	T	■	Y	A	R	N	S	■	S	A	N	D	Y

143

W	A	L	K	S	■	A	B	E	L	■	N	A	T	S
I	N	E	R	T	■	C	L	I	O	■	I	N	I	T
S	T	E	A	L	■	C	A	N	O	P	E	N	E	R
P	I	C	K	U	P	T	H	E	P	A	C	E	■	■
■	S	H	A	K	E	S	■	■	■	L	E	M	O	N
■	■	■	T	E	N	■	B	A	W	L	■	E	R	E
E	S	S	O	■	S	E	R	G	E	I	■	A	B	S
P	U	T	A	F	I	R	E	U	N	D	E	R	I	T
S	I	R	■	R	O	D	E	N	T	■	V	A	T	S
O	T	O	■	O	N	E	D	■	A	L	I	■	■	■
M	E	N	D	S	■	■	■	A	P	O	L	L	O	■
■	■	G	E	T	T	H	E	L	E	A	D	O	U	T
C	U	B	B	Y	H	O	L	E	■	T	O	R	T	E
S	P	O	T	■	O	M	A	R	■	H	E	A	R	S
I	N	X	S	■	R	E	N	T	■	E	R	N	E	S

144

O	A	H	U	■	G	O	O	P	■	D	A	R	N	S
O	L	A	N	■	A	C	R	E	■	E	L	I	O	T
M	I	D	D	L	E	E	A	R	■	P	L	A	T	A
P	B	S	■	A	L	A	N	■	L	O	O	S	E	N
H	I	T	C	H	I	N	G	P	O	S	T	■	■	■
■	■	■	L	O	C	■	■	L	Y	E	S	O	A	P
A	D	E	E	R	■	S	H	E	A	■	■	M	N	O
C	O	F	F	E	E	T	A	B	L	E	B	O	O	K
E	S	T	■	■	L	A	T	E	■	L	O	O	N	Y
D	E	S	P	A	I	R	■	■	A	D	S	■	■	■
■	■	■	E	N	T	R	A	N	C	E	H	A	L	L
M	I	L	L	I	E	■	T	E	C	S	■	W	O	O
A	R	I	L	S	■	F	R	E	E	T	R	A	D	E
R	A	R	E	E	■	A	I	D	S	■	O	R	E	S
K	E	A	T	S	■	B	A	S	S	■	T	E	N	S

145

T	A	R	O	■	A	S	T	A	■	B	A	B	A	S
O	D	O	R	■	D	A	I	S	■	A	M	I	G	O
N	A	S	A	■	O	M	N	I	■	Y	O	D	E	L
S	M	A	L	L	P	O	T	A	T	O	E	S	■	■
■	■	■	■	A	T	A	■	■	H	U	B	■	■	■
A	W	A	R	D	S	■	T	O	E	■	A	S	S	T
C	O	N	E	D	■	M	A	N	I	A	■	H	I	E
T	R	I	V	I	A	L	P	U	R	S	U	I	T	S
O	R	S	■	E	R	I	E	S	■	S	P	R	A	T
R	Y	E	S	■	G	I	S	■	R	I	S	E	R	S
■	■	■	T	O	O	■	■	A	E	S	■	■	■	■
■	■	P	E	T	T	Y	O	F	F	I	C	E	R	S
A	D	U	L	T	■	A	N	T	E	■	A	V	O	W
T	U	L	L	E	■	L	E	E	R	■	L	I	M	A
M	O	L	A	R	■	E	R	R	S	■	F	L	A	T

146

E	R	I	C	■	L	I	L	A	C	■	A	M	E	N
D	A	D	O	■	A	B	O	I	L	■	P	I	L	E
T	H	O	M	A	S	M	O	R	E	■	A	S	I	S
■	■	■	B	U	T	S	■	■	A	O	R	T	A	S
O	B	L	I	G	E	■	D	O	N	A	T	E	■	■
L	E	A	N	E	D	■	R	U	S	T	■	R	T	E
D	A	T	E	R	■	M	A	T	E	S	■	C	E	L
I	T	I	S	■	J	A	P	E	S	■	C	H	A	D
E	E	N	■	H	U	G	E	R	■	R	A	I	S	E
S	N	L	■	A	M	O	R	■	H	A	R	P	E	R
■	■	O	L	D	B	O	Y	■	O	D	I	S	T	S
N	A	V	A	J	O	■	■	A	R	I	L	■	■	■
A	L	E	C	■	J	O	H	N	M	I	L	T	O	N
S	E	R	E	■	E	L	A	T	E	■	O	K	I	E
H	E	S	S	■	T	A	M	I	L	■	N	O	L	O

147

B	E	E	C	H	■	S	A	L	T	■	I	S	A	K
A	D	L	A	I	■	O	R	E	O	■	A	C	R	E
Y	U	M	M	Y	Y	U	M	M	Y	■	G	R	A	D
■	■	■	P	A	A	R	■	■	S	C	R	U	B	S
A	C	T	S	■	N	O	D	S	■	H	E	M	S	■
T	H	A	I	■	K	N	E	E	D	E	E	P	■	■
R	U	S	T	S	■	■	S	T	Y	E	■	T	I	A
I	N	T	E	A	R	S	■	H	E	R	O	I	N	E
A	G	E	■	H	A	H	A	■	■	S	N	O	U	T
■	■	S	T	A	G	E	M	O	M	■	T	U	R	N
■	A	G	A	R	■	A	S	I	A	■	A	S	E	A
A	O	R	T	A	S	■	■	L	A	I	R	■	■	■
G	L	E	E	■	M	M	M	M	M	M	G	O	O	D
R	E	A	R	■	O	B	O	E	■	P	E	D	R	O
A	R	T	S	■	G	A	I	N	■	S	T	E	E	R

148

E	A	G	L	E	■	C	A	M	P	■	R	A	N	K
M	O	R	O	N	■	A	W	O	L	■	O	D	I	E
B	R	A	N	D	O	N	A	M	E	■	M	A	N	Y
E	T	S	■	G	R	E	Y	■	T	H	A	M	E	S
R	A	S	C	A	L	S	■	S	H	I	N	■	■	■
■	■	■	A	M	Y	■	P	H	O	T	O	O	P	S
P	A	S	T	E	■	H	A	I	R	■	F	L	A	T
A	U	T	O	■	B	E	R	R	A	■	O	G	L	E
C	R	A	B	■	E	A	S	T	■	G	R	A	S	P
T	A	B	U	L	A	T	E	■	S	O	U	■	■	■
■	■	■	R	I	C	H	■	C	L	A	M	S	U	P
L	E	N	G	T	H	■	G	O	A	L	■	P	R	O
I	D	O	L	■	B	O	N	O	V	O	Y	A	G	E
A	G	R	A	■	U	R	A	L	■	N	O	T	E	S
R	E	A	R	■	M	E	W	S	■	G	U	S	S	Y

149

H	A	U	L	■	I	R	I	S	H	■	C	H	I	A
A	S	T	A	■	T	A	B	O	O	■	L	O	O	N
S	T	I	C	K	S	H	I	F	T	■	U	P	T	O
N	I	C	E	L	Y	■	■	A	R	A	B	I	A	N
T	R	A	D	E	■	A	C	R	O	S	S	■	■	■
■	■	■	■	E	C	R	U	■	D	I	O	N	N	E
L	I	M	B	■	H	O	E	S	■	A	D	I	O	S
A	R	I	A	■	O	S	C	A	R	■	A	T	I	T
R	A	N	T	S	■	E	A	S	T	■	S	E	R	E
A	N	I	M	A	L	■	R	H	E	A	■	■	■	■
■	■	■	O	N	E	I	D	A	■	C	R	E	M	E
S	O	Y	B	E	A	N	■	■	S	N	A	R	E	S
A	L	A	I	■	P	A	D	D	L	E	B	O	A	T
G	I	R	L	■	E	N	T	R	E	■	I	D	L	E
A	N	N	E	■	R	E	S	E	W	■	N	E	S	S

150

F	O	A	L	■	C	U	B	S	■	O	N	S	E	T
O	M	N	I	■	A	S	A	P	■	V	E	R	N	E
L	E	T	O	■	M	E	R	E	■	E	R	O	D	E
K	N	I	T	T	E	D	S	C	A	R	F	■	■	■
■	■	■	T	I	L	■	■	S	C	H	■	T	H	O
C	O	C	A	C	O	L	A	■	H	E	A	R	O	F
A	L	L	■	■	T	I	M	B	E	R	W	O	L	F
R	E	E	F	S	■	M	B	A	■	E	L	U	D	E
B	A	R	R	E	L	B	O	L	T	■	■	P	E	R
O	R	I	O	L	E	■	Y	I	E	L	D	E	R	S
N	Y	C	■	E	A	R	■	■	E	A	U	■	■	■
■	■	■	I	N	H	A	L	I	N	G	F	O	O	D
H	I	N	D	I	■	J	E	N	A	■	F	O	U	R
A	D	I	E	U	■	A	G	O	G	■	E	Z	R	A
S	A	L	E	M	■	H	O	N	E	■	L	E	S	T